AN END TO INNOCENCE

An End to Innocence

ESSAYS ON CULTURE AND POLITICS

LESLIE A. FIEDLER

STEIN AND DAY / *Publishers* / New York

First published by Stein and Day/*Publishers* 1972
Copyright © 1948, 1949, 1950, 1951, 1952, 1954,
1955 by Leslie A. Fiedler
Copyright © 1952 by Kenyon College
Introduction to the Second Editon Copyright
© 1971 by Leslie A. Fiedler
Library of Congress Catalog Card No. 72-82145
All rights reserved
Published simultaneously in Canada by Saunders of Toronto Ltd
Printed in the United States of America
Stein and Day/*Publishers*/7 East 48 Street, New York, N.Y. 10017
ISBN 0-8128-1478-9

FOR MY FATHER

Acknowledgments

The author wishes to thank the editors and publishers of the following, under whose imprints parts of this book originally appeared:

BEACON PRESS for Preface to *An End of Innocence,* 1955.

COMMENTARY for "Hiss, Chambers, and the Age of Innocence," December 1950; "Dead-End Werther," September 1951; and "Roman Holiday," April 1954.

ENCOUNTER for "Afterthoughts on the Rosenbergs," October 1953; "The 'Good American,'" March 1954; "McCarthy and the Intellectuals," August 1954; and "Images of Walt Whitman," January 1955 (this essay also appeared in *Whitman After 100 Years,* published in 1955 by the Stanford University Press).

KENYON REVIEW for "Italian Pilgrimage," Summer 1952.

NEW LEADER for "Some Notes on F. Scott Fitzgerald," April 9, April 16, 1951.

PARTISAN REVIEW for "Come Back to the Raft Ag'in, Huck Honey!" June 1948; "Montana," December 1949; and "Looking Backward," May-June 1952.

Introduction to the
Second Edition

THOUGH some of the essays included in this volume are now more than twenty years old and none less than fifteen, certain subjects with which they deal have recently come back into the center of everyone's concern, especially that of the young, while others have continuously vexed and titillated all of us during the intervening decade or two.

I myself, for instance, have expanded the central insights first developed in the few pages of "Come Back to the Raft Ag'in, Huck Honey!" into the thousand-page trilogy which begins with *Love and Death in the American Novel*, goes on to *Waiting for the End*, and concludes with *The Return of the Vanishing American*. And these books have become for a new generation of teachers in universities, colleges and high schools, the basis for a new understanding of our classic books and of our culture in general, as well as the model for critical studies which do not even bother to acknowledge their source—as if everyone had always known what was really at issue between Huck and Jim on the raft.

Even more importantly, that erotic archetype which I began to explore in 1948 has come closer and closer to the surface of the nonacademic American mind, appearing quite explicitly as a controlling theme in currently popular novels like Ken Kesey's,

One Flew Over the Cuckoo's Nest, in recent movies like *The Defiant Ones* and *The Fortune Cookie,* and even in presumably unsophisticated television series like *I Spy.* And, finally, during the past year Mark Twain's masterpiece has been rewritten by John Seelye as *The True Huckleberry Finn,* a version in which the line, "Come back to the raft again, Huck Honey," actually composed by me for my own purposes, appears twice over in the dialogue.

Less clearly, but just as inevitably, many of the contradictory impulses memorialized in *Montana; or the End of Jean-Jacques Rousseau*—impulses which led me first to abandon the East, then to criticize the place to which I had come—presently possess the minds of the those young men and women, the children of fathers who unlike me stayed in the Urban East, who are just now abandoning the city and moving into what survives of the West. Such young wanderers constitute a third westward migration which promises to become as significant in the making of American culture as was the mid-nineteenth-century first wave. I can now see my own move as part of a small second wave, whose goals were more ironically and less sentimentally defined than either of the other two since we sought not mining camps (like the first) or communes (like the third) but only universities and colleges, fortresses of culture in a dying wilderness. But we managed all the same to keep alive in a time of paralysis and timidity the notion of heading westward, the dream of getting out.

Most crucial to the moment, however, are my essays on Alger Hiss and the Rosenbergs, since the latter especially are being refurbished as political heroes, noble victims appropriate to an age when leftwing politics has become fashionable once more. There is something touchingly absurd in the attempt to make such devious spokesmen of a movement whose chief aim was to remain invisible into symbols of a proud and courageous resistance to an oppressive system. They sought only to seem like good servants of that system, faithful bureaucrats or loyal technicians —as averse to treason as anyone; and their posthumous recasting as rebels is a function of that ignorance of history which is the special blessing as well as the fatal handicap of the young. What irked me, however, when I first wrote about the Rosenbergs (in what few remember was intended to be a protest against their pointless execution) and Hiss was their refusal of candor and heroism, their failure to stand up in court and define just what it was they had done and just what beliefs had prompted their actions. I like to think that, however current sentimentality may falsify the actual situation of the Rosenbergs, it was precisely such exposures of their cowardice and confusion which make it possible now in a new age of political oppression for defendants like the Chicago Seven to stand up in court and to shout loud and clear just what they are guilty of, rather than to whimper about their innocence and superior patriotic devotion. I hope, in any event, that in the decades to come, even if some of those more candid revolutionaries have to die, none of them will try to seem to die for nothing, to die by mistake, as did the Rosenbergs.

I reread and rethink these essays at a moment when I myself am living through a political trial, and I find it a little uncanny to discover how my imagination has always haunted the courtroom, which has from the first seemed to me not merely a forum but a theater where those uninhibited and courageous enough can perform a kind of drama absurd enough to seem true in a time of total absurdity. I would have preferred not to have been an actor on such a stage, though obviously I have long dreamed myself there in others' boots—as Alger Hiss, as Julius Rosenberg, as the now nearly anonymous victims of Joe McCarthy—dreamed myself, that is to say, failing the chance to say in the spotlight and to a packed house who I really am and for what I am truly prepared to suffer. But circumstances have taken the choice out of my hands so that reprinting the record of such dreams now constitutes a way of making amends in advance for my own inevitable failure to be quite brave or quite true enough.

Preface

Reading over my essays for the purpose of making this collection has been an instructive, though somewhat sobering, experience. Certain phrases that must have struck me once as apt or beautiful I have found not even comprehensible; while certain emphases seem now excessive, and certain declarations of conviction over-rhetorical. I have not hesitated to prune and amend and rewrite where it seemed profitable, though in no case have I made a major change; and several of these pieces I have not retouched at all. I have, as a matter of fact, been pleased to discover how often I have managed to tell what still seems to me the truth about my world and myself as a liberal, intellectual, writer, American, and Jew. I do not mind, as some people apparently do, thinking of myself in such categorical terms; being representative of a class, a generation, a certain temper seems to me not at all a threat to my individuality. As one who dearly loves a generalization (this the reader will soon discover), I relish all that is typical, even me; and I like to think of myself as registering through my particular sensibility the plight of a whole group.

I must hasten to add, however, that the groups for which I think I speak often regard me not as their appointed mouthpiece but as a rather presumptuous apostle to the gentiles; and this (I confess) I do not find *altogether* distasteful. By instinct and training I am polemical — and preaching to the converted has no appeal for me at all. Of course, I do not enjoy being misunderstood, and have suffered in the past when something written in pure rage and love (my Rosenberg article) has been called "gloating." But I will always remember with real joy the cry from the soul of a young man I met for a moment and by chance. Discovering that I had written "Come Back to the Raft," he looked at me reproachfully through a long minute of silence, and then in an impassioned whisper asked: "Why did you *do* it?" This, I suspect, is success.

My essays are not only polemical; they are occasional. I have really a certain uneasiness about committing myself to print, and I certainly do not have the kind of temperament that permits me to make a list of "important subjects" and write on them one by one. It is only when infuriated by some stupid or malicious argument or harried by an importunate editor (usually both) that I can begin to write; and I must express here my thanks to the editors who have harried me out of indolence and silence, especially Irving Kristol, formerly with *Commentary* and now co-editor of *Encounter,* who has persuaded me, protesting and stalling, to get down much that I should regret having left unsaid. The origin of these articles is therefore various; some began life as book reviews or speeches, one as a lecture in Italian to an advanced class in English in a high school in Reggio Calabria. And yet they have common metaphors, common themes, a common center. There is even from essay to essay an occasional repetition of phrase, the reiteration of a key fact, which I have preferred to leave rather than recast the pattern of the individual pieces.

The title of this book is intended not, I trust, to impose but to make explicit the real unity which has been present in my writing over the last several years, and of which I was not until now quite aware. This thematic unity runs, I think, not only through the kind of article to which this selection is limited, but through my stories and poems, as well as my "purely" literary essays. In the three sections of this book, however, the reader will find primarily pieces dealing with political events, the American scene, and literature as a cultural fact, evidence of attitudes and archetypes that shape our relations to each other and the rest of the world. The articles on Fitzgerald and the American novel go beyond this, but in the context I suspect that their sociological aspects will be emphasized out of proportion.

Indeed, I feel just a little misrepresented by a first book so largely political. I think of myself as *primarily* a literary person, though one whose interest in works of art is dictated by a moral passion rather than a cooler technical concern; and I do not hesitate to admit that I write of politics reluctantly, in a world where to ignore them would mean to be less than human. I have no expert knowledge in political matters and am an indifferent researcher; but I have lived (deeply, though somewhat grudgingly, involved) through a crisis in liberalism which seems to me a major event in the development of the human spirit. This crisis I feel peculiarly qualified to describe, precisely *because* I am a literary man, immune to certain journalistic platitudes and accustomed to regard men and words with a sensibility trained by the newer critical methods. It is a "close reading" of recent events that I should like to think I have achieved, a reading that does not scant ambiguity or paradox, but tries to give to the testimony of a witness before a Senate committee or the letters of the Rosenbergs the same careful scrutiny we have learned to practice on the shorter poems of John Donne.

L. A. F.

Contents

PART ONE

AN AGE OF INNOCENCE

CHAPTER ONE

Hiss, Chambers, and the Age of Innocence

You will either aid in moulding history, or history will mould you, and in the case of the latter, you can rest assured that you will be indescribably crushed and maimed in the process. . . . History is not a blind goddess, and does not pardon the blindness of others.

— WHITTAKER CHAMBERS (1931)

Alger Hiss went to prison on March 29, 1951. The last legal judgments have been passed. The decision of the courts stands: guilty as charged — guilty in fact of treason, though technically accused only of perjury. It is time, many of us feel, to forget the whole business: the prison doors have closed; let us consider the question also closed. But history is not so easily satisfied. Like some monumental bore, it grabs us by the lapels, keeps screaming into our faces the same story over and over again. The case of Judith Coplon, the case of Julius and Ethel Rosenberg, the inevitable case of tomorrow's Mr. X — the names change but the meanings are the same, and we protest that we have long since got the point. But have we? Of what was Alger Hiss guilty anyhow?

The statute of limitations protected Hiss against the charge of having passed secret material from State Department files to his accuser Whittaker Chambers, of having placed in the hands of agents of the Soviet Union documents which, whatever their intrinsic value, enabled our present enemies to break some of our most important codes. The transaction had taken place in 1936 and 1937 — a war away, in years we ourselves

3

find it difficult to remember, in years some of us don't want
to remember. It is a painful thing to be asked to live again
through events ten years gone, to admit one's identity with the
person who bore one's name in a by now incredible past. It is
hardest of all to confess that one is responsible for the acts of
that past, especially when such acts are now placed in a new
and unforeseen context that changes their meaning entirely.
"Not guilty!" one wants to cry; "that is not what I meant at
all!"

And yet the qualifying act of moral adulthood is precisely
this admission of responsibility for the past and its consequences, however undesired or unforeseen. Such a recognition
Hiss was called upon to make. Had he been willing to say,
"Yes, I did these things — things it is now possible to call
'treason' — not for money or prestige, but out of a higher
allegiance than patriotism"; had he only confessed in the name
of any of the loftier platitudes for which men are prepared
publicly to admit the breaking of lesser laws — then he need
not even have gone to prison. Why did he lie?

Had Hiss told the truth, the whole meaning of the case might
have been different, might have attained that dignity of tragedy
for which Alistair Cooke* looks through its dossiers in vain.
The defenders of Hiss, and of the generation they take him to
represent, would have been delivered from the intolerable
plight that prompted them, during the trials, to declare at one

---

*Alistair Cooke, *A Generation on Trial.* In addition to Mr. Cooke's book,
a thorough and scrupulous work, though one with many of whose interpre-
tations I disagree, I have used for this article De Toledano and Lasky's
Seeds of Treason, which is marred by a journalistic and melodramatic style,
but contains much valuable background material and sets the Hiss case in an
illuminating context of Communist espionage on two continents. I have
also consulted the newspaper accounts of the case, particularly those of the
New York *Times,* and the printed hearings of the House Un-American
Activities Committee; for the further background, I have turned to the
New Masses for 1931, and various other official Communist publications.
I do not know personally either of the principals in the case, nor have I made
any attempt to communicate with them. I have no private or special sources
of information. What I have attempted in this piece is an analysis based on
publicly available documents, considered in the light of my own experience
and knowledge of that world of values and beliefs out of which the incidents
of the case arose. It is the lack of such experience and knowledge which
makes even Mr. Cooke's careful and subtle book miss what seems to me the
essential point.

and the same time that (a) Hiss was innocent of the charges, the victim of a malevolent psychopath, and (b) even if he was technically guilty, he had the moral right, in those years of betrayal leading to Munich, to give his primary loyalty to the Soviet Union. Why did he lie and, lying, lose the whole point of the case in a maze of irrelevant data· the signature on the transfer of ownership of a car, the date a typewriter was repaired . . . ?

The lie, it is necessary to see, was no mere accident, but was of the essence of the case, a clue to the deepest significance of what was done and to the moral atmosphere that made the deed possible. We can see Hiss's lie now in a larger context, beside the fantastic affirmations of innocence by Julius and Ethel Rosenberg. These were not, after all, common criminals, who plead innocent mechanically on the advice of counsel; these were believers in a new society, for whose sake they had already deceived their closest friends and endangered the security of their country. In the past (and even yet in the present — the Puerto Rican nationalists, for instance), such political idealists welcomed their trials as forums, opportunities to declare to the world the high principles behind their actions, the loyalty to the march of history and the eventual triumph of socialism that had brought them to the bar. They might have been, in some eyes at least, spectacular martyrs; they chose to behave instead, before the eyes of all, like blustering petty thieves.

Not that the avowals of innocence, especially in the case of Hiss, were not affecting. Despite the absurdity of his maunderings about "forgery by typewriter," there was something moving — for a generation brought up on stories of Dreyfus and Tom Mooney, and growing to social awareness through the Sacco-Vanzetti trial and the campaigns to free the Scottsboro boys — in Hiss's final courtroom pose as The Victim. Even now, it is hard to realize how little claim he has to the title. For here was no confessed revolutionary, marked by his avowed principles, his foreign accent, his skin color, as fair game for the frame-up; here was a super-eminently respectable civil servant from the better schools, accused by the obvious outsider, the self-declared rebel and renegade, Whittaker Chambers. Hiss seemed to desire both the pathos of the persecuted and the aura of unblemished respectability. His is, as we shall see, the Popular Front mind at bay, incapable of honesty even when there is no hope in anything else.

After the hung jury, the second trial, the reams of evidence that frittered away the drama in boredom, one thing is quite clear. Twenty of twenty-four jurors, presumably twenty of twenty-four of us, believed that Alger Hiss was guilty of the perjury with which he was charged, of the treason with which he could not be charged.

For many, that verdict may be sufficient; for some, it is not enough. These cannot help feeling that the total issue of the guilt or innocence of Alger Hiss remains still to be solved. The verdict of the courts applies only to the "facts" as defined by precedent and law, a few fragments torn from their rich human contexts and presented to a group of men deliberately chosen for their relative ignorance of those contexts, and for the likelihood of their not being sympathetically involved with the passions and motives which underlay them.

Is there any sense in which Hiss is *symbolically* innocent — in which he may, indeed, have made the mistake of having passed certain papers via Chambers to the Russian agent, Colonel Bykov, but out of such naive devotion to the Good that it is a travesty of justice to find him on merely technical grounds "guilty"? It sometimes seems possible that when a Rosenberg or a Hiss speaks publicly of his "innocence," he is merely using a convenient shorthand for an account of motives and actions too complex to set before an ordinary juryman without completely re-educating him. One of the distinctive features of the recent series of "spy" trials has been that the accused and the chief accusers have been intellectuals, whereas the jury, the lawyers on both sides, even the judges, were not. And since in this country the intellectuals have been notoriously set apart from the general public, living, especially since the Russian Revolution, by different values and speaking a different language, communication is difficult. How can people who do not read the same books, and whose only relationship is one of distrust, arrive at a common definition of innocence and guilt?

One might argue on these grounds that what a jury could have meant by voting "guilty" is ridiculously far from the truth; that Hiss is not what the average mind, brought up on E. Phillips Oppenheim and pulp fiction, means by a "traitor"; that he can surely feel himself neither venal nor skulking, for he has always been faithful in intent to his true fatherland, Humanity; that if in fact he has ended up by helping the interests of just another imperialist power, the Soviet Union, it is not his crime but that of the Soviet Union, which he took in good faith to be the deputy of mankind's best interests.

This was Henry Julian Wadleigh's defense: a minor source of information for Chambers in the pre-war years, and a witness at the Hiss trials, he attempted to declare his innocence and guilt at the same time. With no sign of contrition, he admitted passing secret documents to Chambers but insisted that his course had been justified by history; it had not even occurred to him, he explained condescendingly, as a matter of conscience — though merely joining the Communist party had, and he had finally *not* signed up.

The comic aspects of Wadleigh strike one first — the cartoonist's pink-tea radical, with his thick glasses, disordered hair, and acquired Oxford accent. The articles which he wrote for the New York *Post* are classics of unconscious humor, monuments to smugness and self-pity, and trailers for the novel which (of course!) he was busy writing about his Experience. When Hiss's lawyers found they could not pin on Wadleigh the stealing of the papers Chambers had disconcertingly produced, they were content to make him the butt of their jokes. At several points during his questioning, the judge had to cover his mouth with his hand to preserve the dignity of the court. Wadleigh is the comic version of Alger Hiss.

The clowning of Wadleigh reveals what is not so easily read in Hiss: a moral obtuseness which underlies the whole case. Mr. Cooke tries to make of Wadleigh his tragic figure, but the true protagonist of tragedy suffers and learns. Wadleigh has learned nothing. He cannot conceive of having done anything *really* wrong. He finds in his own earlier activities only a certain excessive zeal, overbalanced by good will, and all excused by — Munich. Was he not a better man for having tried to counter, however ineptly, the shameful appeasement of Hitler? That the irony of events had made him, just in so far as he was more idealistic and committed, more helplessly the tool of evil, he cannot conceive. In the end, his "confession" is almost as crass a lie as the denial of Hiss — a disguise for self-congratulation, a device for clinging to the dream of innocence. He cannot, even in the dock, believe that a man of liberal persuasion is capable of wrong.

It was this belief that was the implicit dogma of American liberalism during the past decades, piling up a terrible burden of self-righteousness and self-deceit to be paid for on the day when it would become impossible any longer to believe that the man of good will is identical with the righteous man, and that the liberal is *per se* the hero. That day came at different times to different people: for some it was the Moscow Trials, for others the Soviet-Nazi pact, and for a good many — including a large number who had, during the war, regained lost illusions — it came on August 17, 1948, when Hiss and Chambers were brought face to face before the House Committee on Un-American Activities.

The facts were clear from the moment of confrontation, but for many the facts did not matter. Chambers stated flatly that Hiss had been a Communist, his associate in the "underground"; Hiss as flatly denied it. Simply to ask *cui bono* would have been enough: which one of the men stood to gain by lying? But somehow such a common-sense approach seemed excluded. The most fantastic psychological explanations were dredged up. One heard via the intellectual underground the unlikeliest proto-Dostoevskian stories to suggest reasons for Chambers' self-vilifying testimony. *Psychopathia Sexualis* was hauled out and Freud quoted glibly by the same skeptics who had laughed at the psychologizing explanations of the Moscow Trials.

But there remained still the detailed circumstantiality of Chambers' memories, the documents stolen from the office in which Hiss had worked, the microfilms taken from the dusty dumbwaiter in Brooklyn and hidden in the famous pumpkin on Chambers' Maryland farm. For all the theatrical instincts of Chambers, who seemed to possess a flair for adding one artistic touch too many to any situation (out of God knows what compulsion), the documents were there — the undeniable goods.

An unbiased look at the proceedings of the House Committee reveals that from the start Hiss quite apparently lied, or, more precisely, half lied and equivocated with the canniness of the trained lawyer. During the trials his version of the events was delivered with great aplomb, but before the Committee one can see him uncertainly feeling his way into the situation, cautiously finding out at each point how much he will have to admit to escape entrapment.

At first, he said simply that to the best of his knowledge (the qualifying phrase hardly seemed significant, a lawyer's habit), he had never met the man Chambers who had named him as one of a Washington cell of infiltrators. There was no mention of espionage, it must be remembered, until Hiss had forced Chambers' hand. Then, advised perhaps of the convincing nature of Chambers' testimony, he began slowly to shift ground, first, however, taking the initiative and charging with increasing surliness that the Committee had been leaking back to Chambers everything he said. At this point the Committee, which had handled him until then with more than normal sympathy, began to press him hard. He could not say for sure, Hiss now testified, but he thought that certainly he had known no one who called himself "Chambers," or anyone who looked very like the photographs he had been shown. They were, however, not very good pictures; so he could not be positive. Indeed, the face on the photograph before him might be that of the chairman of the Committee. It was his last joke.

Finally, he admitted that he had, after all, known the man in question, under a name he had written down on a pad in front of him. It was "George Crosley" (Chambers was later to say that, although he had used many names, he was quite sure he had never used that one), a dead-beat writer whom he had known casually, and with whom he had occasionally talked over possible story material, though he had really found the man despicable. As a matter of fact, he had even once, for certain obscure reasons, let the dead-beat move into his apartment for a couple of days, or was it weeks; and when Crosley had welshed on the rent, Hiss, for reasons even more obscure, had given him a car — just a little old car, it must be understood, with a "sassy" rumble seat, though one, Hiss admitted, to which he had been sentimentally attached. It is a fantastic story, enough to send anyone less well placed to jail without further ado. Later, there was to be a good deal of trouble over the dates of this strange transaction — and records were to turn up proving that the car had never been presented to Crosley-Chambers at all, but apparently to the Communist party!

All the while this amazing farrago was being served up by Hiss, Chambers was patiently building up the story of their actual relationship, born in intrigue and common devotion to an ideal, and destined to end in bitterness and mutual accusation. They had been comrades and close friends, Chambers said, he and the promising young lawyer, whom he was still able to describe as "of a great gentleness and sweetness of character." At first, their dealings were concerned only with dues and reports, but they quickly grew closer together, in the sort of relationship hard to parallel outside the party, the two of them utterly dependent on each other's loyalty, and both betting their self-esteem on the truth of the Marxist-Leninist dream.

They are men who could never have met outside the Communist movement, and even as Communists they were utterly different: Chambers the romantic recruit of the 1920's, hating a world that had rebuffed him at every encounter, and choosing the movement as an alternative to suicide; Hiss, universally respected, and by nature an opportunist, but with a streak of social conscience (personified in his earnest wife, who could not even let a casual visitor call the day "fine" without reminding her of the plight of the sharecroppers), choosing the party to protect himself from a merely selfish kind of success. Different as they were, Chambers had found Hiss a "real Bolshevik," perhaps sensing in him a kind of hardness to which he himself could only aspire, and had defended him against the sneers of their Russian boss, Bykov, who always referred to Hiss condescendingly as "our dear lawyer."

The quality of the feeling that must have existed between the two men is revealed by Chambers' last-minute attempt to draw Hiss with him out of the party, after he himself had become convinced that the Soviet Union was serving not justice but her own selfish national interests. Feeling that he might well be killed by party agents after his desertion (such political murders have occurred even in America), Chambers nevertheless risked exposing himself by a final visit to Hiss's home. But Hiss had stood firm, scarcely listening to the arguments of Chambers, though he had finally wept a little (the scene stays in the imagination, the completely unexpected, uncharacteristic tears), and had given to Chambers a trivial Christmas present for his daughter — "a little rolling pin."

Perhaps, even before the break, Hiss was already tired of Chambers as a person, a little ashamed of his admiration for the shabby writer who wrote nothing, and who had a tendency to remake his experience as he told about it, retouching and bringing up the highlights here and there. Mrs. Hiss had distrusted him from the first, finding him, with a strange inconsistency for a genteel internationalist, "too foreign." They had pretended finally, Alger and "Crosley," that "Crosley" was a Russian, which made him all right, of course; and Chambers had played up to it with all his love of subterfuge.

Whatever the status of their personal relations, when Chambers had come to Hiss with his talk about the Moscow Trials and the betrayal of the revolution, Hiss already could not afford to listen to him. He had by then too much to lose; for, without ceasing to be a Bolshevik, he had become a "success," a respectable citizen. To acknowledge that Russia could be fundamentally wrong would have changed the whole meaning of his own life, turned what had perhaps seemed to him his most unselfish and devoted acts, the stealing of State Department documents, into shameful crimes — into "treason"! Only the conviction that there was no final contradiction between his activities, public and private, could have made Hiss's life tolerable. He must have felt that what he had done as a New Deal lawyer, helping to expose the "munitions makers" in the Nye committee, or working for the AAA in the Department of Agriculture, did not contradict what he tried to do as a member of a left-wing faction in the State Department, urging certain attitudes toward Chiang Kai-shek;

and that what he had sought in both these capacities was merely completed by his "secret" work as a purveyor of information to warn the Soviet Union — his Soviet Union, mankind's Soviet Union — of the forces that worked for and against her in the inner world of diplomacy.

He was not a "traitor"! What the Un-American Activities Committee could not understand, what the two juries were certainly not able to comprehend, is that, to Hiss, his service to the party and the Soviet Union is an expression of "loyalty," not "treason." Before consenting to marry him, Remington's former wife had made him solemnly pledge "not to succeed"; to so many of the generation of Remington and Hiss, the bourgeois success of the American Dream was the final treachery, and each step forward in their personal careers had to be justified in terms of opportunities provided for infiltration. Hiss offered his "espionage" as an earnest to the inner few whose opinion mattered to him (in those days chiefly Chambers, and always himself) that he had not "sold out" to the bourgeois world in which he was making a splendid career.

No wonder Hiss was inaccessible to Chambers' arguments against the party! No wonder he seemed scarcely willing to admit Chambers' existence, refusing him his very name! It was as if Hiss had wanted to shrug off his accuser, not like a real being in the outside world, but like a nightmare. Indeed, the persistent voice of the man he had once admired must have seemed to him to possess the quality of a nightmare, speaking in its characteristic half-whisper the doubts, thrust down in himself, that could destroy his self-esteem.

And so Hiss had spoken out over the condemning voice, protesting his innocence with a vigor that contrasted oddly with Chambers' quiet tone. All the accounts speak of the voice of the accuser as one that, symbolically enough, could scarcely be heard. There is, even in the printed testimony, a sense of a counter-desire not to be heard along with the resolve to speak out. Far from seeming the vindictive persecutor of some accounts, Chambers strikes us as oddly reluctant, willing for a long time to risk perjury rather than reveal the full guilt of his former comrade. What Chambers really seems to be after is a confession of the truth from Hiss; he does not feel he can hide forever what Hiss has done, but he would prefer him to speak out himself.

Hiss, on the other hand, baits Chambers furiously, daring him to become the complete "rat," as if knowing Chambers will suffer in speaking out, as if wanting to shame and punish him. He seems to have felt sure that Chambers could not really harm him. A man does not unflaggingly succeed from high-school days to early middle age without losing something of humility, and forgetting that a single failure of the most superb luck is enough for destruction. When the end comes, when the threat of a suit for defamation against Chambers leads to the disclosure of the damning papers, to the trials of Hiss for perjury, and to the final conviction, one has the sense that both of the men are surprised.

Some of the commentators on the case have spoken of the anti-Red "hysteria" that prevailed at the time of the case, as if in such an atmosphere the cards were hopelessly stacked against Alger Hiss. But precisely the opposite is the case. He is just the type that does not normally get caught in the indiscriminate "witch hunt," which tends to pick out those who look like "witches," the visible outsiders. A woman like Assistant Secretary of Defense Anna M. Rosenberg, for instance, foreign-born and a Jew, is much more likely to be haled up without any evidence against her, while a man like Hiss can slip past the ordinary Congressman, to whom "Red" really means loud-mouth or foreigner or Jew. (Rankin, who was on the Committee when it examined Hiss, apparently spent his spare time thumbing through *Who's Who in American Jewry,* and turned all his fire on — Chambers!)

The Committee did not want to believe Chambers. They were convinced by his, and his wife's, astonishingly specific memories: though some members of the Committee had been eager to "get the goods" on the New Deal, to catch out the State Department at last, they had apparently found it difficult to put much faith in Chambers. It was impossible to like him, as one instinctively liked Hiss for the boyish charm we think of as peculiarly American. Chambers seems to have worn his unprepossessing air (he is the sort of person of whom one believes immediately quite unfounded stories of insanity and depravity) deliberately, as if he had acquired in his revolution-ary days the habit of rebuffing all admiration based on any-thing but his role in the party.

Every word he spoke declared him an ex-traitor, a present turncoat and squealer; and Hiss, sensing his inestimable advan-tage in a society whose values are largely set in boyhood when snitching is the ultimate sin, had traded on his role as the honest man confronted by the "rat." Really, Hiss kept insist-ing, they'd have to call the Harvard Club, say he'd be a few minutes late to dinner — after taking care of this unpleasant-ness. For a while it came off quite successfully, coming from one who visibly belonged, whose clothes beautifully fitted, whose manners were adequate to all occasions.

We learned later, of course, how much the genteel aspect of Hiss was itself a mask, imposed on a background of dis-order and uncertainty not unlike Chambers': the suicide of his father and sister, the undefined psychological difficulties of his stepson, into whose allowance from his actual father, we remember, the Hisses sometimes dipped for contributions to the party. It was as if Alger Hiss had dedicated himself to fulfill-ing, along with his dream of a New Humanity, the other dream his father had passed on to him with his first name — from rags to riches. How strangely the Marxist ideal and the dream of Horatio Alger blended into the motives of his treason. . . .

Any good bourgeois bristles when confronted with Whit-taker Chambers. His years as an editor on *Time* (he is "bril-liant," of course, but the adjective is itself ambivalent), his later role as a small farmer, cannot conceal his real identity as the outsider: the "butterball who could not even learn to play marbles," the writer of poetry for little magazines, the obnoxious young radical expelled from college, the uncomfort-able spirit that either blasphemes or is too religious for re-spectability. At one point, Chambers is asked by a Committee member how he spent his time during a week-long period when he had borrowed Hiss's apartment; and when he says, "Reading . . . ," one feels the troubled silence. How could anyone read so long? It is the suspicious vagary of the kind of man who once believed in Stalin and now believes in the Devil.

After his years in the "underground," he still seems ill at ease in our daylight world; and beneath the guise of the magazine executive (assumed only, we remember, to establish an "identity" for himself as a protection against being murdered by the GPU), the old Chambers persists. Everyone who had known him in his revolutionary days — except Hiss, of course — had no difficulty in recognizing Chambers at the time of the trial.

The jowls and the new teeth do not fundamentally change the face we can still see on the inside back cover of the Communist literary magazine, the *New Masses,* for July 1931. After twenty years, the young Chambers looks up at us still with the sullen certainty of one who has discovered in the revolution an answer to the insecurity and doubt which had brought his brother to suicide, himself to months of despair and near paralysis. In the movement he had found a way out of immobility, a way to join with the other insulted and injured of the earth to change the world which excluded them. To appear in the *New Masses* in those days was not merely to be a writer, but to subscribe to a new myth of the writer, summed up in the blurb under the photograph: "Youth as a periodically vagrant laborer in Deep South, Plains, Northwest. Brief Columbia College experience ending with atheist publication. . . . Joined revolutionary movement 1925. . . ."

Hiss, who really knew Chambers, of course, better than anyone else except Chambers' wife, put his finger on the sources of this myth when he told the Committee that Chambers thought of himself as a kind of Jim Tully or Jack London. To understand Chambers, one must understand the concept of the literary bum as hero that came out of Tully and London, a special Marxist class-angling of the old bohemian ideal. Chambers' once living in the same quarters with an old whore, and his stealing of library books of which Hiss's lawyers and psychiatrists were to make so much during the trials, his name-changing and wandering, were all standard procedure for the rebel-intellectual in those days.

The life style he adopted was perfected in the Communist "Third Period," in the years before 1935, and it is the Third Period we must first of all understand. The term is Lenin's, invented to describe that last stage of imperialism, the age of cataclysmic wars and revolutions; but it comes also to describe the way of life of those who believed themselves the sole carriers of the future in those final days. To the young comrades in their blue work shirts or flat-heeled shoes, there was no need to come to terms with the dying bourgeois world; Marx had told them that the point was to change it. They lived in a fine apocalyptic fury, issuing leaflets to ROTC units in Midwestern agricultural colleges, urging the "peasants and soldiers" to turn their guns the other way; they cried for an autonomous Negro republic to be carved out of the Deep South; and in the few cities where they had sufficient numbers, they were forever rushing "into the streets" to shout their resolve to "Defend the Soviet Union" against their own bourgeoisie in case of war. The only reality in their paranoid world was the Workers' Fatherland, still encircled and unrecognized by our own government. Here is a typical passage from an editorial that appeared in the *New Masses* in 1931, and so might have been written by Chambers:

It is only a question of time until all the imperialist powers mobilize their manpower and hurl its bleeding masses in a rain of steel across the frontiers, to destroy the first Socialist Republic. In this situation what are the intellectuals to do? . . . They realize, however imperfectly, that the Union of Soviet Socialist Republics represents the advance guard, the hope of human progress and civilization. . . . And they desire, the most advanced of them, to employ their minds as weapons in the fight to save the Soviet Union from its reactionary enemies.

Reread in the pages of the old magazine, in the heavy black format that seems to shriek at us across the years, and surrounded by the pen-and-ink drawings with their incredibly depraved bosses and their unbelievably noble workers, the banal paragraph seems merely unconscionably funny, like a bad silent film. But when we remember the universal loss of faith in those years of mass unemployment and of seemingly endless depression, we can appreciate the attractiveness of the Marxist answer, guaranteed by the miraculous existence of the Soviet Union, the last best hope of human culture. We sense, too, the appeal of violence in a world of words — an instant of bloodshed and the whole golden future unfolds!

No Third Perioder could have become, like a later type of Communist, really a "traitor" as distinguished from a mere "spy." How could they betray a world they publicly disavowed? Romantic and ridiculous, they were still revolutionaries, their allegiance single and unconcealed. When such Communists went underground they hid, but they never pretended to be good bourgeois. When the call came in 1932 from Max Bedacht, asking Chambers to disappear as the individual he had been in order to take on "special" work, Chambers seems to have welcomed the chance. He had already sacrificed his will to party discipline, his fate to history. He had little more to offer up beyond his name and the small fame that had become attached to it in the movement: the praise he had received in the Russian press for his stories of Communist life, the popularity of the play *Can You Hear Their Voices?*, based on one of his works, already presented at Vassar and about to be produced in Russia.

Something in his temperament seems to have greeted the prospect of self-immolation; even before he entered what the Communists mean by the "underground," he had been, in the Dostoevskian sense, an underground man, his own enemy. It had apparently pleased him to take the final step, to become one whose death it would be forbidden to notice. What did Mundt or Rankin or Nixon know of Dostoevsky, or those twenty-four jurors of the kind of alienated life that conditioned Chambers? What trick of history brought them and him into the same room, pushed them toward an uneasy alliance?

It was Hiss — the embodiment of the subsequent Popular Front era, as Chambers was the embodiment of the Third Period — who provided the common link: Hiss who had as desperately to look respectable as Chambers had not to. The New Deal had moved American politics left, and had opened the doors of the trade unions and the Washington bureaus to the university intelligentsia at the very moment when that intelligentsia had been penetrated by the Communists, and Communism had undergone two decisive changes: first, the national Communist parties had lost all initiative and internal democracy, coming under the absolute control of the Russian bureaucracy; and, second, world Stalinism had adopted the

Popular Front line of collaboration with the bourgeoisie.

No longer was the ideal Bolshevik the open rebel, the poet-bum chanting songs of protest, but the principled government worker with the pressed suit and the clean-cut look. It was the day of "fronts" and "mass organizations," of infiltrating and "capturing" and "boring from within." As the headlines in the *Daily Worker* declared peace-with-capitalism, a new kind of underground Communist moved into Washington, un-noticed among the purer, pragmatic New Dealers.

Hiss is the prototype of the new-model Bolshevik (Lee Pressman and Henry Collins and John Abt, Noel Field and George Silverman were others) who was the more valuable as he seemed less radical. Far from being urged to sell the party press, he was even discouraged from reading it. These new secret workers had never been open members of the party; they did not merely hide, but pretended to be what they were not. For the first time, a corps of Communists existed for whom "treason," in the sense of real deceit, was possible. These were not revolutionaries but Machiavellians, men with a double allegiance, making the best of two worlds and often, like Hiss, profiting immensely within the society they worked so hard to destroy.

Doubtless some of these new Bolsheviks were able to de-ceive themselves into believing that there was no actual contra-diction between their real allegiance and their pretended one. What helped the self-deception was the rise of Nazi Germany as the chief threat on the world scene, and the changing role of the Soviet Union in international affairs. The blanket phrase "anti-Fascism" covered over conflicts as deep as life itself. On the one hand, the New Deal had finally recognized the new Russian regime; and, on the other hand, Communist Russia had joined the fellowship of nations. In the League of Nations (which Lenin had long before called "a den of thieves"), Lit-vinov was calling for the unity of the anti-Fascist world. The watchword was no longer "Defend the Soviet Union!" but "Establish Collective Security!" The Communists insisted that the interests of Russia and the United States were forever iden-tical, and the majority of liberals collaborated in the hoax — which was to crash with the signing of the Soviet-Nazi pact, be ridiculously revived during the war when we were "allies," and collapse once more at the foot of the Iron Curtain. Here are the words of Earl Browder, written in the first flush of the Popular Front honeymoon:

> In this world movement, there stand out before the peace-loving peoples of the world two centers of resistance to the fascist flood, two points from which leadership and inspiration can be given to the majority of mankind struggling for democracy and peace, two rallying grounds for the hard-pressed forces of progress and culture — the Soviet Union and the United States. . . . The Soviet Union and the United States have common problems, common interests and common enemies. That is a central fact in the new world situation.

The platitudes, read in their context of rallies-for-Spain sponsored by the "big names" from Hollywood and Broadway, seem only a little less old-fashioned and absurd than those of 1931, but we must read them with attention, remembering that they made treason easy. The bureaucrat, busy making himself a niche in the government service while transmitting secret material to the Russians, didn't even have to pose to himself a moral "either-or"; in both his roles, he could consider himself serving what Browder liked to call "the spirit of Jefferson, Jackson, and Lincoln."

Before the Popular Front Communist the ordinary Congressman is helpless, unless there is a "renegade" willing to make revelations. The average legislator pursues ordinarily one of two policies in regard to Communists, springing from his profound inability or unwillingness to tell a Stalinist from a liberal. Either he lumps together as "Reds" everybody left-of-center (and even an occasional right-winger by mistake), or he refuses to recognize as a Communist anyone who denies it. The one kind of Communist likely to be missed by both approaches is the genteel Bolshevik who keeps his nose clean and never even reads the *New Republic*.

That is why the Committee was at first so completely buffaloed by Hiss. When he thundered righteously, "I am sorry but I cannot but feel to such an extent that it is difficult for me to control myself that you can sit there, Mr. Hébert, and say to me casually that you have heard that man [Chambers] and you have heard me, and that you just have no basis for judging which one is telling the truth," Hébert could only stutter lamely something about the degrading necessity of using low "stool pigeons" like Chambers and Miss Bentley.

It is easy enough to understand the shouts of "red herring!" raised in the earlier days of the case by certain old-line Democrats led by President Truman. They did not dissent on principle, but merely on party lines. If a venture sparked by Republicans is admitted to have succeeded, the Democrats stand to lose votes; and one denies anything that might lose votes. But the real liberals, in and out of the Democratic party, from whose ranks most of the actual believers in the innocence of Hiss are drawn, are a different matter. They had not even listened to the earlier testimony, out of a feeling that paying any heed to the House Committee on Un-American Activities was playing into the hands of the enemy, and that, in any event, the personnel and procedures of that Committee made it impossible for it to arrive at the truth. During the trials they paid attention for the first time.

Chambers' documentary evidence was still there, of course, and his circumstantial story was told again; but by this time Hiss was able to make a better showing than he had, taken unawares, before the Committee. He was imperturbable and glib in his testimony; and his lawyers were able to make Chambers seem more than ever a "moral leper," turning his very virtues (the lies and half-revelations by which he had attempted to protect Hiss) against him, and mocking his new-found religion. All the world distrusts a convert, but no part of it does so more heartily than the liberals. Finally, there were the psychiatrists, prepared on the basis of courtroom observation to call Chambers seriously unbalanced.

But, most important of all, there arose to stand beside Hiss, one by one, a series of respectable character witnesses, an elite corps, as it were, of the New Deal, distinguished civil servants and honored judges, until it seemed as if the whole movement that from 1932 on had swept the country out of fear and toward prosperity was staking its very reputation on the innocence of this single man. We know the character witnesses did not deliberately lie. But if they were not liars — as they certainly were *not* — they were, in some sense, fools.

It is not an easy admission, certainly not for them, but not even for those (among whom I include myself) who have admired in them a vision of national life that still appears worth striving for.

Even the wisdom of Franklin Roosevelt, the final culture hero of our liberal era, is brought into question. For he seems personally to have pooh-poohed the suspicions, relayed to him in 1940 by Ambassador Bullitt, about the reliability of Hiss. How could he have done otherwise? Was not Hiss one of those young men, mocked by the reactionary press as "brain-trusters," it had been his special pride to bring into political life? The big-city bosses, the unprincipled "experts," and the party hacks he had been forced to carry with him for expediency's sake; but these young idealists he had supported for the sake of principle. Superficially, the history of Hiss is the prototypical history of the New Dealer at his best: the distinguished years at Harvard Law School, the secretaryship to the almost mythical Justice Holmes, the brilliant career that began in the Nye committee and culminated at Teheran.

Certainly, a generation was on trial with Hiss — on trial not, it must be noticed, for having struggled toward a better world, but for having substituted sentimentality for intelligence in that struggle, for having failed to understand the moral conditions that must determine its outcome. What is involved is not any question of all or most of the younger New Dealers having been, like Hiss, secret agents of the GPU, but the question of their having been so busy denying that there was a GPU, or that it mattered, that they could not identify an enemy of all the values in which they most profoundly believed.

They cannot even flatter themselves on having been fooled by master tricksters. Hiss was, perhaps, an extraordinarily accomplished dissembler; but what of the Pressmans and the Wadleighs, more obvious in their intended deviousness? Lest the New Dealers seem "Red-baiters," they preferred to be fools. Even in the case of Hiss, disquieting reports were transmitted to his superiors from time to time, and it was noticed, on at least one occasion, that information which passed through his hands had an odd way of leaking out.

At one point A. A. Berle, after a conversation with Chambers, had gone to Dean Acheson, then Hiss's immediate superior, to report the rumor that "the Hiss boys" were members of a secret Communist group; and Acheson called in Donald Hiss to ask him if he and his brother were really Reds.

The naïveté of the thing is monumental! He asked Donald Hiss, and when Hiss said *no*, Acheson was "satisfied." After all, he had known "the Hiss boys" since they were children; they had gone to the same schools, belonged to the same clubs, could speak man to man. Dean Acheson simply could not bring himself to believe that if the Hisses, who were gentlemen, were also Communists, they would as a matter of course lie. One thinks of Mrs. Roosevelt, under somewhat similar circumstances, calling the leaders of the American Student Union into her drawing room, asking them please to tell her the real truth: were they Communists?

In part, the lack of realism shared by Acheson and Mrs. Roosevelt came from belonging to a world in which liberals and conservatives (and even radicals) are assumed to share the same moral values, the values of the old Judeo-Christian ethical system, however secularized; but, in another sense, it arises from long conditioning of the public mind by the "front organizations" of the late 1930's, through which the bulk of the liberals learned to maintain the paradox that (a) there were really no Communists, just the hallucinations of "witch hunters," and (b) if there were Communists, they were, despite their shrillness and bad manners, fundamentally on the side of justice. After all, the Communists are "left," and everyone knows that only the "right" is bad. This absurd metaphor of "leftness" managed to conceal from men of good will and some intelligence the essential fact that the Communists had ceased to subscribe to a political morality universally shared, whatever its abuses, until 1917. How many victims of this confusion were able to spend years moving in and out of Communist fronts and say blandly in the end, "To the best of my knowledge, I have never known an actual Communist"!

Seen in this larger context, the half-deliberate blindness of so many decent people, which is a vital part of the total Hiss case, explains itself. The erstwhile defenders of Hiss's innocence show a growing tendency to remain silent; but their silence does not mean, alas, that they are finally convinced. Looking through Carey McWilliams' book *Witch Hunt,* for instance, one is startled to discover, in a study of the rising tide of accusations of Communism, no mention of the name of Alger Hiss — nor, indeed, of Klaus Fuchs. So significant an oversight must mean, if not active skepticism about Hiss's guilt, a feeling that his case is somehow less relevant than those in which charges of Communism have not been substantiated.

We must clearly understand that the failure of Hiss to confess, far from casting doubt on his guilt, merely helps to define its nature. If Hiss's guilt is of the sort I have tried to indicate, it is clear that, without some change of heart or values, he could not possibly have confessed. One has only to think of the recent trial of the twelve members of the national committee of the Communist party. Even these avowed and open leaders of the movement, whom one had perhaps expected to cry out their faith proudly before the tribunal, could only plead — so ingrained had the Popular Front lie become — in the teeth of the evidence of their own early writings, that (a) they had never advocated revolution and (b) by God, it was their inalienable right as American citizens to do so. What could one expect from Hiss?

If there is a note of tragedy in the case, it is provided by Chambers, the informer driven to mortify himself and to harm those he still loved. The Third Perioder, still pursuing the absolute, makes a tragic final appearance as the scorned squealer; the Popular Fronter can only exit in the role of the hopeless liar. It is difficult to say what factor is most decisive in cutting Hiss off finally from the great privilege of confession; opportunism or perverted idealism, moral obtuseness or the habit of Machiavellianism — they are all inextricably intermingled.

In the end he failed all liberals, all who had, in some sense and at some time, shared his illusions (and who that calls himself a liberal is exempt?), all who demanded of him that he speak aloud a common recognition of complicity. And yet, perhaps they did not really want him to utter a confession; it would have been enough had he admitted a mistake rather than confessed a positive evil. Maybe, at the bottom of their hearts, they did not finally want him to admit anything, but preferred the chance he gave them to say: He is, we are, innocent.

American liberalism has been reluctant to leave the garden of its illusion; but it can dally no longer: the age of innocence is dead. The Hiss case marks the death of an era, but it also promises a rebirth if we are willing to learn its lessons. We who would still like to think of ourselves as liberals must be willing to declare that mere liberal principle is not in itself a guarantee against evil; that the wrongdoer is not always the other — "they" and not "us"; that there is no magic in the words "left" or "progressive" or "socialist" that can prevent deceit and the abuse of power.

It is not necessary that we liberals be self-flagellants. We have desired good, and we have done some; but we have also done great evil. The confession in itself is nothing, but without the confession there can be no understanding, and without the understanding of what the Hiss case tries desperately to declare, we will not be able to move forward from a liberalism of innocence to a liberalism of responsibility.

CHAPTER TWO

Afterthoughts on the Rosenbergs

Since the execution of the Rosenbergs, it has become possible to see clearly what was for a long time obscured: that there were *two* Rosenberg cases, quite distinct though referred to by a single name; and that this ambiguity made it difficult for the pro- and anti-Rosenberg forces ever to engage in a real dialogue. How often we were talking about quite different things under the same label!

The first Rosenberg case, which reached its climax with their trial in March 1951, involved certain questions of fact about the transmission of secrets to the Soviet Union, culminating in the handing over of sketches for the detonating device of the atom bomb. Implicated in this first case were: the brother of Ethel Rosenberg, David Greenglass, who made a full confession; Morton Sobell; Anatoli Yacovlev, the Russian vice-consul who had got safely out of the United States in December of 1946; and the notorious Communist "drop," Harry Gold. Through Gold, the Rosenberg case was linked with those of the confessed espionage agents, Klaus Fuchs and Allan Nunn May, woven inextricably into a context against which their guilt appeared clear beyond doubt. The denials of the Rosenbergs seemed merely the mendacious pleas of two people fighting for their lives in the face of overwhelming evidence.

In this initial open-and-shut case, scarcely anyone was very interested. In the United States, it did not stir up nearly as much discussion as the Hiss-Chambers affair, or even the trivial business of Judith Coplon. In Europe, it was ignored or meagerly reported, so that the European defenders of the

25

Rosenbergs tended to be happily ignorant of the first or factual case in its real interconnections; and this ignorance in many cases they fought desperately to preserve. The Communists themselves maintained a strange official silence about the Rosenbergs for more than a year after their arraignment, wary, presumably, about identifying themselves with a pair at once so central to their whole espionage effort and so flagrantly guilty; and baffled, no doubt, at how to defend two comrades who had been underground for six years and who refused to admit their party membership in court.

The second, or legendary, Rosenberg case was invented, along with the Committee to Secure Justice in the Rosenberg Case, at the end of October 1951 in Knickerbocker Village, a housing settlement in New York City. The place of the double birth seems almost too apt; the Rosenbergs themselves had once inhabited that melancholy block of identical dwelling units that seem the visible manifestation of the Stalinized petty-bourgeois mind: rigid, conventional, hopelessly self-righteous — the mind which dreamed the odd parody of the martyr which was the role of the Rosenbergs in their second case.*

The Rosenbergs stood alone in the new version of their plight — alone except for certain honorable ghosts. Gone were the real accomplices: Yacovlev and Sobell, Harry Gold, Klaus Fuchs and Allan Nunn May, though "Davy" Greenglass, recruited to the Movement at the age of twelve by his nineteen-year-old sister, remained to play the shadowy villain — replaced by the evoked figures of Sacco and Vanzetti, Tom Mooney, the Scottsboro Boys, and, especially, Dreyfus. The cue had been given by the "progressive" *National Guardian,* which had opened the defense campaign with a story headlined: "Is the Rosenberg Case the Dreyfus Case of America's Cold War?" The revised Rosenbergs were no longer spies, but "political prisoners" in the European sense, victims of the class struggle and the Cold War, defenders of the peace, a perse-

---

*The Rosenbergs of the second case possess a certain kind of immortality; that is, they will continue to live in the official history and art of the Communist Movement, until, for one reason or another, their particular segment of history is forgotten or refalsified. But not yet! In 1954, the hit of the season on the Warsaw stage was a play called *Ethel and Julius.*

cuted minority — these very people, it must be remembered, who would not confess their political allegiance in court, and who for six years had been under instructions not even to appear "progressive."

The long-drawn-out process of appeal in the American courts had made it possible to set up the symbolic Rosenbergs in place of the real ones; between the first exposure of two spies and the appeal of the "framed up victims before the bar of world opinion" came the year (soon two, and three) of separation and imprisonment and real suffering. The Communists banked on this stretch of time to screen their sleight-of-hand; and it worked. Even those who had followed the first trial carefully found it difficult to keep it in mind; and the maintenance of the anti-Rosenberg position soon fell largely into the hands of those who countered liberaloid sentimentality and rancor not with facts but with their own even more wretched "Down with the Communist Rats — God Bless America" sentimentality and rancor. The second, the legendary, Rosenberg case possessed the imagination of the world.

It is that second case which I wish to discuss. There is no point in rehearsing the first; as far as I am concerned, the legal guilt of the Rosenbergs was clearly established at their trial, and it is from an assumption of that guilt that I begin. What I want to examine (and this, after all, is the enduring point of the matter) is why the Rosenbergs, for all their palpable guilt, won their second case before the world; why there arose such a universal condemnation of their sentence; and why so many, in the teeth of the evidence, even believed in their innocence.

One can say in a general way that in the second case the Rosenbergs were not tried at all, but that by a bit of prestidigitation they, too, disappeared along with Gold, Yacovlev, and the rest; and that we were called upon to judge in their places Sacco and Vanzetti or Dreyfus. And how did they get in? Through the evocation of these almost traditional victims, a kind of moral blackmail was practiced on us; the flags of the gallant old causes were unfurled, and we were expected to respond by revivifying the battered belief that the political dissident (but in what sense is the present-day flag-waving Communist a dissident?), the proud rebel (but in what sense were the Rosenbergs, peering slyly out from behind the Fifth Amendment, rebellious or proud?), the Jew (but in what sense were the Rosenbergs Jews?) is always framed, that the guilt is always on the other side.

What a relief to be able to reassert that simple-minded article of faith after Fuchs and Nunn May and Hiss, and after the thousand betrayals of the Soviet Union. The fact that the Rosenbergs were remarkable chiefly for their difference from the older martyrs, that the whole point of their affair lay in that difference, was hardly remarked; scarcely anyone wanted to see them as they were, but merely to *use* them for self-exculpation — for joining together once more the ranks that had marched unbroken for Vanzetti, but had since fallen hopelessly apart.

And yet the question remains. Why this occasion rather than another; why this improbable pair; and why (outside of the United States itself) so nearly unanimous a response to their plight? To disentangle the motives that found a focus in the pro-Rosenberg movement is to write a thumbnail moral history of our time.

One must begin, I suppose, by separating out the absolute cynics, the Communist bureaucrats who used the case coldly when it was convenient to use it, as they had ignored it calmly when it was convenient to ignore it; and who knew that they could not lose in any event. For if the freeing of the Rosenbergs would have been for them a minor victory, their death was a major one in the struggle against the United States. After a certain point, the energies of such functionaries were patently directed at insuring that clemency would not be granted. I do not want to seem to make master-minds out of shabby Communist bureaucrats, but surely a certain elementary cunning rather than mere stupidity led them to do everything that would infuriate official American opinion, make any revision of the death sentence seem an admission of a judicial error.

It is no accident, I think, that the only plea which came near saving the Rosenbergs was prompted by an outsider who had been expelled from both the Communist party and the Communist-controlled defense committee. The suffering and death of the Rosenbergs were *willed* by the makers of Communist opinion and relished by them, as every new lynching in America, every bit of violence against the Jews, is willed and relished as further evidence that they are right! These are the professional accomplices of calamity; and if they cried "innocent," it was because they thought that the greatest possibility of disaster lay in such an assertion.

These conscious exploiters of the case were a tiny minority, yet one which had ready to hand a mass of naïve communicants already trained to believe, sincerely and even fervently, what that minority decided they should believe. In this sense, one can think of the bacterial-warfare campaign and the various "peace" petitions as preparations for the Rosenberg case, as the Rosenberg case in turn is no end in itself but a rehearsal for the next real or manufactured issue on the Communist agenda. This prefabricated public is made up not only of the naïver party members, activists to whom ideas are unknown and the mute attenders of meetings, but also of fellow-travelers and the "innocents" who read nothing but the Communist press, or even only the Communist posters (knowing, of course, that all other sources of information are "bought"). For such believers an event does not even *exist*, much less have a significance, until it is recognized by their journals; and so for them there had simply been *no* Rosenberg case until the party had given the go-ahead signal after months of discreet silence. For them, only the legendary case was real.

The Communists have long controlled in Europe large numbers of "advanced" workers, peasants, and petty bourgeois by manipulating a mythology inherited from a hundred years of political struggle: the belief that the state and its courts are always wrong; that the bourgeoisie is always wrong; and especially that the United States, the bastion of capitalism, is always wrong* — with the corollaries that no Negro, Jew, or "progressive" (i.e., Communist or sympathizer) can ever be anything but innocent. This group was joined by an even larger periphery, stalinized to the extent of not believing its own

---

*Only the notion that priests are always wrong could not be exploited in the Rosenberg case; otherwise it was a perfect ritual expression of the sub-Marxist catechism.

press and of accepting in critical instances the opinions screamed in the piazzas by those whom they consider more "devoted" and "unselfish" than themselves, because they are louder and more assured. Together these formed a sizable public which appears really to have believed that the Rosenbergs were innocent in the basic sense of the word, guiltless of the crime with which they were charged. This they knew, not from scrutinizing the record, but from consulting the opinions of those who had always defined for them the truth. They would have believed it quite as firmly if there had been no such people as the Rosenbergs — as, in a sense, there were not.

Such a rank and file, stalinized at second and third remove, did not exist in the United States, which possesses in their place a mass of people politically innocent and merely indifferent to such affairs in a way no European can understand. To this oppositely corresponding American group, the *second* Rosenberg case had no existence; so that between them and their European opposite numbers there was not even ground enough for real disagreement.

In both Europe and America, however, a substantial minority of intellectuals shared a third position which asserted the innocence of the Rosenbergs, or at least maintained the final irrelevance of their guilt. This position combined in varying proportions two complementary attitudes: the *wish* that the Rosenbergs might actually be innocent; and the conviction that they were *symbolically* guiltless whatever action they may have committed. The first feeling led to an incantatory declaration of the Rosenbergs' guiltlessness, based on the belief that what these intellectuals repeated with truly unselfish fervor could not help but prove true; and, in any event, the Rosenbergs *couldn't* have done it, couldn't have committed treason — or these intellectuals, too, might have been guilty of as sordid a crime when in their own heedless youth they also had been Communists or had at least defended in perfect self-righteousness their Communist friends against the "Redbaiters."

But, even if the Rosenbergs *had* performed the act, this line of argument continues, treason was not what they had meant; they had been acting for a better world, for all Humanity (i.e., for the Soviet Union, whose interests all the more enlightened had once known were identical with those of mankind); and, anyhow, Russia had been our ally when the Rosenbergs gave them a helping hand, standing with us side by side against the Nazis; and, after all, Russia had not yet used the Bomb, will never use it, never, never, *never* (to stop believing this would mean having to rethink their whole lives), so that sharing the atomic secret in this somewhat unorthodox fashion was really a blow for world peace: just look at the present *détente,* etc., etc. In light of all which, isn't it better simply to declare that the Rosenbergs are "innocent," as a kind of shorthand for an analysis too complicated to explain to the uninitiated without re-educating them completely.

How near the conscious surface such reasoning was carried on must have varied from case to case; but in almost every instance it led to the by-now-customary double bookkeeping of the Communists' friends, the exploitation of a vocabulary which makes it possible to say, at one and the same time, "They didn't do it at all; it's a frame-up!" and, "After all, they had a right; their hearts were pure!" This is a fantastic enough position in any event, but when held by the accused themselves (and it *was* held by the Rosenbergs, as I shall show), it becomes utterly fantastic, the obverse of those equally absurd "symbolic" declarations of guilt in the rigged Russian trials.

Finally,* one is left with those who cried only for mercy, for the conversion of the death sentence, "even if they were guilty as charged." It is difficult to disentangle the position itself from those who maintained it; to redeem it from the scandalous way it was used by the Communists, who sought to confuse hopelessly the two kinds of protest, to make every cry for grace seem an assertion of innocence, and more: a condemnation of the United States, the Atlantic Pact, the European Army, and God knows what else. One is so ap-

---

*I am relegating to this footnote the "diplomatic" advocates of mercy — those who urged a revision of the sentence in order to "placate world opinion" or in order "not to give the Communists a martyr." This was not an important group, and the point of the whole case is precisely that the Rosenbergs were *incapable* of becoming martyrs.

palled at the cynicism of many of the exploiters of "mercy," with their own record of political executions without appeal, without trials — and after the most ignominious of self-degradations — that he is tempted to discount the whole movement.

Even where the Communists played only a secondary role, there was evident in the shrillness of the cries of horror (rising from countries where only a little while before the lynching of political enemies was considered an act of virtue) a desire to celebrate the fall of America from innocence, to indulge in an orgy of self-righteousness at our expense. There is no political act (and the simplest cry for clemency was inevitably a political act) that is not marred these days by the obsessive envy and anguish of the Europeans in our regard. If the Europeans could only have believed as firmly as they pretended that we had utterly yielded to hysteria and persecution, the balance of guilt that tilts so annoyingly in their direction would have been righted; and they might have loved us more, not less. But they could only *want* to believe this, not really credit it — any more than they have been able to really accept the stories of germ warfare in Korea. In a Europe that tends to admire where it is horrified, and to be overwhelmed by the fascination of ruthlessness, even our approximate innocence, or the mere inefficiency at terror that is its equivalent, is a reproach.

Yet, allowing for all that was stage-managed or disingenuous in the pleas for clemency; discounting the rather professional nature of some of the ecclesiastical protests; allowing for the sob sisters who are ready to howl bitterly at the sentencing of the most sadistic wretch; setting aside the pleading based on a general condemnation of the death penalty, which does not bear precisely on this case; and discounting the almost mechanical reflex of those to whom since Hitler any threat to any Jew seems a recrudescence of the old horror, one comes to a residual protest that cannot be explained away, and in the face of which we must as Americans admit a real, a perhaps tragic, failure of the moral imagination.

The final protest that existed behind all the others based on stupidity or malice or official dogma was the humane one. Under their legendary role, there were, after all, *real* Rosenbergs, unattractive and vindictive but human; fond of each other and of their two children; concerned with operations for tonsillitis and family wrangles; isolated from each other during three years of not-quite-hope and deferred despair; at the end, prepared scientifically for the electrocution: Julius' mustache shaved off and the patch of hair from Ethel's dowdy head (and all this painfully documented by the morning papers in an America that can keep no secrets); finally capable of dying. This we had forgotten, thinking of the Rosenbergs as merely typical, seeing them in the context of a thousand other petty-bourgeois Stalinists we had known, each repeating the same shabby standard phrases. That they were individuals and would die they themselves had denied in every gesture — and we foolishly believed them. In the face of their own death, the Rosenbergs became, despite themselves and their official defenders, symbols of the conflict between the human and the political, the individual and the state, justice and mercy; and this symbolic conflict only those who knew they were guilty could fully appreciate.

It is, in the end, no mere matter of protesting an excessive sentence, but of realizing that they *count,* these people moved always like puppets from above, that they count as *human,* though they committed treason in disregard of all real human considerations in the name of an intolerably abstract "Humanity." It is wonderful in a way that two individuals did still count to so many people in a world as accustomed as ours to mass slaughter and injustice become mere routine.

There is no sense in becoming enraged at the fact that these two, our *only* two victims, should have stirred up the response that could not be brought to focus for the millions of victims of Soviet firing squads; that most of the world should have been crying out for the lives of two American spies, convicted by due process, at the very moment when Willy Goettling and a score of nameless others were being summarily shot in Soviet Berlin. We should rather be flattered that as a nation we continue to act on a plane where moral judgment is still possible; elsewhere assertions of human value seem merely pointless, and the only possible protest is silence, the resolve at least not to hail institutionalized murder as social justice.

Some Americans have, indeed, felt flattered at being among the last peoples to whom real protest is still conceivable, not merely permitted by law, but possible to the uncorrupted moral sense; and they have been willing to stop there, arguing that this very fact sanctions the execution of the Rosenbergs, by proving it the sort of exceptional act we can still morally afford when political considerations demand it. But the point is surely that clemency to the Rosenbergs was what we could *not* afford to deny. The world had turned to us (that part at least still not hopelessly stalinized) for a symbolic demonstration that somewhere a government existed willing to risk the loss of political face for the sake of establishing an unequivocal moral position. A minority at least understood that the Communists were doing everything in their power to make any concession on our part seem a cowardly retreat; but they hoped we would have the courage to seem in that sense cowardly. I cannot help feeling that even among the rank-and-file Stalinists there existed on some deeply buried level the shadowy desire for someone somewhere to assert that the political man was not all of man, that our humanity is neither fictional nor irrelevant.

This opportunity we let slip away from us, in part because of our political innocence, in part through a lack of moral imagination, but also through a certain incapacity to really believe in Communists as people. In the official declarations of Eisenhower, one senses behind the cold reasoning from cause to effect, and the shaky conclusion that the secrets transmitted by the Rosenbergs unleashed the Korean War, the failure of the military mind to see beyond a justice defined in codes. In the justifications of Judge Kaufman, on the other hand, one feels a personal hysteria — a fear of Communism magnified by the sense that in the United States, where so many Stalinists have been Jews, the acts of the Rosenbergs were an attainder of the whole Jewish population. But the Rosenbergs were not, after all, excessively punished merely because their fates happened to rest in the hands of a military man and a Jew, but because mass opinion in America, in so far as it took notice of them at all, *wanted* their deaths, as an example and token.

When counter-pickets to the Rosenberg defenders carried

placards demanding "Death to the Communist Rats!" there was involved, beyond an old American metaphor for spies, a wish to believe that the enemy is subhuman, an animal to exterminate rather than a man to confront. Needless to say, the Communists themselves need no lessons in this sort of manoeuver; we have only to remember the words of the Rosenbergs' lawyer before the White House on the eve of their death: "I don't know what animals I am dealing with, but I know that I am dealing with animals." Yet we have no right to let ourselves be provoked into answering the Communists with equivalent strategies; differently from them, we still have much to lose; and in trying to dehumanize our opponents we may end by dehumanizing ourselves.

When the news of the Rosenbergs' long-delayed execution was announced before the White House, the counter-pickets cheered. A critical episode in the moral and political coming of age of America had reached its climax; the hopes for a world of equity and peace that had moved the more sensitive and intelligent in the 1920's and 1930's, had been used as camouflage by a brutally imperialistic power and had ended by leading two undistinguished people into a trap of lies and espionage and death; and the counter-pickets *cheered!* One is tempted to echo the words of Irwin Edelman* just before he was chased out of Pershing Square by an irate crowd: "If you are happy about the execution of the Rosenbergs, you are rotten to the core!" But, if this reaction seems the final indignity, there is much worse to come.

Our failure placed in the hands of the Communists the

---

*Edelman is one of the most extraordinary figures in the whole affair. Thrown out of the Communist party in Los Angeles in 1947 for advocating more inner party democracy, and expelled from the official Rosenberg defense committee as a heretic, he nonetheless provided the nearest thing to a legal out for the Rosenbergs. His pamphlet, *Freedom's Electrocution,* inspired two rather eccentric lawyers to make the plea which brought into special session the Supreme Court, which had recently reviewed a case against Edelman himself on a charge of vagrancy. He enters and exits from the affair in a style that provides a real contrast to the Rosenbergs' sly, maddeningly mendacious conduct. He seems a survival of the old-fashioned American radical, refreshingly honest beside the new "underground" models. One would bid those who think the Rosenbergs were killed for being radicals to notice that in a presumably hysterical America it was the real radical who was free to come to their aid.

advantage of being able to exploit the very human considerations that they were least capable of feeling. And there was an additional advantage in their cynicism itself, which left them able to *use* the Rosenberg children, the coincidence of the electrocution date with the fourteenth wedding anniversary of Ethel and Julius, their frustrated love, and the shocking physical details of their death with a complete lack of squeamishness. On the hoardings of the whole world, the embraces of the Rosenbergs and their approach to the Chair were turned into clichés, occasions for public orgies of sentiment. The Judaism of the condemned pair was played on tearfully by the same activists who had screamed for the death of the Russian Jewish doctors until the line was changed; and the believers that religion is the opium of the people cried out against executing the Rosenbergs on the Sabbath.

But all this, it must never be forgot, was not until the leaders of the party had decided it was *safe* to be sorry — safe for the party, of course, and not for the Rosenbergs. The disregard of the Stalinists for the individuals whose causes they support, their willingness to compromise their very lives for the sake of making propitious propaganda, has been known to everyone since the days of the Scottsboro boys. But unlike those boys, or Tom Mooney, or the other classic cases, the Rosenbergs were actual comrades. This did not mean, however, that there was any more real desire to save them; indeed, as enlightened and disciplined members they would be expected to approve the tactics that assured their deaths in order to blacken the United States in the eyes of the world. Their actual affiliation was, in fact, an embarrassment, something not to be played upon but concealed. The Manchester *Guardian* and other liberal journals might talk of "making martyrs for the Communists," but the Communists, victims of the frantic game of hide-and-seek they had been playing with themselves ever since the dawning of the Popular Front, expended a good deal of energy to hide the fact that these martyrs were "theirs."

"Death for the Rosenbergs Is a Victory for McCarthy!" the posters read, and who, in Europe, at least, remembered that McCarthy had never had anything to do with the affair? Surely the chief evil of McCarthyism consists in branding honest men as Communists out of malice and stupidity. But how does this concern calling a Communist a Communist, or with deciding by legal process that a spy is a spy? These creatures of Soviet foreign policy were labeled the defenders of all "freedom-loving peoples," sacrificed to nothing less than their love for "American Democracy."

There were no limits to the absurd masquerade. A hundred marching Communists in London put flowers at the foot of a statue of Franklin Roosevelt, with an attached card reading: "That Roosevelt's Ideas May Live the Rosenbergs Must Not Die!" Not Marx or Lenin's ideas, please note, but Roosevelt's. It is all of a piece. Julius draped after his death not with a red flag but with the ritual prayer shawl of the Jews; not "The Internationale" sung but "Go Down, Moses" and the Psalms; the American flags flying brazenly over the cortege and the rabbi to intone unbelieved-in prayers at the grave. But the hoax would not quite hold to the end, for the crowd at the funeral parlor booed when a rabbi invited for the sake of camouflage, reminded them that the Jewish religion teaches forgiveness of enemies. In an instant, the fake piety and humanity had disappeared from the carefully prepared faces, and those who had cried for mercy a little while before hooted down the mention of its name.

But there was worse yet. I was in Rome when the news of the Rosenbergs' death came through, and I can speak only of what I actually witnessed; but there, at least on the faces of the Communist crowds surging and screaming before the American Embassy, I saw evidence of *joy*. They were glad, these young activists, that the Rosenbergs were safely dead; for a little while they had been afraid that some last-minute reprieve might cheat them out of their victory celebration, that they would be unable to go through the streets in their Sunday best chalking up "Death to the Killers of the Rosenbergs!" and to sit afterwards over a bottle of wine content with a good day's work. But even this is not the utterest obscenity.

That the American public should deny the humanity of their enemies is terrible enough; that the Communists should deny the humanity of their comrades much worse; but that two people should deny their *own* humanity in the face of death is the ultimate horror, the final revelation of a universal moral calamity. For even at the end the Rosenbergs were not able to think of themselves as real people, only as "cases," very like the others for which they had helped fight, Scottsboro and Harry Bridges and the Trenton Ten, replaceable puppets in a manifestation that never ends. There is something touching in their own accounts of reading each issue of the *National Guardian* (not the frank *Daily Worker,* but the crypto-Communist sheet) to share in the ritualistic exploitation of themselves. But even before the "progressive" journal had begun to spread their story, they themselves had written to each other the foreseeable platitudes of the propaganda on their behalf. From the start, they had not been able to find any selves realer than those official clichés. If there is a tragedy of the Rosenbergs, this is it.

The persistently evoked image of Sacco and Vanzetti had led many to expect in the correspondence of the Rosenbergs some evidence of an underlying honesty, some frank and simple declaration of faith; but they could not hit upon any note that rang true. Reading the "death-house letters" of the Rosenbergs, one has the sense that not only the Marxist dream of social justice but the very possibilities of any heroism and martyrdom are being blasphemed. It is a parody of martyrdom they give us, too absurd to be truly tragic, too grim to be the joke it is always threatening to become.

Ethel's last appeal to President Eisenhower was the first of their letters I read; and it is surely among the most embarrassing, combining with Ethel's customary attempts at a "literary" style, and the constitutional inability to be frank which she shared with her husband, a deliberate and transparent craftiness. She, who had already been writing about Eisenhower in private as "our gnaedige Gauleiter," refers in a painfully adulatory beginning to that embarrassment "which the ordinary person feels in the presence of the great and famous" and which has kept her from writing to the President before. Only the example of Mrs. Oatis,* who "bared her

---

*The evocation of the Oatis case raises problems which demand another article: the prefabricated stalinoid public's celebration of Oatis' re-

heart to the head of a foreign state," has led Ethel, she explains, to look for "as much consideration from the head of her own." She has been unable to avoid the note of reproach in this comparison of mercy on either side of the Iron Curtain, but to take off the curse she hastens to protest her ignorance, in the typical gesture of the Communist who has felt obliged to praise, however mildly, something publicly identified with his real allegiance. "Of Czechoslovakia I know very little, of her President even less than that. . . ." This unconvincing avowal, however, does not satisfy even her, so she tries the alternative gambit of gratuitous flag-waving, announcing quite inconsequently that for America she "would be homesick anywhere in the world."

She then reminds Eisenhower that before he became President he was a "Liberator," but it is not really a congenial memory to her who has still ringing in her ear her own cry of "gauleiter" and the conventional Communist characterization of the American general staff as "heirs of the Nazis." The transition to this note is easy: her execution will be, she charges, "an act of vengeance," and not the first, she reminds Eisenhower, identifying herself and her husband with the 6,000,000 hounded Jews of Europe, and the President with the masters of Buchenwald — those "ghastly mass butchers, the obscene fascists," who are presently "graciously receiving the benefits of mercy," while "the great democratic United States is proposing the savage destruction of a small unoffending Jewish family. . . ."

At last she is at home. The hatred, the obvious irony, the ready-made epithets of the Communist press are released like a dog's saliva at the *ting* of a bell. How happily she forgets that she has been defending the concept of mercy, and using the word "democratic" of her own country without sarcasm. But "a small unoffending Jewish family" — it seems incredible that anyone could speak so about herself, her own children.

---

lease as an unparalleled act of generosity; his own attitude toward himself and his sentence; etc. Here I would like to note merely how neatly this reference joins together two problems that are really one. Why do the guiltless confess on the other side of the Curtain, while the guilty protest their innocence here? In both cases, "symbolic" truth-telling, a shorthand for the uninitiate, is at stake.

At last she is ready for the final series of elegantly unctuous appeals: in the name of "fealty to religious and democratic ideals," as "an offering to God," in the name of the President's wife who will "plead my cause with grace and felicity," or of "the province of the affectionate grandfather, the sensitive artist, the devoutly religious man." And the rhetoric reaches its high point with the reminder that "truly the stories of Christ, Moses and Gandhi hold more sheer wonderment and spiritual treasure than all the conquests of Napoleon." Against the shadow of these names the alternating venom and flattery seem especially evident; and we are left astonished at the self-righteousness that dared evoke them.

The letters which the Rosenbergs wrote to each other from their cells in Sing Sing seem at first glance superior at least to this. Ethel, to be sure, is still hopelessly the victim not only of her politics but of the painfully pretentious style that is its literary equivalent; but Julius, more the scientist in his view of himself, manages from time to time to seem sincere and touching. One is moved by his feeling for his wife, which is more than love — an almost frantic dependence and adulation; and by the tears that stand in his eyes after the visits of his children. But even these scenes, we remember, were, if not staged, at least edited for publication; published in a context of the most banal thumbnail editorials ("I was horrified to read . . . that our government is planning an accord with Spain . . . to ally ourselves with the most reactionary, feudal, and Fascist elements in order to defend democracy . . . something is very rotten in Denmark . . ."*) at the wish of the Rosenbergs themselves.

In part, their self-exposure was aimed, as they declared, at raising money for their children; but, in part, it must have been intended to make political capital out of their own misery and frustrated passion. Finally, the letters are incomprehensible either as genuine expressions of feeling or as partisan

---

*The reader checking these quotations against the English text of the letters will find certain discrepancies, for I am translating them back from the French text of the *Figaro Littéraire,* the only one available to me. There is however, a certain justice in this procedure; for the documents of the legendary Rosenberg case were intended primarily for Europe, and should be seen backward through Europe to be truly appreciated.

manifestoes, since they consist almost equally of intimacies which should never have been published, and lay sermons which should never have been written to each other by a husband and wife confronting their deaths. The line between the person and the case, between private and public, had been broken down for them long before and could not be redrawn even in the extremest of situations. A single logic connects the Communist hating on order the person he has never seen; the activist ignoring on the street yesterday's best friend who has become a deviationist; the wife leaving her husband the day after he is expelled from the party; the son informing on the father; the accused in Russia slavishly vilifying themselves in court — and the Rosenbergs exploiting their final intimacies to strike a blow in the Cold War.

It is in light of this failure to distinguish the person from the cause, the fact from its "dialectical" significance, that we must understand the lies (what are for us, at least, lies) of the letters. The most flagrant, of course, is the maintenance by the Rosenbergs of the pose of innocence to the very end and *to each other!* We have grown used to Communist spies lying in court with all the conviction and fervor of true victims; there was the recent example of Alger Hiss, to name only one; but we had always hoped that to their wives at least, in darkness and whispers, they spoke the truth. Yet the Rosenbergs played out their comedy to the end; and this we should have foreknown.

Some, I recall, advocated a conversion of their sentences on the tactical grounds that they might in the long run confess; and some have even been shaken by their consequent persistence in the cry, "We are innocent!" An occasional less-convinced Stalinist, bullied into complicity like David Greenglass, can be bullied out again into a frank admission; but the true believer believes above all in his own unimpeachable innocence. Precisely because the Rosenbergs could have committed espionage as they did, they could not ever confess it. A confession would, in a certain sense, have shed doubt on their complicity.

They were able to commit their kind of treason because they were incapable of telling treason from devotion, deceit

from honesty. It was not even, though this would be easier
to accept, that they chose deliberately between rival allegiances: the Soviet Union versus the United States. They did
not know that such a choice existed; but believed in their own
way what they continued to assert, that they had always loved
and served "American Democracy." It is misleading to think
of them as liars, though their relationship to everything, including themselves, was false. When Julius, who had stuck
up in his cell a copy of the Declaration of Independence
clipped out of the New York *Times,* refers to it as if in passing
so that all the world will know he is really a misunderstood
patriot, one is tempted to call him a poseur and a hypocrite;
but he is something much more devious.

When he and his wife carefully observe the coming of each
Jewish holiday and sentimentalize over their double heritage
as Americans and Jews, they are not deliberately falsifying,
though they neither know nor care what Judaism actually is
about; they will use as much of it as they need, defining it
as they go. "In two days," Julius writes, "it will be Passover,
which recalls the search of our people for liberty. This cultural heritage has for us a special significance, because we are
imprisoned . . . by the Pharaohs of today. . . ." And in
another place he remarks that "the culture of my people, its
fight to liberate itself from slavery in Egypt" is astonishingly
like "the great traditions in the history of America" — and,
one understands though it is left unsaid, like those of the Communist party.

Ethel, typically, insists on defining her enlightened position
more clearly. Thrilled by the sound of the shofar, she thinks
of the Jews everywhere hastening to the synagogues to pray
for a Happy New Year, but hastens to remind them via her
husband that "we must not use prayer to the Almighty as an
excuse for avoiding our responsibilities to our neighbors . . .
the daily struggle for social justice." And she concludes, astonishingly, with the appeal: "Jews and non-Jews, Black and
White, we must all stand together, firm, solid, and strong."
It is like the curtain line of an *agit-prop* choral production at
the combined celebration of *Rosh Hashanah* and the anniversary of the Russian Revolution.

Judaism happens to lie closest to hand because of the accident of the Rosenbergs' birth, but any other tradition would have done as well — and does. Not only the Christ, Gandhi and Moses of Ethel's letter to the President, but Roosevelt and "Butch" LaGuardia in their letters to each other — the list might be extended indefinitely. For they have been told, and are prepared to believe a priori, that they are the heirs of all the ages: Lincoln, Washington, Jefferson, Isaiah, Confucius, Leonardo da Vinci, Ivan the Terrible, Charlie Chaplin, and Christopher Columbus have all contributed to their patrimony.

They even like to think of themselves as sharing in the peculiarly American mana of the Brooklyn Dodgers. "The victory of the Dodgers," Ethel writes, "over the Phillies quickly restored me to my customary good spirits," and one takes it for a relatively harmless example of the pursuit of the popular and folksy that led Ethel to sing folk songs in the death house. But she cannot leave it at that; the editorial follows the next day, between declarations of love: "It is the Dodgers' unconquerable spirit which makes people love them. But where they have especially covered themselves with glory is in making an important contribution to the rooting out of racial prejudice." We have moved from melodrama to comedy, but the point is always the same. What is involved is the system of moral double bookkeeping invented to fool the Examiners, but so successful that it has ended by bamboozling the bookkeeper himself.

Nothing is what it seems: the Communist parties advocate revolution, and they do not; the Communist International has been dissolved, but it exists; one commits crimes, but he is innocent. Anyone can call war peace, or lies the truth; but to believe such assertions so that one will face death for them requires a trained will and imagination. For such belief, the Rosenbergs had been in training ever since they had combined wooing with the study of Communist literature; and they had finally reached a degree of perfection which enabled them to attain the final stage of subterfuge, to go "underground."

To me, even more extraordinary (for it seems on the face of it *pointless*) than the assertion of their innocence is the Rosenbergs' stubborn silence about their political affiliations.

In court, they had refused to speak on constitutional grounds; in their letters to each other, these "martyrs of the Communist cause" never mention the word "Communism," unless in quotation marks as an example of the slander of their enemies; while the name of the Soviet Union is, needless to say, avoided like a dirty word.

The expurgation goes sometimes to fantastic lengths, of which the most amusing example occurs in a letter of Ethel's written on June 21, 1951. "My beloved husband," she begins, "I feel so discouraged by this unjustifiable attack on a legally constituted American party! The specter of Fascism looms up, enormous and menacing . . ." But she does not identify the party beyond labeling it "American"; and the explanatory note attached by the defense committee in the published volume is equally coy. "Seventeen men and women had been arrested and convicted in New York under the recently passed Smith Act." If one already knows that those otherwise unqualified "men and women" were the leaders of the Communist party, all well and good. If not, it is apparently better to persist in one's ignorance.

The upshot of the whole business is that the Rosenbergs were quite incapable of saying in their last letters just what it was for which they thought they were dying. Not only had they excluded themselves from the traditional procedure of the old-style radical, who rises up in court to declare that he has acted in the teeth of accepted morality and law for the sake of certain higher principles; they could not even tell the world for what beliefs they were being framed. Beyond the cry of frame-up, they could only speak in hints and evasions; so that they finished by seeming martyrs only to their own double talk, to a handful of banalities: "democracy and human dignity," "liberty and peace," "the greatest good of our own children, our family, and all families," and finally "the interests of American Democracy, of justice and fraternity, of peace and bread and roses and the laughter of children."

To believe that two innocents had been falsely condemned for favoring "roses and the laughter of children," one would have to believe the judges and public officials of the United States to be not merely the Fascists the Rosenbergs called them, but monsters, insensate beasts; and perhaps this was partly their point. But one must look deeper, realize that a code is involved, a substitution of equivalents whose true meaning can be read off immediately by the insider. "Peace, democracy, and liberty," like "roses and the laughter of children," are only conventional ciphers for the barely whispered word "Communism," and Communism itself only a secondary encoding of the completely unmentioned "Defense of the Soviet Union." The Defense of the Soviet Union — here is the sole principle and criterion of all value — and to this principle the Rosenbergs felt that they had been true; in this sense, they genuinely believed themselves innocent, more innocent than if they had never committed espionage.

The final pity was that they could not say even so much aloud — except in certain symbolic outcries of frame-up and persecution, and only through the most palpable lies. It is for this reason that they failed in the end to become martyrs or heroes, or even men. What was there left to die?

Yet despite all this, *because* of it, we should have granted them grace. The betrayal of their essential humanity by their comrades and themselves left the burden of its defense with us. This obligation we failed, and our failure must be faced up to. Before the eyes of the world we lost an opportunity concretely to assert what all our abstract declarations can never prove: that for us at least the suffering person is realer than the political moment that produces him or the political philosophy for which he stands. Surely it is not even a paradox to assert that it is our special duty to treat as persons, as real human beings, those who most blasphemously deny their own humanity.

CHAPTER THREE

McCarthy and the Intellectuals

Tell the truth or trump, but take the trick.
— PUDD'NHEAD WILSON'S CALENDAR

Recently a major wire service carried the story of a man released from prison after more than fifty years, who confessed to never having heard of Joe McCarthy. The implication of the article was clear: the *only* man in the United States, the last man in the world still unaware of the Junior Senator from Wisconsin . . . It is a hyperbole, of course, but a modest one, almost the literal truth. McCarthy, McCarthyism — the two names have become familiar in most of the tongues of the earth. Choose a passer-by at random in any of the great cities of the world and ask him to identify the "X" in the following quotation: "Beware, Commies, spies, traitors, and foreign agents! X, with all loyal, free men behind him, is looking for you, ready to fight until the last one of you is exposed for the yellow scum you are."

"McCarthy," he will tell you, "Joe McCarthy, of course," though he might be incapable of saying whether the actual lines were a publicity release from McCarthy's supporters or a parody of such a release by his worst enemies. Actually, the name for which I have substituted an "X" is "Captain America," and the warning is taken from a comic book for small boys. But the implied commentary is apt: in our world, what seems to one group a howling travesty strikes another as a clarion call to action; and a legend has become confused with a man.

Here is the clue to the many paradoxes that surround Mc-

Carthy: the discrepancy between his reputation and his accomplishments; between the special aura of fear which surrounds him and the banality of his personality; between the real terror which has spread and the equally real freedom with which the terrified speak of being gagged; between his disavowal by the whole respectable press and his continuing popular support; between the piety and assurance of his attackers among themselves and their hedging before his committee; and finally, between the millions of words written about McCarthy and the sense that he has not yet been explained.

Even to himself McCarthy is apparently a double man; his way of referring to his official self in the third person is well known; and there appears to be a real difference between "McCarthy," the public presence, humorless and vindictive, and "Joe," the private person who jokes and sets up the drinks and has managed to make lifelong friends even of some whom the political "McCarthy" betrayed. Being his own legend has become a full-time job, so that the real Joe comes to have, not only less and less relevance, but less and less time to exist. Somewhere along the line, he found time to marry Jean Kerr, who had been his assistant, but he has never managed to unpack his wedding presents; and one sees him camped among the unopened boxes, his palsied head trembling, his throat closing with what may be a cancer of the larynx, as if his body and his voice rebelled against the role into which they are forced. One can almost feel pity for the man who has become as vividly unreal as a political slogan, or as the newspaper headlines that reinvent him daily.

To make matters more confusing, there are not one but two legendary McCarthys, the first of which he has defined himself: the figure scarcely distinguishable from "Captain America," the embodiment of an "Americanism that is ready to stand up and fight Communism." The other has been created by the Communists in their pose of abused "progressives," and has been adopted by many liberals and some conservatives: McCarthy as the spirit of "warmongering hysteria and the witch hunt." There have been other aspirants for this two-faced legendary status: William Randolph Hearst and Martin Dies, Father Coughlin and Captain Patterson and a score of others; but only Hearst has ever stirred the archetypal hatred which McCarthy compels, and even he did not flourish at so apt a moment. It is a time for nightmares and the need to project them: the traditional enemies of the hyper-patriot in confusion at the final revelation of the perfidy of the Soviet Union; America learning to face up for the first time to endemic frustration and to loneliness, as the whole world threatens to desert us out of hostility or cowardice or indecision. The Red Scare which for years remained a journalistic luxury, a Hallowe'en false face for bored chauvinists, comes to resemble more and more the bad dream from which we cannot awaken, the bad dream of history.

Those who believe, on the one hand, that there are *no* Communists or spies (I suppose this is the final implication of crying "witch hunt" in an age of enlightenment) or, on the other, that everyone who challenges middle-class orthodoxy is a lackey of Russia have been long trying to make their stereotypes flesh. They have evoked McCarthy; the rest of us merely suffer him. But for all of us he comes into existence at the same moment, some time just after 8 P.M. on the evening of February 9, 1950. From the moment he rose before the Women's Republican Club of Wheeling, West Virginia, McCarthy's history has been in the public domain. What most people know of his earlier career in the Senate — his opposition to sugar rationing and public housing; his leading though unofficial role in saving from the death sentence German storm troopers convicted of shooting down 250 American and Belgian prisoners at Malmédy in 1944 — all this has been reinterpreted in light of the unbroken series of charges and counter-charges that have followed the Wheeling Lincoln Day address.

McCarthy on the one side; the State Department, the Democratic party and international Communism on the other; a threatened America between — this is our modern *East Lynn,* a melodrama (but about who is the hero, who the villain, we cannot agree) played over and over with an almost mindless persistence and lack of variation, in the newspapers, on the radio, on television. The names and dates change, but the meaning of the play is always the same: the conspiracy exposed, the "liberal" revealed as camouflaged Communist or understrapper of the Communists; or, alternately, as the traduced innocent, rounding on his tormentors in all the radiance of his virtue. Sitting in the same playhouse, the two audiences see two quite different plays acted simultaneously by the same cast: John Carter Vincent and Owen Lattimore and Philip Jessup and Edward G. Posniak or Theodore Kaghan or . . . In the end, one can no longer remember who is in the title role.

From the very first the plot, the tone were set, half-comic, half-terrifying: the attack without warning, wild, self-contradictory, almost random; and never better documented or better prepared really, merely better prepared *for* with the press conference that announces another press conference at which the hyperbolic accusation is launched in the conspiratorial setting, as McCarthy raps a pencil against the mouthpiece of his telephone, turns on the water in the sink. He is surrounded by dictaphones, one is given to understand, spied on and harried. No matter how often the performance is repeated, the air of improvisation is never lost, the sense of one who rides the tiger, driven endlessly to defend and justify the indefensible first statement by an indefensible second, the indefensible second by a shameless diversion: "a list of 205 known to the Secretary of State as being members of the Communist Party . . . still working and shaping policy . . ." "I do not believe I mentioned the figure 205. I believe I said 'over 200' . . ." "I told him three times. I read the speech to him. I told him I said there were 57 Communists in the State Department . . ."

We hesitate between laughter and exasperation, until we realize that some are neither annoyed nor amused, that our buffoon and villain is someone else's hero, certainly his own hero. Against those who harass him, he strikes out with a holy rage possible only to one convinced he is justified. Indeed, he is at his most ferocious against the relatively innocent who merely challenge his exposés of his first targets: General Marshall, because of a demurrer in favor of Jessup, became the victim of a 60,000-word attack on the floor of the Senate, later transformed into a book; while Senator Tydings, whose committee investigation of the Wheeling charges ended in an indictment of McCarthy, was stalked and slandered and defeated at the polls; and Secretary of the Army Stevens has recently had to fight a series of engagements after a rather modest protest over McCarthy's publicity on presumable Communist infiltration in the Army Signal Corps. Finally, President Eisenhower himself, for siding with Stevens, has become a target of abuse. The process begun at a venture becomes institutionalized and self-perpetuating, like the Russian treason trials, and can end only with universal capitulation or universal accusation.

Against opponents whom even he would not call Communists, McCarthy displays his notorious willingness to edit stubbornly unrevealing facts to make clear hidden truths: a composite portrait of Tydings and Earl Browder, or a picture of Secretary Stevens and McCarthy's former assistant, G. David Schine, emended by the discreet use of scissors — these appear to McCarthy legitimate enough weapons to use against an enemy who he is convinced is ultimately backed by the Soviet secret police.

But it is vain to attempt to gather the historical *facts* about McCarthy; in simple truth, there are no such facts, only issues. McCarthy does not deal in documents, he deals in polemics; and it is impossible to get behind them. Regret it as we may, we have to admit finally that there *is* no behind; McCarthy and McCarthyism exist only on the surface — that is to say, in the newspapers. It is not the recorded proceedings of the Permanent Subcommittee on Investigations or the remarks on the floor of Congress that we read and remember, but what the daily paper chooses to tell us, what the radio considers it good editorial policy to excerpt.

Many people have deplored what they consider to be the excessive attention paid to McCarthy by our press, and some have even suggested trying to ignore him out of existence; but bad economic reasons have helped to preserve us from such a censorship of good intentions, since McCarthy apparently does more to sell newspapers than newspapers do to sell McCarthy. In an annual poll taken among the political reporters in Washington, McCarthy has more than once been voted the worst of the ninety-six Senators by those who do most to spread his name and fame, and only thus can make amends to themselves. Between McCarthy and the press in general there is a state of chronic feud, which erupts from time to time into particular squabbles with editors like William Evjue and James Wechsler, columnists like Drew Pearson, and radio commentators like Edward R. Murrow; and yet he has the best press in the country. It is a minor paradox among the major ones that define his meaning, and is simply enough explained.

The very reporters who as men despise him, as reporters recognize in him the newsman's blessing, the story that writes itself. His statements do not have to be touched up or toned down to make good journalistic fare; McCarthy may have babbled in headlines as precociously as certain poets are said to have lisped in numbers. His releases have that swollen, emotion-ridden air, that immunity to documentation, of the journalistic statement at its lowest level; and his legend has been dreamed by the kind of mind to which the press habitually condescends. It is not a matter of politics at all; the rhetoric which makes McCarthy kin to the rightist Chicago *Tribune* also relates him to the late communoid *PM*.

But McCarthy is not his only press agent; he has also the Communist party, which by a simple act of inversion turns his own hyper-patriotic image into one of *their* stereotypes; and this in turn is adapted by the vague anti-capitalists all over the world who borrow from official Soviet propaganda whatever depreciates America. It is easier, however, to forgive the foreign manipulators of the meaning of McCarthy than the American ones; for it requires at this juncture, when we are an embodiment of the least palatable necessities of history, superhuman virtue to love us from abroad. But the motives that make most Americans recast the doubleness of McCarthyism into some easy singleness are less creditable. Whether we be hyper-Americans or doctrinaire liberals, to assess McCarthyism justly means to admit that good and evil are divided, though not evenly, between ourselves and our enemies; that there is not an entirely innocent "we" opposed to an absolutely guilty "they." It is easier to slip into the one-sided platitudes that preserve our self-righteousness and identify us like a campaign badge: "whitewash" and "willful coddling" on the one side; "witch hunt" and "putrid slander" on the other.

The Tydings investigation is a case in point. Any approximately objective study of the relevant documents reveals that *two* things are true at once. First, the investigation itself was partisan and inefficient, a mere token glance at the questions raised, and its official report misrepresents what the committee did, or rather failed to do. From its title page on, the Tydings report is dubious, for it claims to be a report of a whole committee to which it was never submitted — as, indeed, it was not even submitted before release to the minority (Republican) members of the subcommittee actually involved. Moreover, the findings of the Tydings committee have been falsified in discussion ever since, as they are for instance in the McCarthy issue of the *Progressive,* where Senator Lodge is quoted as having said that the investigations found no Communists in the State Department, but where his qualification that most of the case material was insufficiently followed up to *prove anything either way* is misleadingly omitted, as is his specific comment that "sufficient evidence was not developed with regard to Mr. Lattimore to enable me to clear him or not to clear him."

On the other side, a mere glance at the documents makes clear how shifty and unreliable a witness McCarthy was, uneasily dodging from number to number, completely contemptuous of dates, and unwilling, despite boasts to the contrary, to strip himself of senatorial immunity and take the legal consequences of his statements. It must be said finally that, on the one hand, McCarthy has never attempted to claim the $25,000 Tydings offered in 1950 if McCarthy could convict anyone in the State Department of being a Communist; but that, on the other, at least 11 persons named by McCarthy on his final list of 81 were subsequently removed from their positions or resigned under fire. Interestingly enough, one of the cases in McCarthy's original list was that of William Remington, who was, of course, in the Department of Commerce rather than the State Department (departments mean even less to McCarthy than numbers) but who certainly is not above suspicion.

In the same way, it is easy enough to talk horrifiedly of "book burning" in condemning McCarthy's campaign against the libraries of the United States Information Service, or to snicker at his advocating the removal of detective stories by Communists as sources of infection; but it must be observed that on the shelves of our own propaganda libraries at a moment when we were presumably engaged with Russia in a struggle for the minds of Europe there were political tracts by Earl Browder and William Z. Foster — and even a book by Ilya Ehrenburg. To find in such choices evidence of treason is, of course, absurd; if traitors do not keep themselves better occupied than that, they are not worth their hire. What the selection of these books indicates is an uncertainty about what Communism is and about its relationship to the American tradition — a feeling, perhaps only half confessed, that there is no *real* contradiction between the particular goals of the Communists and the general aspirations of the democratic world.

The case of Owen Lattimore, in its interconnections with *Amerasia,* the Institute of Pacific Relations, and State Department policy, must do as a final example chosen from an embarrassing overplus. McCarthy has almost succeeded in completely obscuring the facts of the Lattimore case in his attempt to remake a self-righteous party-line professor into a "top espionage agent." Most people do not even realize that at the present moment Lattimore stands indicted on three counts of perjury (there were originally seven) for his testimony before the McCarran committee, because his appearance before the grand jury fell between the premature rejoicing of almost the whole liberal world after his clearance by the Tydings committee, and a comic coda in which McCarthy "discovered" a completely invented plot to get Lattimore out of the country. Those who sprang so quickly to Lattimore's defense on the simple grounds that, if he was accused by McCarthy, he *must* be innocent, should be required to read through Lattimore's testimony, and writhe with him as he tries to explain how, when he uses the word "radical," he means it in its pure etymological sense, or why, after he had informed our ambassador that Outer Mongolia was a state completely independent of Russia, he applied for a travel visa to that unfortunate country at the Russian Foreign Office. We must recognize finally that

Lattimore is not a hired spy in a melodrama, but simply a defender of the Moscow trials as a higher form of justice; not an official "high in the State Department" but yet a person of considerable influence on the policymakers in that Department.

To write off the whole desire to learn the role of Communist influence in shaping our late mistaken China policy as a bugaboo scared up by the "China Lobby" is as facile and wrong as to interpret that policy to be the fabrication of disloyal or suborned officials. The notion of the Chinese Communists as "agrarian reformers" or "the representatives of a nationalist revolution" or "at least preferable to the corrupt Chiang Kai-shek" is merely a particular development of a widespread liberal willingness to see a better side to expanding Communism even where it did not exist. To label that impulse harmless and blameless is to the advantage only of the Communists; to indict it as utterly stupid or perverse is only to McCarthy's; but to see it in all its ambiguity is to the advantage of all whose first allegiance is to the truth.

We must, I am convinced, see this ambiguity or become its victims; and it is difficult to be sufficiently on guard. I do not mean, of course, that we must moderate our fight against McCarthyism in an excess of scrupulosity; merely that we must understand what it is that we are fighting, so that we do not waste our energy in stalking the enemy where he is not. It is better, I am sure, to fight windmills than not to fight; but where there are real monsters it is a pity to waste one's blows on windmills. Even the rallying cry which seems superficially most sound — the contention that McCarthyism, on whatever half-truths it may be based, has by its methods created an atmosphere of suspicion, a stifling pressure of conformity — is only one piece of a double truth.

It can be asserted with almost equal justice that there is nothing easier in America at the present moment than to speak ill of McCarthy. In academic circles, for instance, particularly in the East, it is generally the pro-McCarthy position which occasions resentment and even ostracism; while in the country's major newspapers and on the chief radio networks the majority opinion, quite openly expressed, is unfavorable to the Senator from Wisconsin. For intellectual respectability (and one can understand "intellectual" in its broadest possible scope), it is required that one consider McCarthyism a major threat to liberty. I doubt that there has ever been gathered together a broader or more articulate united front than the one which opposes the tactics of the former chairman of the Permanent Subcommittee on Investigations. Aside from the Communists and their more intimate friends (actually well aware that it is to their best interests that McCarthy continue to spread confusion), this front includes socialists and libertarians, Old Guard and New Deal Democrats, leading spokesmen for Jewish, Protestant, and liberal Catholic groups, and a strong representation of Republicans, including apparently the President and Vice-President of the United States.

It need hardly be said that such a group has little trouble in making itself heard; the daily press and the radio are open to their statements; their books are prominently and favorably reviewed, whereas the partisans of McCarthy find a certain resistance not easy to overcome. McCarthy is notoriously well covered by day-to-day reporting, to be sure, but I do not find in the *Book Review Digest,* for instance, a single notice of his book *The Fight Against Communism;* and the recent favorable study of McCarthy by Buckley and Bozell has received comment almost universally hostile. It is instructive, in this regard, to look through the additional material included in the Appendix to the *Congressional Record,* in which the opponents of McCarthy are able to quote from the leading newspapers of his own state and from journals ranging from the social-democratic *New Leader* through the Jesuit *America* to the Republican *Time,* while he and his friends can eke out the Hearst and McCormick press only with excerpts from the scarcely literate editorials of back-country weeklies.

And yet the statement made in article after article by the attackers of McCarthy, a statement repeated by the commentators and re-echoed by commentators on the commentators, is that McCarthyism threatens if it does not actually bludgeon into silence the hostile press. From one end of the country to another rings the cry, "I am cowed! I am afraid to speak out!" and the even louder response, "Look, he is

cowed! He is afraid to speak out!" In my own town, where
it proved almost impossible to turn up a pro-McCarthy speaker
for a recent forum, and where no library contains a copy of
McCarthy's major book, though Lattimore's version of his
encounter with the McCarran committee is available, I have
been told over and over that there is "something" now in the
air which makes one swallow unsaid what he might once have
spoken without a second thought.

One is tempted to laugh at first, to find only comedy in this
constant frightened twittering back and forth among people
who are in almost universal agreement, and who rise, with all
the air of Christians entering the arena, to address those who
listen with the set jaw of Galileo muttering, *"Eppur si muove!"*
And yet — and yet, it was only with difficulty that I refrained
from adding a parenthesis to the last sentence of the preceding
paragraph, to read: ". . . needless to say, our librarians are
far from being Communists." The "needless to say" would
have been only a sop; obviously there was some need to say,
some nagging fear that a careless reference *under the circumstances* might get the unimpeachable guardians of our books
into trouble. I am convinced that the intellectual community
has been an accomplice to this situation of fear, compounding
it out of pride and guilt; but it has been an accomplice after
the fact. There have been reprisals against the holders of ideas
unpopular with McCarthy: some nervous regents have dropped
instructors in universities and colleges; in the public-school
system, there has been an occasional firing; sponsors on the
radio, cowed by an advertising-agency legend of public
opinion, have been particularly jittery; and in certain government agencies there has been a real terror, as McCarthyism
has combined with the standard vagaries of bureaucratic administration and the usual rumormongering of bureaucratic
underlings.

Even if we attribute to McCarthyism a whole atmosphere
of suspicion of which it is a symptom rather than a cause, it
can be said that its effects (I do not mean the firing of proven
Communists, in which many anti-McCarthyites would concur,
but the intimidation of all unorthodoxy and especially of the
outspoken critics of intimidation) have been small in propor-

tion to the anxiety they have created. I should suppose that the excessive fear of the "intellectuals," in so far as it is more than a tic of anxiety, is based on the suspicion that McCarthy represents not merely himself, his own ambition and chicanery, but a substantial popular hostility, immune to argument and logical proof, to their own *raison d'être*. Certainly, it was disconcerting to discover not many months back that the majority of the American people were favorably disposed toward McCarthy, despite the fact that the larger part of their semi-official spokesmen were bitterly opposed to him. In a certain sense, McCarthyism not only flourishes in but *is* this hostility between the community and its intelligence. An occasional intellectual apologist, whether an embittered "premature anti-Communist" like James Burnham or a black young radical like Buckley, makes little difference. The price of supporting McCarthy is self-abnegation, and there is no reward.

The forces that McCarthy really represents (I mean his mass support, not the Texas millionaires of whom so much is made; anyone who persists in politics in America, whether he be right or left or center, McCarthy or the Communists or F.D.R., can get himself a millionaire or two) find their expression in the resolutely anti-intellectual small-town weeklies and in the professionally reactionary press, which continue to say in his name precisely what they have been saying now for thirty-five years. To realize this is to understand that McCarthyism is, generally speaking, an extension of the ambiguous American impulse toward "direct democracy" with its distrust of authority, institutions, and expert knowledge; and, more precisely, it is the form that populist conviction takes when forced to define itself against a competing "European" radicalism. McCarthy is a new voice for these forces though scarcely a different one, with his automobile salesman's pitch, his proffering of inaccuracy and the inability to stay on a point as evidence that he talks the customer's language. The astonishing thing about McCarthy is his closeness to a standard kind of Midwestern political figure, usually harmless and often comical. What defies analysis is the aura of fear which surrounds him.

Certainly, the facts of McCarthy's early life add scarcely
anything to a comprehension of the phenomenon for which
he stands. There is so little in his career sinister or even
calculated, and so much clearly banal and accidental, that
one who dislikes him finds himself tempted to overinterpret
unfavorable data in a way embarrassingly reminiscent of Mc-
Carthy himself. There is a quality in the man that makes
McCarthys of us all, unless we are content to accept a paradox
for our conclusion. He is not (though it would be comfort-
ingly simple to believe so) any of the things we ordinarily
mean by the word "Fascist"; and comparisons with Huey Long
are beside the point. McCarthy is not, to begin with, a spell-
binder in the Hitlerian sense, but almost anti-rhetorical in his
effect, confidential and bumbling, an expert harrier of witnesses but a mover of masses only in a queer, negative way.
Certain crowds seem to find his very lack of glibness an assurance that he is their voice — and quite inexplicably they
roar; but an even mildly sophisticated audience finds it easy
to laugh him down. He is not a racist, and, indeed, in the
early days of his career was opposed by the old-school, anti-
Semitic native Fascists. Though more recently he has been
hailed and even supported by known anti-Semites,* he has
himself never been recorded as playing on the racist fantasies
common enough among his own constituency; and his association with certain clearly identifiable Jews like Cohn and
Schine works in quite another direction. Indeed, when the
latter two were on their famous quick European investigation
tour, one sensed in certain of the adverse comments on them
(the comparisons to Gallagher and Shean, for instance) the
faintest and most polite undercurrent of anti-Semitism working
in the anti-McCarthy direction. Moreover, one of the bitterest
McCarthy onslaughts against the Voice of America was for
cutting down its Hebrew broadcasts at a point when it might

---

*The case of which the most has been made by those who would find
McCarthy an anti-Semite is that of Mrs. Anna Rosenberg, whose appoint-
ment as Assistant Secretary of Defense he challenged. There is no doubt
that leading racists closed in like vultures during the affair, among them
Gerald L. K. Smith; but the original charges, though unjustified, seem to
have been made in good faith (on the basis of a confusion of identities) by
one who far from being an anti-Semite was actually a Jew.

have been possible to make capital of the anti-Semitic tone of the Slansky trial in Czechoslovakia. Because it baffles a convenient stereotype if McCarthy is not a racist, the charge continues to be made, and American Jews as a group were in the middle of 1953 the only section of the population to oppose McCarthy by a large majority; but the verdict is at least: unproven.

Certainly, he has left behind the backwoods doctrine which identifies the Elders of Zion with the International Bankers, and the Bankers with the Bolsheviks; for McCarthy, Communism is no diabolic expression of an outcast race, but quite simply the foreign policy of the Soviet Union. It would be ridiculous to claim for McCarthy (as he occasionally does for himself when visiting easy scorn on some innocent Army intelligence officer who cannot distinguish between Marxism and Marxism-Leninism) any real theoretical understanding of Communism; he keeps a stock of experts on hand for such matters, satisfactorily repentant ex-Communists and an occasional amateur like G. David Schine, who once prepared a brochure on the subject for circulation in his father's hotels. McCarthy seems, however, to have been twice victimized by Communist *agents provocateurs,* once in the almost prehistoric days of the Congressional debate on the Malmédy massacre, when he was completely duped by a German Communist called Rudolf Aschenauer, who apparently supplied McCarthy with manufactured evidence that American interrogators extorted confessions from German storm troopers by torture; and once when he was taken in by a young American Negro, Charles Davis, who offered faked evidence to prove that John Carter Vincent was in contact with Soviet agents. When McCarthy refused to recognize Davis, after the latter had been deported from Switzerland, Davis filed a suit for libel, confessing in the course of the proceedings that he had been a member of the Communist party. The combination of naïveté with an eagerness to accept any evidence against an enemy as true has made McCarthy the victim of almost as many frauds as he has himself perpetrated.

But it needs no sophistication to understand Communism in 1954; history has defined for anyone with a sense of political fact what Marxism-Leninism has become — namely, the rationalization and defense of that which Russia or its agents do for the sake of expansion or self-defense. In the light of this, it is a little disingenuous to complain, as some critics have done, that McCarthy never defines in his books and speeches his key term, "Communism." In the formal and academic sense, he certainly does not; but it is hard to deny that the term has been defined for him, as for all of us, with distressing clarity.

The story of McCarthy's life is at first glance disconcertingly the rags-to-riches idyl of campaign literature: the son of a poor Wisconsin farmer, he worked hard from childhood on, taking from his father a small section of land that, single-handed at the age of sixteen, he made into a paying poultry farm. Indeed, he seemed on the very verge of prosperity when he broke down from overwork; and, when he recovered, his ambitions had changed. He began the slow movement toward the big city which he has followed ever since, transferring first to the little town of Manawa, Wisconsin, where he became not merely the successful manager of a grocery store but the town's darling. Deciding that he needed an education to fulfill the hopes he had aroused in his fellow-townsmen, Joe finished an entire high-school course in the single year before he reached twenty-one, alternating extraordinary feats of memorization with equally fervent bouts of physical activity; and went on to Marquette University, where he soon switched from engineering to law, though he was a shy and awkward speaker in public.

In college, McCarthy became a boxer of considerable ability, learned painfully to debate, was elected president of his class, and was graduated without particular academic distinction. After two years of law practice, he entered a political campaign for the first time, being defeated for Shawano County attorney on the Democratic ticket, and decided, though he had glowed earlier with a hatred for Hoover in particular and the Republicans in general, that his future lay in their party. In 1939, at the age of thirty, he was elected judge of Wisconsin District 10, winning an utterly unforeseen victory. All his early political activity was characterized by an incredible willingness to take pains, a complete contempt for expert predictions, and a fantastically unflagging energy.

As a judge, he proceeded immediately to wipe out in a matter of months an apparently permanent backlog of 250 cases and never dropped behind in his calendar again, though keeping up meant holding court in session past midnight on many occasions. When the war came, he took a leave of absence from his judicial post to enlist in the Marine Corps, where he served as an air intelligence officer behind the front lines, volunteering from time to time to accompany bombing flights as an unofficial tailgunner. Before the war was over, he left the Marine Corps to enter national politics, making a first vain bid to get the Wisconsin senatorial nomination away from Alexander Wiley in 1944. He was finally elected to the Senate in 1946, after taking, in a victory that characteristically astonished everyone but himself, the Republican nomination from an overconfident Bob LaFollette, who had scarcely troubled to campaign.

Superficially the record is a cliché, embodying only too patly the Pluck and Luck of the legend; but one must accept as real the unquestioning will to victory (across his tent in Guadalcanal McCarthy hung a banner reading: "McCarthy for U. S. Senate," though he was willing to pass it off as a joke) and the compulsive drive toward hard work, which led McCarthy after his election to slip off anonymously and work in the wheat fields. He is an American instance, and must be understood in terms of our myths and compulsions rather than in adapted European terms.

It has often been alleged that McCarthy lacks principles; and certainly he is immune to most of the traditionally noble ones, desiring to succeed chiefly for success' sake and loving the feel of overextended strength as an end in itself. To punish and be punished, to yield voluptuously to the fury of struggle — these *are* his principles, the fundamental values to which he is devoted. "I don't claim to be any smarter than the next fellow," he told a reporter after his election to the Senate, "but I do claim to work harder." One has the sense that he is reciting a part rather than making a statement. Though, as his name indicates, McCarthy's background is Irish and

Catholic, he has none of the amiable fecklessness one associates with his stock; he is the puritan we all tend to become, with the puritan's conviction that the desire to win is the guarantee of being chosen, the gift of energy a sign of salvation. He has apparently never doubted this, though he was for a while uncertain of what end he had been chosen for, aside from the important one of being Joe McCarthy. But his discovery of the Communist issue settled his doubts quickly, giving to his undefined conviction of a mission a sanction at once religious and political. His notorious shopping around for a cause up until 1950 must, in the light of this, be considered something far more complicated than simple opportunism.

A closer look at the record reveals the shoddy underpinnings of the American legend — but this also is typical. From the start, McCarthy's career has been marked by broken promises and betrayals of confidence (his very first office was obtained behind the back and at the expense of his law partner, who had similar ambitions); and by a series of "deals," petty or large (beginning with the trivial episode of the high-school teacher wooed into making possible his record secondary-school career). His appearance of simple virtue goes to pieces under the most superficial scrutiny; though he has been able all along to establish legal innocence of various charges against him, he has emerged always morally indicted. In his early campaign for the judgeship, he apparently overspent the statutory allowance and in campaign literature consistently misrepresented his opponent's age; and even in his famous clearing up of the docket he turns out to have shown more haste than discretion. He connived in a series of astonishingly quick divorces for friends, personal and political, though it meant by-passing the divorce-counsel system of which Wisconsin likes to boast; and he attained special notoriety for not only acquitting the Quaker Dairy of unfair price practices on the odd grounds that the law involved would go out of date in six months, but also destroying a vital part of the court record. He seems also to have contravened the clear intent of a Wisconsin law forbidding judges to run for public office while maintaining tenure on the bench; he could not be convicted because he was running for federal rather than state office.

McCarthy's whole subsequent career has followed the same pattern: from the production of a pamphlet on housing for which he was paid $10,000 by Lustron, a private manufacturer of prefabricated housing, much interested in the legislation before McCarthy's housing committee; through his tangled relations with sugar consumers that earned him the nickname of the "Pepsi-Cola Kid"; to his long history of alleged misrepresentation and barely legal accommodation in preparing his income-tax reports.

It would be foolish to portray McCarthy as extraordinarily corrupt in these respects. He is a hopelessly ordinary politician in all things: his manipulation of his finances, his willingness to "arrange" matters behind the scenes, his barely legal maneuverings to escape uncomfortable restrictions. This is the standard procedure of the standard elective official, and is standardly revealed from time to time in standard investigations; but between such orgies of exposure and righteousness the ordinary American voter not merely condones but applauds evidence of such minor duplicity in his representatives as a sign of political acumen.

McCarthy has been shown up, too, in another favorite practice of the politician: the refurbishing of his own record and the blackening of his opponent's by the discreet manipulation of truth. McCarthy's election as judge at the age of thirty is not considered striking enough: it must be made twenty-eight; his enlistment as a first lieutenant in the Marine Corps must be revised for public consumption into enlistment as a private who then worked his way up through the ranks. A job as an intelligence officer must become an assignment as tailgunner; a leg smashed up during horseplay aboard ship must be turned into a combat wound, recognized with the Purple Heart — and finally metamorphosed into "ten pounds of shrapnel" carried with an exaggerated limp. It is possible that McCarthy does not even consider such conventional accommodation of facts to be lying; he seems especially proud of his own truthfulness, and whenever he and some opponent come into absolute conflict over a question of fact, he typically cries out for a lie-detector test with all the air of a much-abused citizen turning to science to redeem him.

He practices in addition the college debater's device (I can dimly remember my own debate coach recommending it to me with a wink) of waving about irrelevant papers as he makes some especially undocumented statement. This is a clue, I think, to his whole attitude, the "plain man's" conviction that figures are useful only for bolstering after the fact an intuitive judgment or insight. Despite his extensive research staff, and his recent willingness to do a little homework on his charges, McCarthy seems still incapable of believing that it *really* matters whether there are 200, 205, 81, or 57 Communists in a certain branch of the government. He appears clearly convinced that those of his opponents who concern themselves with such discrepancies are stupidly or insidiously trying to divert attention from what truly matters: are there *any* Communists in the department concerned?

It is tempting to identify McCarthy's lying with the Big Lie of Hitler; but it seems more closely related to the multiple little lies of our daily political forum, to a fact of our national life too often ignored by those looking for analogies instead of roots. McCarthyism is, in part, the price we pay for conniving at or ignoring the alderman's deal with the contractor, the mayor's boast that he was always labor's friend. Yet McCarthy's distortion of the truth is not merely a particular development of the cheap politician's hyperbole; it is also the courtroom lawyer's unchallenged device for "making a case" rather than establishing a fact. The politically naïve citizen called for jury duty in any town in the United States begins by being horrified at what seems to him at first a contempt for the truth, but is revealed later as the lawyer's assumption that *there is no truth:* that guilt and innocence are matters, not of moral judgment or even of established fact, but of a decision arrived at inside a devious technical code of procedure. But the naive are never horrified enough.

I do not place McCarthy in this context to justify him, but rather to condemn the system of which he is a pathological symptom. Anyone unwilling to believe how *like* most other lawyers McCarthy is should volunteer to serve on a jury; or, short of that, should read the reports of other Congressional investigations, preferably of those with whose ends one is in general sympathy — of war profiteers, say, or of organizers of anti-labor violence. It would suffice, perhaps, to read through the report of the Tydings subcommittee which condemned McCarthy to see how clearly such investigations distinguish between looking into facts and proving a case. To change the rules of *all* Congressional investigating committees so that at least the safeguards of the courtroom will be provided for what has become a judicial procedure, to insist on the right of confrontation, representation by counsel, etc. — all this will help; but it will not solve the underlying problem I have tried to define. In certain ways, it would seem more desirable to make the proceedings of Congressional investigation *less formal*, less like trial procedure, leaving to the courts the business of establishing technical innocence or guilt, and reserving for the legislative branch, as our national conscience, the task of seeking the truth of morality and feeling. One can imagine no person less equipped for such a task than the run-of-the-mill lawyer trained in the cynical school of the community courtroom.

But there remains in McCarthy's handling of the truth a more sophisticated and "modern" use of the lie than the politician's or the lawyer's. It is a concept of "symbolic" truth-telling, which has, of course, always existed, but which has entered into public life with especial vigor in recent years. It is tempting to call it a "totalitarian" concept, for it has been much exploited by Communists and Fascists; but it is, alas, a favorite device of hard-pressed liberals and conservatives; once the process is begun on either side, the other seems forced to respond in kind. A McCarthyite will say, for instance, "There are hundreds, thousands of Communist espionage agents in the State Department," meaning merely that the influence of Communist ideas, at one remove or another, has helped determine State Department policy for the worse. To this the liberal will answer, "There is not a single Communist in the State Department and there has never been one," meaning simply that, in so far as men and notions influenced by Communists have played a role in the State Department, they have been "idealist" in inspiration, and therefore have done more good than harm.

Or, on a more specific level, a McCarthyite will howl, "Lattimore is the top espionage agent in the United States," which translated means that Lattimore's ideas coincide remarkably with those of the Communists; to which the liberal answers, "He is entirely innocent, a good man," or decoded, "Well, whatever his ideas, they were ones that some quite close friends of mine agreed with once, etc." The Communists themselves have a "scientific" way of saying all this, making the charge, for instance, that the Jewish Social Democrats were "objectively" on the side of Hitler.

McCarthy, of course, is not capable of distinctions between objective and subjective allegiance, any more than he can distinguish between ends and means; but his intellectual and proto-intellectual supporters are quite willing to sustain him on these grounds both publicly and to themselves. There is no doubt in my own mind that Robert Taft, for instance, supported McCarthy (despite waverings and reservations) because he himself had long been convinced that "objectively" socialists were no different from Communists, and leftish New Dealers no different from either; so that calling any supporter of the "welfare state" a Communist might be rude and impolitic but was not actually wrong. Still, Taft was always a little *uncomfortable* about it all, as the handful of more intellectual fellow-travelers of McCarthyism continue to be uncomfortable.

The simple-minded McCarthyite, however, has no trouble at all; he is not disturbed about the problem of whether a lie can be objectively true, because a political lie does not seem to him to be morally reprehensible. McCarthy's position depends not at all upon fair play or respect for conscience, whereas the moral *raison d'être* of his opponents is their scrupulousness; and it is for this reason that these opponents, once betrayed into playing his game of symbolic truth-telling, are at a disadvantage. They find themselves in a terrible dilemma in this regard; granted the discrepancy between their values and that of the vast public, even the non-McCarthyites, they can hardly ever be quite candid without seeming to confess a guilt they do not feel; and, granted their own morality, they cannot trifle with the truth without feeling a guilt they do not confess.

How have the intellectuals fallen into such a plight? Even ten or fifteen years ago, they would have stood up proudly to hoot down McCarthy's equivalent; and that equivalent, bold enough among his own buddies or on the floor of Congress, would have been on the defensive, shouting a little, enraged before the superior tittering of an audience that sympathized with his heckler. The defeat of J. Parnell Thomas, one-time head of the House Un-American Activities Committee, made a laughingstock and finally convicted of petty crime, symbolizes the older state of affairs; the apparent invulnerability of McCarthy the new. As the nation's current Grand Inquisitor, McCarthy is perhaps a good deal smarter than Thomas, but he is not otherwise notably different. What has happened? Chiefly, the main body of liberals has recognized that the Soviet Union, once considered a rallying point for the opposition to Fascism, has replaced Fascism as a symbol of social evil; and that, therefore, "Red-baiting" when directed against real Reds is far from a certain sign of indecency.

The typical confrontation by McCarthy of his witnesses (when those witnesses have not been Communists, open or concealed) has been the legendary confrontation by the Hundred-Percent American of the Enlightened Internationalist at the moment of discomfiture for the Internationalist. There has always been a greater or lesser split in the United States between the Ordinary Voter and the Man Seriously Interested in Politics; but this difference was exaggerated and specially defined in the years between the triumph of the Russian Revolution and the Great Depression. Unlike Western Europe, where a gradually Marxianized people and intelligentsia have found a way of neutralizing old tensions in their attitude toward the Soviet Union, in America the influence of Marxism, however remote, has served only to separate the intellectuals decisively from the mass of people.

The intellectuals, including brighter college students, newspaper reporters, lawyers, and professional people, as well as artists and political theorists, have had as a typical initiation into the intellectual community (the case of Oppenheimer, recently much bruited, is a classic though untypically belated instance) a brief bout of membership in the Communist party, fellow-traveling, or at least the experience of collaboration and friendly intercourse with Communists and fellow-travelers. Communists and liberals seemed in those days to be bound together not only by a passionate revulsion from war and the inequities of capitalism, but more positively, too, by certain tastes in books and in the arts, by shared manners and vocabulary — and especially by the sense of moral engagement that used to be called "social consciousness." From this fellow feeling, the great United Front organizations of the late 1930's were forged, in the teeth, as it were, of the ordinary voter, who, immune to all this, identified not only the Communists but their most distant friends with free love, looting, and general bloodshed; and who were condescended to majestically by the enlightened, thus storing up a special resentment for the hour of disillusion.

To the stereotyped cry of "Red!" the intellectual, who was above stereotypes, shouted back "Fascist!"; and on both sides the notion of two irreconcilable camps grew. From the time of the Sacco-Vanzetti case — that is to say, from 1927 — until 1946 (when those unshaken by Spain and the Moscow trials and the Soviet-Nazi pact were jarred loose by the Cold War), it seemed that America had chosen sides in a bloodless civil war. To the liberal-intellectual,* "we" consisted of the supporters of trade unionism, social security, and the rights of Negroes, Jews, and other minorities, including socialists and even Communists ("rude but on our side"); while "they" consisted of "Red-baiters," readers of Hearst, supporters of Franco, Pinkertons, and *ad libitum* members of the Catholic hierarchy, William Green and the A.F.L., Southern Senators and football players, American Legionnaires, etc. The questioning of Reed Harris, deputy administrator of the Interna-

---

*I cannot in all honesty resist defining this term, though I should have preferred to leave its meanings implicit. To describe the allegiances of the group is to define it sufficiently; but it is perhaps wise to forestall objections by stating explicitly that I use the word "liberal" (and "intellectual" is, for better or worse, historically synonymous with it in America) to mean all those who believe or believed Sacco was innocent, who considered the recognition of the Soviet union not merely wise strategically but a "progressive" step, and who identified themselves with the Loyalist side during the Spanish Civil War. It is perhaps unnecessary to say that I consider myself one of this group.

tional Information Administration, illustrates the difficulties such a conventional categorizing can occasion years later. Despite his subsequent record of loyal service in government, Harris was quizzed at length over a book he had written when just out of college called *King Football;* and the McCarthy committee thought it worthwhile to quote, as a presumable example of disloyalty, Harris' identification of someone as "a sadistic butcher who is now probably the commander of some American Legion post." The complicated innocence of such a remark made in the 1930's is almost impossible to explain to someone whose proudest boast has always been his membership in the Legion.

It is perhaps worth adding that anti-Stalinist leftists of all kinds, especially Trotskyites, were most usually included in the liberals' "they," and that in a strange way a distaste for energetic anti-Communists often survives any sympathy for Communism and the Soviet Union. Often enough, the reconverted liberal, though prepared to grant the decency of A.F.L. organizers, American Legion post commanders, and members of the Kiwanis club (at least in public), feels no qualms about expressing contempt for such "traitors" as Whittaker Chambers or Louis Budenz or Benjamin Stolberg, even though what they have "betrayed" is what he now believes to be evil. There is a sizable minority of non-Communist liberals to whom the "hysterical anti-Communist" (which is to say, *all* anti-Communists) and the "professional informer" (which is to say, anyone who exposes even the most flagrant traitor in the Communist party) are objects of almost irrational horror. This is the last negative persistence of the belief in the Soviet Union as a touchstone of human decency — not a conviction really but a tic, which leads to a compulsive closing of the eyes before the evidence that would make, say, a Chambers right and a Hiss wrong.

I do not want to exaggerate even polemically the Communist influence on American life; in a political sense, the movement was a failure in the United States, for it never appealed to any large number of the workers and poorer farmers to whom it presumably spoke most directly. Indeed, it never won the total allegiance, much less the actual adherence, of the intellectuals; but it *did* manage to establish itself in the intellectual community as an acceptable variant of the liberal-humanistic tradition — and, even more, made its acceptance as such a variant the test of political decency. This established confusion not only enabled such party members as Hiss to regard their activities as the expression of a higher loyalty to "humanity," but even made it possible for others like Wadleigh, too "liberal" to join the party, to commit espionage on behalf of the Soviet Union. And it has bequeathed to us the bewildering concept of an undefinable "left" which obscures for us the actualities of the political situation.

The liberal-internationalists found presumable justification for their self-righteousness in the knowledge of their own superiority to the practicing politician in personal morality. Bribery and logrolling, patronage and "fixing," were as exceptional among the liberals as they were common among those who hated them. Besides, the liberals knew that they were immune to platitudes and conventional rhetoric; that they were more intelligent, read better books, liked superior music and pictures; could use the vocabularies of advanced thought. Certainly intelligence in itself is an advantage, and surely the majority of the intelligent were on the liberal side; but intelligence is not synonymous with virtue nor is it a specific against either political error or malice. The intelligent do not make the same mistakes as the others, or at least they do not make them for the same reasons; but even when they are buttressed with good will they do make mistakes. And they were wrong, drastically wrong, about the most important political fact of our time. The unpalatable truth we have been discovering is that the buffoons and bullies, those who *knew* really nothing about the Soviet Union at all, were right — stupidly right, if you will, accidentally right, right for the wrong reasons, but damnably right.

This most continuing liberals, as well as ex-Communists and former fellow-travelers, are prepared to grant in the face of slave labor and oppression and police terror in the Soviet Union; but yet they, who have erred out of generosity and open-mindedness, cannot feel even yet on the same side as Velde or McCarthy or Nixon or Mundt. How desperately they wish in each case that the Hiss, the Lattimore who speaks their language might be telling the truth; that the hyper-patriot who combines the most shameless stock phrases of nationalism with behind-the-scenes deals, who distrusts litera-ture and art and intelligence itself, might be lying

How happy the liberals are when McCarthy out of malice or ignorance miscues, traducing the innocent or bullying the merely timid. How gratefully they welcome his contempt for legal safeguards and elementary fairness; but, despite all, they cannot convince themselves that these are the *whole* issue. They know that McCarthy is sometimes right or half-right, and even then (perhaps then even more) they resent his charges for reasons they are no longer prepared to defend, feeling, against all reason, their side, themselves, somehow indicted. It is hard to say this precisely without seeming to accuse honest people of conscious duplicity; but no one who shared once the liberal concept of an innocent "we" and a guilty "they" can appear before an investigating committee without a double sense of guilt: over having once lived his past and over being now obliged to betray it.

Some try to evade the problem by simplification: either choosing silence on the grounds of the Fifth Amendment and thus avoiding the second guilt completely; or identifying them-selves with the investigators and atoning publicly for the first. But the non-cooperators find themselves in the company of the Communists who, like McCarthy, want to perpetuate the confusion of liberals and "left" totalitarians; and, in so far as they know that the human spirit is offended and maimed wherever Communist governments exist, they bear the burden of having chosen to shelter as a "lesser evil" the enemies of all they most love. They tell themselves in vain that the *particular* Communists they knew and once worked with may have long since changed their political convictions; and that they were, at any rate, "idealists" who would never have committed espionage or condoned terror. But they know that Klaus Fuchs or the Rosenbergs seemed to some intelligent people of good will equally "idealistic" and harmless.

Meanwhile a very few ex-liberals or repentant radicals find not peace but further exacerbation in acknowledging publicly

the rightness of those they long despised. They become either
superior apologists for McCarthy in journals that most Mc-
Carthyites never read, or else employees of investigating committees, to which they supply the minimal information about
Marxism that their employers are capable of understanding.
Aside from one another, they find few sympathizers with their
course; those they work for cannot really communicate with
them, while the majority of their intellectual compeers regard
them as unclean. Actually, the intellectual informers range
in reliability and basic decency through the normal spectrum;
but some find themselves trapped in the need to continue informing, and end by substituting fantasy for memory in the
effort to justify themselves from day to day. In any case, their
shrillness betrays a nagging sense of guilt which no public
accolade can allay.

Between the evasion of the non-cooperaters and the over-
cooperation of the confessers lies a troubled and difficult
course: what seems to me the truly liberal one. Such a course
has been variously followed before one committee or another
by Robert Gorham Davis and Stewart Alsop and James
Wechsler. Naturally, it seems to do no *immediate* good, to
satisfy neither side. When such a witness speaks out bluntly
in opposition to something which McCarthy believes, he is
charged by the hyper-patriots with being a stooge or even a
secret member of the Communist party; and when he identifies
for the investigators the utterest scoundrel in the pro-Soviet
camp, he finds himself scorned and ostracized by the kind of
"sincere" liberal who gasps horrifiedly: "He named names!"
— as if to "rat" were the worst of crimes. It is not, however,
really the boys' code of not squealing which is at stake, but the
whole dream of an absolute innocence.

The honest witness's worst enemy will be finally neither the
hyper-patriot nor the sentimental liberal but himself. The
opportunities for self-deception will be many, and even his
most legitimate strategy may turn out to be a trap. He may
be tempted to begin by making clear his present opposition
to the Soviet Union, to bid against McCarthy in terms of the
fervor if not the priority of his convictions: to produce, perhaps, out of McCarthy's own past naïvely favorable statements

about Stalin or refusals to reject Communist votes. But especially he will feel compelled to boast: "I also am opposed to . . ."; "I have always fought against totalitarianism . . ." Such statements can be made in bland good faith by those who have simply forgotten that once, of course, "totalitarianism" did not for them include the Soviet Union. One would be wrong to call this falsification; it is the scarcely conscious adjustment of fact made by the happily married man asked fifteen years later about a disreputable love affair.

Too much of what the witness wants to say is forbidden to him: not only cut off by the ridiculous yes-and-no questioning, the setting up of leading questions for quotable answers, though this is a source of exasperation and dismay; but barred to him by the impossibility of communicating in his own language. He wants to say, perhaps, that having been inoculated with philo-Communism once, he is now immune; that his former allegiance is a special guarantee of his present integrity. He may even have the mischievous impulse to declare: "Just as we glory in what made us wrong in 1936, though we deplore our wrongness, so you should be thoroughly ashamed of what made you right then. You were opposed to Communism then, and are still, for reasons which make us enemies and not allies!" But these things remain unspoken, because speaking them would be unpolitic before a committee to whom they would seem a confession of treason; and because the witness is not quite sure how far or in what sense he really believes them himself. Even James Wechsler, by far the most effective witness ever to face McCarthy, got himself into trouble in this way. I quote this passage in the hearing not to detract from the honor due Wechsler, but to illustrate the difficulty of candor and communication under the best circumstances.

Though Wechsler began his testimony with the air of one determined to expose with the weapons of frankness and forthrightness a procedure that had thriven on the fear and deviousness of previous witnesses, he himself fell into equivocation on three main issues: Had he ever written favorably of any ex-Communist? Had he ever approved of *any* chairman of an investigating committee? Had he voluntarily submitted to the FBI a list of former associates after his presumed break with Communism? Confronted with these three shibboleths, the turncoat, the "Red-baiter," and the cop — unchallenged heroes to all his inquisitors and villains in the legendary melodrama he had believed in as a youth — Wechsler hedged and squirmed. He seemed especially unsure on the issue of the FBI, and his questioners, scenting weakness, closed in on him, McCarthy and Roy Cohn hammering away by turns, six, seven, eight, nine times.

Now, did you go to the FBI, after you broke with the movement in 1937?

No, I did not go to the FBI, but over a period of years . . . I was visited at times by FBI men. I was visited . . .

Have you ever in your editorial columns, over the last two years, praised the FBI?

Well, sir, I would have to go back and read our editorials for the last two years. I did not understand that I was being called down here for . . .

Did you at any time . . . go to the FBI and offer to give them what information you might have to aid them in their fight against Communism. . . ?

I did not go to the FBI . . . I was visited on several occasions by FBI men . . . I answered freely and to the best of my knowledge. . . .

Mr. Rushmore since he broke with the movement has been of great assistance to the FBI. . . . This is the first time Mr. Wechsler has given a list of names.

That statement, sir, is not consistent with the facts!

Did you give a list of names before?

I was not asked for it.

The unspoken point is clear, though Wechsler does not feel it politic to make it. In his generation and in the world in which he moved, one simply did not "give a list of names" in any case, and certainly not to the FBI, who seemed an especially insidious form of the Enemy. It is hard to re-create that world in a time when coeds inform on suspicious boy friends to the proper government agency; but one raised in it can never recover completely from its assumptions. Wechsler has, indeed, come a long way, being prepared now to admit that the FBI "does not deserve to be denounced as it has been de-

nounced in some quarters as a Fascist-Gestapo agency"; but
this concession is less than meaningless to those who have never
had any doubts about the virtue and wisdom of J. Edgar
Hoover.

What Wechsler did not succeed in declaring openly — that
the FBI is in some of its aspects comic; that its men are often
incapable of telling who is a Communist; that its immunity
to criticism is a menace to freedom — these convictions are
quoted from his published writings as evidence of perfidy.
And yet how could he have declared what he truly felt to a
group which shared not at all the central experience of his life;
and which, at its friendliest, felt the need to assert in the words
of the Democratic member, Senator Symington: "First, I want
to say that nobody believes in the FBI more than I do, and I
am sorry if Mr. Wechsler has criticized the FBI."

No wonder that baffled witnesses (and most are considerably
more baffled than the alert and articulate Wechsler) seek to
right the balance outside of the committee room, crying out
"corruption" and "reckless charges" and retailing in print circumstantial descriptions of the bullying, intimidation, and
misrepresentation they have endured. The epithet "Fascist!"
is shouted and the image of Huey Long evoked; the sincerity
of McCarthy's anti-Communism is impugned, and it is suggested variously that he is self-seeking, an unwitting tool of the
Communists, and/or a creature of the Texas oil men and the
Catholic hierarchy (though at the same time it is pointed out
how many influential Catholics oppose him). The whole
arsenal of liberal mythology is drawn upon, until what began
as a genuine bill of particulars ends as paranoid speculation,
paranoia answering paranoia: McCarthyism of the left and
center, McCarthyism of the right.

Just as McCarthy is incapable not only of believing that
those who disagree with him may be right, but even of granting
that they may be wrong through misjudgment or normal stupidity; and as he is convinced that behind the opposition to
him there is a conspiracy or plot; so his opponents fall into a
similar belief. The plot discovered is the finding of evil where
we have always known it to be: in the *other*. But the final
joke and horror of the situation is that there *are* in our days

conspiracies which baffle common sense. Even the most fantastic accusations of McCarthy are lent a certain plausibility by the revelations of the Hiss case, in which it scarcely matters whether you opt for the Communist-espionage-ring theory of Hiss's guilt, or the equally fantastic forgery-by-typewriter theory of his innocence. What an absurd world we live in where only half the audience, or less, laughs aloud when Mc-Carthy charges that James Wechsler himself wrote the Communist editorials attacking him.

But the Red-baiter and the liberal do not really charge each other with equal conviction. The liberal is uncertain even when, closing his eyes in desperation (but all the time, he *knows*), he repeats ritually: "Lattimore is pure; Hiss was framed; the Rosenbergs are a mirage; there never was a Klaus Fuchs; Harry Dexter White was maligned . . ." And as a final charm: *"No harm has been done, no harm has been done, no harm has been done!"* The McCarthyites, however, answer with more certainty (their eyes have always been closed and they do not even suspect it) and equal ritual insistence: "Yalta and China, Hiss and Marzani and Harry Dexter White; treason and the coddling of treason: *guilty, guilty, guilty!"*

It is no use protesting that McCarthy himself has revealed no dangerous hidden Communists; that the Marzanis, the Hisses, and the Rosenbergs of whom he boasts were turned up by other agencies, before the opening of McCarthy's much-advertised campaign. In so far as Joe McCarthy is an individual, he has proved little beyond the foolishness and uncertainty of many who have appeared before him; even his single prize, Lattimore, is no "espionage agent." But in so far as McCarthy is the personification of a long-inarticulate movement, of the sullen self-consciousness of a sizable minority, he *begins* with a victory that he cannot fritter away, no matter how many errors he makes or how many downright lies he tells.

The emergence of McCarthy out of the wreckage of the La Follette Progressive movement in Wisconsin is a clue to what he represents. He inherits the bitterest and most provin᾿ cial aspects of a populism to which smooth talking has always meant the Big City, and the Big City has meant the Enemy. Traditionally that enemy has been identified with "Wall Street," but from the mid-1920's there has been a tendency to give an equal status to the non-native rebels who claim also to oppose the bankers. Indeed, Robert La Follette, Jr., had gone so far in the latter direction that in 1946 the Communists, through the Wisconsin CIO council, supported McCarthy against him. It was not until 1950, however, that McCarthy discovered a symbolic butt in the State Department "Red," the "Park Avenue Pinko," capable of welding together the fractured Populist image of the Enemy. In light of this, it is just as important that McCarthy's initial attack was directed against the State Department under Acheson (and against Harvard behind him) as that it was directed against the Communists. Acheson is the projection of all the hostilities of the Midwestern mind at bay: his waxed mustache, his mincing accent, his personal loyalty to a traitor who also belonged to the Harvard Club; one is never quite sure that he was not invented by a pro-McCarthy cartoonist.

With something like genius, McCarthy touched up the villain he had half-found, half-composed, adding the connotations of wealth and effete culture to treachery, and topping all off with the suggestion of homosexuality. McCarthy's constant sneering references to "State Department perverts" are not explained by his official contention that such unfortunates are subject to blackmail, but represent his sure sense of the only other unforgivable sin besides being a Communist. The definition of the Enemy is complete — opposite in all respects to the American Ideal, simple, straightforward, ungrammatical, loyal, and one-hundred-percent male. Such an Enemy need not be *proven* guilty; he is guilty by definition.

It is interesting by way of comparison to see how much less sure McCarthy is before even a scoundrel who shares his own "American" prejudices. Certainly, no traduced liberal has ever faced him down as he was faced down by Isador Ginsberg, a war profiteer and former leader of a veterans' organization, who appeared before McCarthy when he was on the housing committee. "I want to say, sir," the grey-marketeer cried out in the midst of the questioning, "Ginsberg is as proud as McCarthy. I don't believe you can possibly pass legislation to prevent me, and honest men like me, from making a fair profit. Only in Russia can that be done!" And McCarthy, an "honest man" like Ginsberg, after all, and no friend of Russia, had to confess he was right: that only the enemies of profit and the defenders of Communism were outside the pale.

But the Enemy for McCarthy is not only a dandy, a queer, an intellectual, and a Communist; he is (or was, at least, in the beginning) a Democrat or a Democrat's friend. The struggle between the liberal intellectual and the old-line Red-baiter has been absurdly confused with the contest for votes between the Democratic and Republican parties. This seems, in part, clearly accidental. McCarthy himself was, for a while at least, a Democrat (his chief counsel Roy Cohn still proudly declares himself one); and at the start his charges were taken up largely as ammunition to be used against the ins, who happened to be Democrats, by the outs, who happened to be Republicans. It was possible at first to believe that there was no anti-Communist conviction at all behind McCarthy's campaign against the State Department, but merely a desire to slander his opponents and advance the fortunes of his own party; but one senses in him the happy coincidence of conviction and strategy. Blessed is the man who can at the same time gather in votes and vent the fear and hostility that the encroachments of Soviet imperialism have stirred in most American hearts!

Does the Republican party have any right to claim the mantle of Communist-hunting as its own? Certainly, there have been leading "Red-baiters" in both parties; and dupes of the Communists in both, too. Everyone remembers, I suppose, that among the friends of Alger Hiss was not only Acheson but also John Foster Dulles. Yet it is true that the Democratic party had become, in the early days of the New Deal, not liberal perhaps, but certainly liberal-colored; finding a place in its ranks somewhere between the big-city bosses and the Southern reactionaries for communoid and liberaloid professors, left-wing CIO trade unionists, and especially for a new kind of practical politician who had learned in Depression times to adapt the vocabulary and attitudes of the true liberal to his own constant opportunism.

Roosevelt himself was a representative of this group, and his own approach to the Soviet Union (the recognition of which became a leading slogan of the party), to England, and to China, for example, were deeply conditioned by the stereotypes and conventional allegiances of the liberal, at a point when the liberals were most victimized by illusions about the Soviet Union. The influence of such attitudes on our military activity in Europe and Asia and on our diplomatic activity as at Yalta and Potsdam, as well as the actual presence of Communists or sympathizers in key spots at key moments, have been documented and are outside the scope of this essay; but perhaps a word should be said about F.D.R.'s Vice-President, who symbolized the various stages of the liberalization of the Democratic party.

There is a shift of revolutionary scope between Garner, who represented an assurance to the right wing of the party that Roosevelt did not intend to go overboard in a radical direction, and Henry Wallace, who stood for an exactly opposite assurance to the left. Wallace is the blindly "idealist," hands-across-the-sea approach to the Soviet Union made flesh; and his symbolic role reaches a climax in his famous junket to Soviet Asia, under the partial tutelage of Owen Lattimore, during which Wallace failed to see anything blameworthy though he passed through one of the larger slave-labor camps. Later, he was to plead that he had been taken in by the wily camouflage of the Soviets, and (most interestingly) that he had been instructed not to look too hard for negative evidence, but to concentrate on what might bind us to our ally in amity. The ditching of Wallace for Truman meant on the surface a counter-gesture of reassurance to the right; but it actually represented the final penetration of the new ideology into the party, with the emergence of the liberalized party man, who makes unnecessary the window-dressing principledness of Wallace. Truman is basically the old-style politician, brought up inside the Machine, where fixes and deals are the order of the day, and where party or personal loyalty is ranked above the "reformer's" morality; but he has learned, on the one hand, to dedicate his political craft to liberal ends; and, on the other, to sanction his means by the pious evocation of those ends. It is no accident that it was Truman who cried loudest at the charges of Communist infiltration into his party's ranks: "Red herring!"

It remains to be added that the Roosevelt administration pushed the safeguards for labor and provisions for social security to the verge of what Republican conservatives like to call the "welfare state"; and, though the latter cannot, of course, undo such progressive measures, they can deplore them or condemn the "philosophy" behind them; which is to say, they can call liberal-colored improvisation a philosophy, and name it "creeping socialism." The spokesmen for this ideological opposition to the New Deal were tempted to use the exposure of real or alleged Communists in the Roosevelt bureaucracy as objective proof of a kinship of ideas between left-wing Democrats and Bolsheviks.

Whatever the justification before the fact for the Republican identification of the Democratic party with the liberal intellectuals and the Communists, they found in the jittery and uninformed reactions of men like Truman more fuel than they had hoped for. Fearful that granting any truth to the Republican charges might lose them votes, the Democrats arrayed themselves in strict party lines over every issue from the Tydings subcommittee report (when the anti-New Deal Tydings found himself backed by those who had tried to defeat him in the previous primaries) to the Army-Schine squabble. Once the Democrats had put themselves in the absurd position of denying Chambers' allegations about Hiss, and of screaming, every time Harry Dexter White's name was mentioned, that he was *dead* so loudly that they never heard the evidence against him, the way was open to make the whole New Deal seem nothing but a cover-up for Communist infiltration and espionage.

In the polemics which have followed, it has become impossible to speak of the sense in which the New Deal *did* put into positions of trust a few men with a double allegiance, and *did* encourage many colleagues of such men to look on that double allegiance as no more than an annoying foible, without seeming to ascribe to the "realistic" New Dealers more stupidity or Machiavellianism than they deserve. It would be foolish to accuse the Democrats, who under Truman launched a creditable program of opposing Communism abroad, with any real desire to protect Communists at home; but they did often choose to deny what they knew to be true in the interests of vote-getting; and after a while they came to speak of hysteria and "witch hunts" as if the danger of Communist espionage were not merely exaggerated but non-existent.

It was a strange and embarrassing opportunity for the Republicans, who found themselves on the popular side of an issue for the first time since 1932. In America anti-Communism has never been an exclusively bourgeois attitude; indeed, the only sizable group ever to challenge it was completely bourgeois. It has always been strongest among farmers, unorganized workers, and the lowest level of the middle class; and, once McCarthy had brought into the open a problem which opposed to the People the Intellectuals rather than "the Economic Royalists," a new kind of Republican was needed to assume leadership, the kind of Republican represented on varying levels of respectability by Nixon and McCarthy. This Senator Taft, for instance, appears to have sensed; perhaps he knew all along that though he was called "Mr. Republican" he could not make the populist appeal. Certainly, in this light his otherwise inexplicable support of McCarthy, his willingness to tout him in speeches dedicated to "political morality," makes a kind of sense.

The votes which clinched McCarthy's first senatorial victory came not only from the wealthier Catholic farmers of Wisconsin but from the working-class districts of Kenosha and Racine and Milwaukee ordinarily considered safe for the Democrats. If there is a blackness in McCarthy, it is not the reactionary blackness of the oil interests or of the Catholic Church, but of something in the American people which grows impatient with law and order, with understanding and polite talk, when it feels it has been betrayed. The ordinary American who has for years thundered in his Legion post against Reds cannot understand why, at a time when we are being baffled by Reds on three continents and are actually committing troops to battle against them, there should be a single Communist or defender of the Communists in a position of trust. He is only enraged when one speaks to him of safeguards and due process; of the difficulties of adjusting from a period in which the Communists were not only a legal party but our allies; of the actual equivocal status of Communists under the law. The Army, caught up in the toils of its own involved legality, finds itself forced to promote a Communist dentist before it can discharge him; and those who always have equally distrusted red tape and Reds scream in anguish through McCarthy, who is their mouthpiece.

The spirit that speaks is fundamentally a lynch spirit, the cry of those convinced that recognized evil cannot be touched by the law: "Let's get them before it's too late. Let's do it now!" But the lynchings have been only verbal so far, moral lynchings, which compared even to the reprisals against radicals that followed the First World War appear relatively calm and sane. The fight against McCarthyism must be carried on, but those who wage it must be aware that they are fighting a whole section of our people unable to understand a situation in which moral condemnation of a group has far outstripped the community's legal procedures for dealing with them. It is therefore hard to undercut McCarthy, especially because most of those who attack him have always been considered by his supporters to be their natural enemies; and because, more and more, the picture is established in the minds of his adherents of Joe the Giant-Killer — a limited but dedicated man, fallen among fast-talkers and slickers.

In light of this, the constant hope of the already enlightened that McCarthy's following can be split away if only some forcefully written exposé could be got into the right hands, or if only someone would stand up to him boldly enough at the hearings, is revealed as fantasy. Equally chimeric is the dream that "given enough rope he will hang himself," that some lie revealed, some exceptionally absurd accusation hastily dropped, will damn McCarthy in the eyes of his fondest followers. It is this sort of eternally deferred hope that leads to final despair: the Dorothy Kenyon case, the Wechsler case, the Benton charges, the Army scandal — each hoped-for blunder, each eagerly awaited revelation, finds McCarthy unshaken and assured, his pathos more firmly established for his supporters.

I am not trying to suggest that McCarthy cannot be dislodged from his place of power. I am sure that, if the Republican National Committee cuts him off unequivocally, those of his adherents who are allured only by the aura of success will depart, even some of those to whom he represents the triumph of principle. A glance at the decline of McCarthy's vote from 1946 to 1952 indicates how much damage can be done even by the defection of a few influential people inside his own party; and certainly the opposition to McCarthy continues to grow in Republican ranks: even those who seem at first glance closest to him begin to edge away. Vice-President Nixon is the representative figure; himself an inquisitor (he must get the chief credit for Hiss's exposure before the House Un-American Activities Committee) and an exploiter of anti-Communism as a campaign issue, he has nonetheless a yearning for intellectual respectability. "This is just a note," he wrote to James Wechsler in January of 1950, "to tell you that I thought your editorial on the Hiss case . . . was one of the most able and fair appraisals of a very difficult problem I have ever seen. Since you probably have me categorized as one of the 'reactionaries' . . . I thought you might be particularly interested in my reaction." This letter to one whom McCarthy finds it politic to call a concealed Communist reveals clearly the difference in Nixon's approach that must force him to a final break with the traducers of the anti-Communist position as he understands it.

Most recently, McCarthy has created a new kind of resentment with his defense of the "young officer" who transmitted to him for use against the Department of Defense a classified FBI report on Communists in the Army, and his assertion that all government employees "are duty bound to give me information even though some bureaucrat may have stamped it secret." Under a Democratic administration, his Republican colleagues might have found it possible to ignore the positing of a "higher" allegiance, embarrassingly reminiscent of Communist theory; but with their own man in the White House they have felt forced to take a stand. Attorney General Brownell set the tone by blasting publicly "an individual [coyly unnamed] who may seek to set himself above the laws of the land"; and even some of McCarthy's staunchest supporters hastened to dissociate themselves from his position. But most leading Republicans were apparently not yet sure that McCarthy could be disavowed without losing votes, and on second thought they shifted from attacking him to accusing the Democrats of plotting to split the Republican party on the McCarthy issue.

The melancholy conclusion is that, whatever personal resentments or principled differences may exist within the Republican party, McCarthy will not be cast off until it is politically expedient. Perhaps what will sink him in the end is a rather personal quirk, the almost compulsive hatred of the Army and its brass which has led to his most unpopular moves: the investigation of the Malmédy massacre, the (since-repented) attack on MacArthur, the book-length onslaught on General Marshall (with unfavorable side-glances at Eisenhower); and the tongue-lashing of General Zwicker which helped precipitate the Army-McCarthy hearings. This is an age of generals, and McCarthy's distaste for them may eventually compromise him, though liberals will be able to find small comfort in such a dog-eat-dog defeat.

But none of this will touch the hard core for whom McCarthy establishes in history the nightmare they have dreamed in private; and that group which preceded Joe McCarthy will survive him, as McCarthyism itself, whatever new name it bear, will outlive the death of its present form. The fight against McCarthyism is more than the fight against McCarthy; it is a struggle against the outlived illusions of the left as well as the distortions of the right, against the superciliousness of the intellectuals as well as the resentment of those to whom they condescend. It is the fight against our own comfortable lies as well as the disquieting ones of our enemies, against self-righteousness as well as slander. It is a war for the truth we cannot help betraying even as we defend it; and in this war each victory is only a new way to begin.

A Postscript

Though the Army-McCarthy hearings did not, of course, produce a clear-cut condemnation of the Senator from Wisconsin; though they did not, indeed, even raise the issues everyone felt to lurk behind the superficial question of who was lying, McCarthy or the Army (or, more precisely, who had lied first and more egregiously), they have in an indirect and unexpected way led to the partial collapse of McCarthy's prestige. His double defense of, on the one hand, portraying himself as the champion of the legislative branch against the executive, and, on the other, revealing with what unclean hands his presumably high-minded opponents came against him, was only too successful. As far as his mass support is concerned, any exposure of the incidental lack of virtue on his part remains, as I have tried to show above, beside the point. The convinced McCarthyites, his scarcely articulate admirers, who applaud him almost more for bucking his glib upper-class opponents than for blasting Communists — these have not been touched.

And yet, at the end of the late televised hearings, everyone but those *lumpen* advocates was left with a sense of shame, a feeling that he had been personally besmirched by the whole ignoble affair. It was not only that nobody directly involved in the circus managed to perform with distinction or tact, but that even those not directly implicated, the nation itself, sat transfixed for weeks before their television receivers in a voyeuristic orgy — unable to turn away from the often vacuous bluster of Jenkins, the somewhat oleaginous piety of Welch, the surly and unprincipled "cleverness" of Roy Cohn, the aggrieved smugness of McCarthy himself. Supporters of one side or the other tried hard to find moments for enthusiasm; but as the affair wore on, as Secretary Stevens weakly stumbled (with a last-minute, useless kind of courage) from point to point, as any semblance of order and coherence disappeared and the "actors" preened for the cameras, the reigning feeling in most hearts was self-contempt for being unable simply to turn off the sets and go away to useful work or decent play.

Never before had television revealed itself quite so clearly as the electronic keyhole from which it is impossible to remove one's eye no matter what disgustingness is being played out behind it. Never before had the underlying triviality, the small dirtiness behind the large statements of McCarthyism, been so patent. In the morning after the orgy of the hearings, it became clear to many that no one could join McCarthy's ranks or even combat him on issues of his own choosing without being degraded. The dignity of the nation and the government seemed at stake.

It is in light of this morning-after revulsion that the recent report of the Watkins committee must be read. The function of that committee was not so much to investigate certain particular charges against McCarthy for behavior unworthy of the Senate, as to redeem the total dignity of that body. It is for this reason that the procedure of the committee has been as important as its findings: its decision to forego the more grotesque excesses of publicity, its refusal to lose all coherence in a welter of irrelevant "points of order." But it is also for this reason that the accusations against McCarthy sustained by the Watkins committee are so uncentral to the problem of McCarthyism. He has been found guilty not of failing to fight effectively the enemy against whom he blusters, Communism; not of attacking civil liberties; not even of setting loyalty to himself above government regulations and the standard procedures for handling confidential material. The latter conflict he managed to put in the light of a struggle between legislature and the executive, and the committee chose to evade it.

No, the charges sustained against him are the use of vile language to fellow-Senators and his refusal to testify before an earlier legislative committee on the score of financial matters. What McCarthy says in self-defense is, of course, deplorably true: that on these points (the use of vituperation and the discreet manipulation of income-tax reports) he is scarcely more guilty than many other legislators. It is a little like the case of the gangster whose kidnapings, assaults, and murders cannot for one reason or another be proved against him, and who is finally jailed for income-tax evasion.

The Democrats on the committee really found, *as* Democrats, McCarthy guilty for stealing the Communist issue and hence votes from their party; the Republicans, *as* Republicans, for disrupting the unity of their party and sniping excessively at their administration; all of them as Senators for his public besmirching of the upper house by behavior common enough in milder form but unforgivable in this flagrant version. In McCarthy, what is for other Senators incidental vice becomes published as public virtue; and this, in a country still in a residual sense puritan, is unpardonable. McCarthy will not pay vice's customary tribute of hypocrisy to virtue; and in the end it is for his sullen honesty in dishonesty that he has been condemned.

Besides which, time has run out on the Senator. So many of his colleagues in both parties have for so long been joined with him in rooting out Communist influence, both real and fancied, in all branches of government, that there no longer appear to be any spectacular unexplored areas. The great diversionist finds himself at the moment of his supreme discomfit without any diversion at hand; the man who has based his whole claim to regard on the constant harrying of Reds is fresh out of Reds. It is not merely a matter of being distracted from his hunt, as McCarthy keeps declaring; much of the game has been flushed and bagged. No wonder he has recently retreated to the hospital, overwhelmed by the respiratory ailment that nags him like a reproach; and that the face he raises on current television shows is that of a man badly hurt if not beaten. No wonder he begins to boast of his own impending defeats as voluptuously as he once forecast his victories. McCarthyism, the psychological disorder compounded of the sour dregs of populism, the fear of excellence, difference, and culture, remains still a chronic disease of our polity; but its acute form, our most recent attack, seems to have passed the crisis.

PART TWO

INNOCENCE ABROAD

CHAPTER FOUR

Italian Pilgrimage: the Discovery of America

For shipboard reading en route to Italy, I took along with me *The Marble Faun*. It was a toss-up between that and *Innocents Abroad*. There seemed no use in trying to kid myself — no American just goes to Italy; he makes willy-nilly a literary journey, and his only choice is between melodrama and comedy. Hawthorne or Mark Twain? You pays your money and you takes your choice — if it is a choice; for after all each writer confesses, according to his own conventions, the same meanings of the voyage: a Pilgrimage to the shrines of an idea of man (or more accurately, I suppose, to the visible forms of a culture in which that idea is entombed) and a Descent into Hell. Moreover, both books agree in telling us, what we might have guessed anyhow, that the Descent into Hell is for us the real pleasure of the venture, while the Pilgrimage threatens always to become a bore.

Even the distinction between comedy and melodrama is not final. With Hawthorne's romance of terror clutched firmly in hand, two generations of Innocents Abroad dutifully followed in the steps of the writer who had in turn dutifully followed in the steps of his wife. And I, once arrived, dutifully followed at third hand the now fashionable itinerary of those foolish and innocent ghosts, standing before the "Faun" on the Capitoline, and in the dim innards of the Church of the Capuchins looking at the insufferable St. Michael of Guido Reni. It is a lesson in humility to contemplate such works of

91

art, once extravagantly admired; though no one ever quite believes that his own enlightened preference for Caravaggio and the figures on Etruscan tombs will seem one day as inconceivably and nostalgically ridiculous.

The comedy of the journey is no more final than the melodrama. One forgets too easily that *Innocents Abroad* is one of our saddest books. At first glance, shipboard life had seemed to promise passages of pure comic Twain, and things threatened to reach a hilarious climax when we disembarked briefly at Barcelona to make our first penetration of Europe. We had only a few hours ashore and everyone piled into the sightseeing buses at the dock. I found myself just behind a large, enthusiastic lady, almost purple with the strain of being an American. She had thrust eagerly down the gangplank but, getting her first whiff of the Old World, had begun holding her nose in ostentatious and growing disgust, until finally, in the shadow of her first cathedral, she had turned to all of us, imploring us to join in "God Bless America!" It was impossible to laugh; she was so obviously afraid.

The setting of comedy is conservative, and one can still play Mark Twain straight, but the décor and personnel of melodrama have changed drastically, and hell itself has been refurnished and completely recast to suit our shifting taste. To Hawthorne, Italy had seemed a Gothic inferno, an underworld familiar and traditional for all its terror, with the Wandering Jew making a not-unexpected appearance in the catacombs, and the legend of the Cenci once more evoked. For us, however, Italy has become a politicalized, a "neo-realistic" hell; it is the comic-tragic shade of Mussolini that haunts our underground (half the Jack Oakie of Chaplin's *Great Dictator,* and half the bloody, head-down corpse of the obscene newsreel shots that fade indistinguishably into the montage of a handful of recent Italian movies). Beatrice Cenci walks no more; and instead of the print of that tragically theatrical face we are likely to take home with us the image of the latest twelve-year-old rape victim from some seedy suburb; not the figure of classic incest and terror, but of mechanical lust and meaningless violence. The malaria is gone, and we who know all about mosquitoes and germs can believe no longer in a curse, a miasma arising from the almost timelessly compounded evils of Empire and Papacy. But there is still overcrowding and poverty and hunger raised to the power of the exotic; and, to delight the liberal Protestant imagination, the vision of a land harried by evil landlords and by a clergy which can no longer kidnap and torture but which, by opposing birth control, continues its dastardly work.

No, Italy is hell enough for us still; what is disconcerting, however, is the realization that for many Italians we do not seem the gingerly visitors from an upper world that we appear to ourselves, but refugees from our own authentic and ultimate inferno. America has become the hell of its own favorite hell! This is the most disturbing and diverting thing I have learned thus far in Italy. I have had the unexpected sense of Italy as a mirror, a distorting mirror to be sure, one of those diabolical things from a Coney Island Fun House, that gives you for the laughs a brutal caricature, at once a nightmare and a joke, a travesty and a disturbing criticism of yourself.

I am never able to doubt that the portrait of America I find reflected here is a portrait of my own America. Unfair, I may find it, even occasionally dishonest, but it never seems to me the limning of someone else. I have, indeed, felt here as I have never felt before that there is only *one* America. To be sure, an occasional homegrown speaker, visiting under the auspices of the United States Information Service, and reviving the familiar banalities about the infinite variety of our land and the misrepresentations of writers like Faulkner, will arouse in me a suspicion that the monolithic America the Italians dream is a hoax. But, at this distance and inside another view, I see clearly my own ironies and dissents as a necessary part of an overall pattern; and this does not upset me. I have come across occasional detached Americans who seem eager to attest, by loudly certifying the Italian picture of their country, their own dissociation from that picture. "Yes," they declare, "it is true of those others, but we, on the other hand . . ."; and they devote themselves to exposing unfortunate American influences in current Italian movies and novels. These are our last true Innocents Abroad, the last claimants to what seemed once our unquestioned birthright. For whoever admits his complicity in the existent America, down to the crassest Philistine, avows a sense of guilt.

The Italian attitude toward our country is, however, not really available to the innocent expatriate, still linked to us, strain as he will, by a bond of ennui, the last vestige of familiar love. There is no tedium in the Italian's view; he may tremble in hatred before his own image of our civilization, but his connection is essentially passionate and desperate — as if we were, indeed, a *femme fatale*. We have become quite absurdly the blonde Dark Lady, the Beatrice Rappacini of the Italian world. It is ridiculous, one keeps wanting to cry out: the roles are reversed, the drama miscast!

And yet, if the mythic America has seemed for the Italians an inferno, it has also seemed to them a symbol of salvation. But this is, of course, no real contradiction; for why else does one descend into hell, except to find his way home or to heaven or to the promised fatherland, which is to say, into his own yet unravished margins of consciousness. Within the last twenty years, America has come to stand to the Italians for a new idea of man, a humanism beyond their official Humanism, lost in a compulsive rhetoric and captured by the makers of Fascist propaganda. Italian intellectuals had remained strangely immune to the earlier idyllic Americas of the French; though Cooper in translation made a popular success, there never was an Italian Chateaubriand, much less an Italian Crèvecoeur. Not out of the expurgated forests of *Atala* or *The Last of the Mohicans,* but out of the ravaged landscapes of *Sanctuary* and *Winesburg, Ohio,* the Italians have contrived a utopia. Imagine the wit and desperation necessary to such a conceit!

But this is the final America of Italy, the America of its present poets; and one must come to it last of all, through the other Americas which greet the initial glance of the uninitiated traveler, who sees first the apartment houses of the fashionable quarters and the newsstands everywhere: the imaginary America of the upper bourgeoisie, complete with steam radiators and nylons and electric refrigerators, enshrined in the resolutely un-Roman, the really inhuman, "functional" architecture of the Parioli district; and the popular America of comic books, illustrated periodicals, detective stories, and movie magazines. Perhaps there is no other really popular culture except our own. Certainly, no one in Italy seemed capable of filling the vacuum of expectation left after the civil war. The traditional guardians of Italian culture had compromised themselves by coming too easily to terms with Fascism; and the bright young men, who at first flocked almost unanimously to Stalinism, could only *talk* of a new people's culture, at once generally available and uncompromisingly complex. While they chattered and debated, a debased popular literature, made in the image of our own, simply grew.

On every street-corner kiosk, one now sees displayed side by side a half-dozen Italian imitations of *Life* and *Look* and *Pic,* reducing all events through the camera lens to the same values and consequence — the monotone of the spectacle. And, in contrast to their slick black and white, the colored comic books (colored only on every fourth page, one discovers, for Italy after all is not as rich as some countries) translating the adventures of Pecos Bill and "Jane Calamity," of Donald Duck and Mickey Mouse. Mickey especially, rebaptized Topolino in Italian, is everywhere: lending his name to a caramel penny candy, a new Canasta set, a movie house for children — and providing an affectionate nickname for the midget cars that tear through the Roman streets with all the abandon and pace of a Disney cartoon. Only the Superman type of comics have not taken, whether because the sock in the jaw means little in Italian symbology, or in simple reluctance to adopt an urban mythology, I can't say. Certainly, the Romans seem to prefer to linger in the legendary Far West with "Jane Calamity," and they even insist on Mickey Mouse being sent week after week to their own tormentingly lost "Far West," the jungles of Africa.

The translation of American *gialli,* murder mysteries, is a major industry; and, along with the equivalent films, such works provide on the popular level the vision of America as the utopia of violence ("At least your country is young, exciting!") which the intellectuals derive from Erskine Caldwell or William Faulkner. Indians, outlaws, and gangsters flow together with Communist-inspired versions of the American G.I. (on every wall during the recent NATO conference, a

death's-head or a thug's face under a swastika-marked helmet
— and *Via Americani!* Americans Get Out!) into a single
image of the Tough Guy, infinitely repulsive and infinitely
alluring — an ambivalent image of potency.

But the movies provide other Americas, too, Americas of
luxury: the oversize purring automobile, the long-legged girl,
the penthouse towering above the swarming streets; and it is
the movies in their endless repetition that are decisive in the
end. Whatever political paper a man may read, his myths
are made in the dark before the screen; and the Italians are
still moviegoers with an intensity and enthusiasm that has
been gone from America for fifteen years. The provincial
opera house, which once sustained a local art, now shows *Tea
for Two* and *All About Eve,* and the outraged cries of the
nostalgic grow weaker and weaker. Two-thirds of the pictures
one sees advertised on the hoardings are American films, despite the excellence of the Italian product and the substantial
fine which an operator must pay if he does not show a certain
proportion of Italian movies. For most Italians the voyage to
America is a cinematic one — a ritual more honored than
the Mass.

What is hard to see at home, where we are oppressed by the
real vulgarity and triviality of our ordinary films, is the exu-
berant confidence they manage to convey to a society as
anxious and unstable as Italy's. The Italian moviegoer can
only conceive of our life in terms of strength; and it is in this
sense that he finds it easy to reconcile his double view of us
as a Land of the Heart's Desire (the old-fashioned notion of
Golden America has survived the reality of our Depression
and thirty years of Fascist and Communist "revelations") and
as a threat to peace and prosperity. The average moviegoer
would vote Communist, of course; but his willingness to vote
for Togliatti does not mean that he would not be delighted to
emigrate to the United States — to join himself to our mana,
our potency.

The "American" in a quite wonderful current Italian comedy, *Guardie e ladri* ("Cops and Robbers"), is the incarnation
of present Italian stereotype: a bureaucrat, bluff, hearty, a
little overfed, but offensively strong in his checked overcoat

— he is fair game for the Italian con-man, despite the fact (perhaps, after all, because) he has come over to distribute food packages to poor children. Though he is temporarily hoaxed, he is never defeated; though he is blustering and ridiculous, his unassailable confidence and health still overwhelm both the Italian policeman and the crook, who serve or undermine a state in which they cannot believe and inhabit bodies on whose livers they cannot depend. Liver trouble and sexual failure — these are the calamities that fill the columns of Roman newspapers with advertised cures. *Povera Italia!* In America, similar space is occupied by minor anxieties about B.O. and dull teeth. After a while, one cannot help seeing in the eternal newspaper offers to cure impotency a symbolic expression of a general fear of failing virility, from which the rhetoric of Mussolini was able to deliver the Italians for a little while.

Our political "friends" do not challenge the picture of us our enemies cherish; they merely assess it a little differently. A Roman daily newspaper that has supported the Atlantic Pact, describing our crop-headed, ignorant young soldiers with condescending enthusiasm, assures its readers that Stalin would hesitate to attack if he could only see our strength (these strange giants who are capable of washing down a huge meal with ice water!), and ends by assimilating us to a myth of Imperial Rome — a civilization of luxury hedged about by its Praetorian Guards, who fortunately (though quite by accident) became also the guardians of Western European civilization.

We have moved now to the middling level of Italian culture — to the essay on the third page of the daily newspaper with which the serious writer and the professor still manage in Italy to meet the mass mind. The nearest thing to "third page" style, at its not infrequent worst, is to be found in American life in the kitschy program note, which, you may be sure, also flourishes over here. Elmer Rice's *Dream Girl* was playing in Rome when I first arrived, in an Italian version called *Sogno ad occhi aperti* ("Dream with Open Eyes") — and the program note attempted to make clear to its audiences exactly how Rice's trivially amusing, philistine piece was a political lesson of great importance (Americans should continue to dream with eyes wide open and with "the Declaration of Rights in their fist"), and a revelation to America of its own true self. Both the style and the attitude are typical enough to bear quotation. In Rice's work, we are told, we are to find "an expression . . . made in U.S.A. . . . athletic and muscular, well adapted to drawing rooms and martinis . . . a revolt against the labels on canned foods, the black journalism of Hearst, and the fame of Coca Cola." And in Georgina Allerton, the heroine of the play, we are to see not the mad romantic she might seem at first, "riding her European despair like a Lady Godiva," but a true-blue American girl capable of throwing over Freud for the Sane Living of Doctor Hauser. (If the last reference baffles you, you can look up Doctor Hauser in your nearest bookstore, or order the Italian version, if the American edition is exhausted.) The general philistinism of Rice is taken as a special plea to Americans to give up the false pursuit of culture (all the Italians' own weariness with European culture is being projected continually and savagely upon us) and to reveal themselves as what they truly are: lovable noble savages, who "dance the boogie, secretly read the comic strips, are in love with Clark Gable, and walk along Fifth Avenue in all the glory of their long-limbed bodies."

It is the long-limbed blondness of a Georgina Allerton which defines the erotic image of the modern Italian; it is hard for us, for whom the sexually potent primitive tends to be thought of as dark, to understand the Latins' blonde dream — testified to by the outrageously unconvincing peroxided heads one is forever passing in Rome. The American woman is no longer, if indeed she ever was, a "Snow Queen" for the Italians, but a sexual mana-object like her male counterpart, to whom is also attributed a mythical sexual allure. In a recent scandalous murder case, the mother of the child victim turned out to be a whore, "honest," however, the papers all assured us, until she was corrupted during the war by "anglo-saxon" troops; and the unhappy woman who only last week slashed her wrists in a seedy hotel room had been, of course, abandoned by "an American diplomat." There is a popular movie actress called Tamara Lee, with pale-gold hair and legs of extraordinary length, who appears in film after film as the Anglo-Saxon *femme fatale,* scarcely speaking, merely moving across the screen to register her archetypal self. And it is one of those symbolic and inevitable "accidents" that the foremost Italian "Americanist," a poet and translator, committed suicide a year ago, apparently as the result of an unhappy affair with "an American moving picture actress." A posthumous volume of his poems had just appeared, some written in English and dedicated to the beloved "C." — yet another record of the pursuit of the elusive image which is America and death.

It is only on a more serious literary level, however, that the relationship of contemporary Italy to America has come to full consciousness. The confrontation of Italy and America is of recent origin — though it is not as recent as our awareness of it in the United States. We are likely to think of the encounter as a post-World-War-II phenomenon, a result perhaps of the actual penetration of Italy by our troops — a function of an enthusiasm for us as "liberators." Nothing could be further from the truth. The relationship of the Italian intellectuals to our culture begins in horror and disgust, at a point when Italy is in the midst of Fascism and we are at the beginning of our greatest Depression.

It is not the image of a triumphant and flower-crowned army that presides over the start of Italian interest in us, but a vision of soup kitchens and bowery bums, bloody corpses of gangsters and lynched Negroes. *America amara* ("Bitter America") — that is the title of the almost legendary travel book by Emilio Cecchi, "its assonance," as he says, "most exact in every sense," the book which transformed America from a geographical and social entity to a fact of the Italian imagination. The Cecchi volume did not appear until 1938, and it had been preceded in 1935 by Mario Soldati's *America primo amore* ("America, First Love"), the story of an emigration that failed. But Cecchi had already been registering his impressions in the earliest 1930's; and Soldati's book, the work of a very young man, unequal and marred by self-pity, has tended to fuse its meanings into those of the more expert and coolly bitter exposé of Cecchi. In both, after all, there is the same vision of a land ravaged by senseless violence, ruled by women, and presided over intellectually by professors who despise ideas and love bridge; and in both there is the view of a desperate materialism brought to the edge of despair, though the New Deal, by Cecchi's time, is trying to resuscitate the American dream of happiness, that "joy of the child about to collapse into tears."

In Cecchi and Soldati the journey to America becomes literature; and in Cecchi, at least, there is a clue to the next step, in which literature is to become a journey to America. In the midst of the desert of American life, Cecchi finds the unexpected fact of American literature, despising and despised by America. Watching American women in a cafeteria, eating with their curious coldness "a few peas and an ice," Cecchi thinks that on just such a diet Ligeia must have subsisted; reading the account of a particularly repulsive crime in the South, he reflects that America does not have to read Faulkner to imitate him; and, entering New York, he remembers the frantic night journey of Pierre and Isabella into the city. Poe, Faulkner, and Melville — in the phrase of D. H. Lawrence, the minority of ardent and sorrowing spirits lost in a vast republic of fugitive slaves — they are welcomed by the Italian essayist as witnesses against their own civilization, whose barbarity he feels as a threat to his own.

It is important to keep sight of the fact that the contemporary Italian interest in American literature begins with a search for documents to justify a revulsion, to explain an enemy; that it ends in finding a utopia and a cue for emulation is a splendid irony, and betrays perhaps an ambivalence in Cecchi himself, a secret hunger for the madness and primitive rage he chose to read into America. At any rate, whatever his intentions, his essays on American literature (collected in *Scrittori inglese e americani* in 1935) helped release an interest in American writing which burgeoned beyond all foreseeing; and which eventually led to a belated revolution in Italian prose style (the so-called "neo-realism" of Pavese, Vittorini, etc.), with which Cecchi has found it hard to sympathize; and which even contributed to the anti-Fascist movement a motivating myth, though Cecchi himself is a self-declared sympathizer with "cops on horses."

Since about 1930, there has taken place in Italy one of the most extraordinary feats of translation and assimilation in the history of culture; hundreds of American books have been turned into Italian, provided with prefaces, critically discussed, and, most important of all, read with a fantastic eagerness. The figures of Poe, Melville, and Whitman, Hawthorne, Hemingway, O. Henry, and Faulkner have become real presences to the Italian imagination — living and important figures available even to the commonest reader, who will find from time to time in his daily newspaper stories by the older writers, even pieces by Saroyan or Eudora Welty. A new language has been invented — an Italian remade by American prose rhythms (a hybrid like the Mayakovsky-English of the Communist poets in the 1930's), a sometimes deplored idiom, common to the translations and the latest "neo-realistic" novels. If America welcomes warmly the flood of new Italian fiction (and the closely related pseudo-documentary films), it is welcoming itself, a deliberate reflection of its own moods and stylistic devices. What Italy itself had been to England in the Renaissance, what Germany to Europe when Romanticism was beginning — America is (or has been until only yesterday) to contemporary Italy.

In the ten years from 1930 to 1940, the literary discovery of America was made twice over. History has moved so fast, and events have so tended to blur, that for a while the double discovery seemed one. Ten more years, however, have sufficed to show clearly the differences between the two experiences, essentially contradictory, even inimical: the discovery of a barbaric culture and its literature, a new Ossian, by a generation of cultivated and tolerant humanists, who managed to live at peace with Fascism and whose own style was never touched by the American example; and the rediscovery of a land that was at once its particular self and a myth of deliverance. Emilio Cecchi is, as we have seen, the leading figure of the first group; Vittorini and Cesare Pavese and Giaime Pintor, typical figures in the second.

It is both odd and just that the Italian double vision of the journey to America corresponds part for part to the American double vision of the journey to Italy: a Descent into Hell, and a Pilgrimage to the shrines of an idea of man. For the generation of Cecchi, the American experience is the pure Descent into Hell. In his introduction to *Americana,* a thousand-page analogy of American prose, edited by Elio Vittorini,* Cecchi remembers a phrase of D. H. Lawrence which he has already quoted in *America Amara;* of certain documents of American life, Lawrence said: "They seem more terrible than the Oedipus or the Medea; and beside them, Hamlet, Macbeth and King Lear are eyewash." Lawrence is for the Italians the Virgil of their infernal descent. It is impossible here in Italy to pick up a book or listen to a lecture on American literature that does not draw on *Studies in Classic American Literature,* that shrill, self-indulgent, insightful book so little honored still in American universities. After all, it is "unscholarly," as Cecchi was told in 1930, when he read from it in an attempt to persuade his students at the University of California to rediscover Melville! To an Italian, of course, the rhetoric of Lawrence's book (so committed and uncorseted and disturbing to the professor with a pipe) is an earnest that he is *simpatico,* on their side; and so their classic American literature, their Melville and Hawthorne and Cooper, are to this very day essentially Lawrence's.

But Cecchi is not, after all, quite prepared to grant to American writing the tragic status which Lawrence's remark seems to imply. For all their fragmentary brilliance, American prose and poetry are from the beginning "demented and shaken by a St. Vitus dance," and, indeed, it tends to become more and more frantic as a civilization, never dedicated to anything higher than "well-being and material felicity," collapses in its hour of crisis into "hopeless disillusion." To be heard among the exhortations of "the medicine men and Jewish grey eminences of the New Deal" and the baleful cries of American women harrying their men to bed to celebrate orgies of a "frozen and frenetic paganism," the American writer must scream louder all the time. The dialog between him and his public comes to be more and more like that between Hamlet

---

*Apparently, Vittorini had written a too-friendly introduction — and the intervention of the Facist censors prompted the last-minute substitution of the Cecchi essay, a rehash of his earlier pieces.

and Laertes in the grave of Ophelia, a contest of imprecation; and he ends in a kind of sadist *concettismo,* a baroque of the horrible.

As if he were a little afraid of his own yearning toward the madness of American literature, Cecchi keeps reminding himself that, after all, the Hemingways and Faulkners may well turn out to be the Macphersons and Radcliffes of our time, "primordial romantics," forerunners of little intrinsic merit — interesting finally only as documents, as "social and historic testimony" of a culture already sick to death in its youth.

This point of view is met head-on by Cesare Pavese, the brilliant novelist and translator of *Moby Dick.* His collected essays have just appeared posthumously, not only the studies of American literature, but a fascinating series developing a new theory of the relation of myth and literature. In his earliest pieces, written between 1930 and 1934, he boldly spurns the comforting official theory of the American artist as the enemy of his own culture, the foe of that upstart "puritan" system of values, which the Fascist press was always discovering in the act of "threatening our 2000-year-old culture." (Like two boys fighting, Pavese says, one of whom boasts, "I'm the son of a general!") In his studies of Whitman and Dreiser, Sinclair Lewis and Edgar Lee Masters, Pavese sets himself the task of showing how certain works which, read as satire or polemics, create an anti-America, read as poetry, reveal an essential, positive America, America's consciousness of itself; a complex and ironic affirmation, which must also be taken into account along with the strikes, the lynchings, the "materialism," and the "emancipated women" that are its occasions.

To a writer like Pavese, the facts of life in the United States as perceived by Cecchi matter only in their whole context, in which they come to seem minor components of an astonishing attempt to come to terms with the modern world in all its immediacy; to find words for dealing with motives and passions whose very existence a tradition-ridden Italian official culture denied. This search for an anti-rhetorical rhetoric and the honesty which prompted it were essential to America, and not the "babel of clamorous efficiency," "the cruel, neon-lighted optimism," which, after all, were precisely what the Fascists would have liked for Italy — "granted always a civilized veneer of Roman hypocrisy." In the mirror of America, the young Italian intellectuals recognized themselves, their deepest longings, which the official culture wanted to persuade them were spiritual vices. "America was not another country . . . but only the giant theater where with greater candor was played out the drama of us all."

Though the leaders of the Italian state were never willing openly to oppose the interest in American culture, the young soon came to feel each act of criticism or translation, the simple reading of an American text, as symbolic revolutionary acts, secret heresies. Years later Pavese wrote of this period: "It can be said frankly that the new mania for American writing helped not a little to perpetuate and nourish the political opposition. . . . For many people the encounter with Steinbeck, Caldwell, Saroyan, or even with the old Lewis . . . aroused the first suspicion that not all the culture of the world ended with the fasces."

There is in a great deal of the critical writing about American literature under Fascism a sense of an intended ambiguity, a deliberate double-entendre; the young Italian writers (for the Americanists were also the leading novelists and poets) talked about "style" and "expression" — as if, in Pavese's words, they were studying "the past, Elizabethan drama or the poetry of the *stil nuovo*" — but one understands that they are really interested in the living drama, the myth, the problem of America. And the literary attacks on the "hermeticists" and "aesthetes" must be understood, in part at least, as a veiled political foray against the social system with which the older generation of "aesthetes" had made their peace. A revolution of the word that aimed at changing the world! Whatever they may have intended, however, the young intellectuals accomplished a vital renewal of language which is still bearing fruit — whereas the political revolution of which the literary one was to be the type appears to have been stillborn. There is little vital democracy in Italy today, but there is "neo-realism." If this is a wry kind of joke, it is also a real achievement.

It is worth noting, by the way, that the very literature from which our best young writers have been seeking to be delivered, the post-Dreiserian tradition, particularly in the forms it took in the 1930's, has been for the Italian fictionist precisely a means of delivery. Cecchi, to be sure, deplores the mean catalogs of Dreiser, the ephemeral slang of Hemingway; but for the contemporaries of Pavese a kind of practice which impresses us with its exhaustion provided exemplars of a passionate fidelity to the brute given world, of a language that tries impatiently to be things, and of a tradition that exists only in being sought.

In the light of the uses they have made of our literature, it is possible to understand certain Italian estimates of our authors, so different from our own. Masters and Dreiser, Anderson and Sinclair Lewis, and, oddest of all, O. Henry, have seemed to them central; while the "bourgeois and Europeanizing" James has appeared irrelevant for all his undeniable merit — and Eliot, though he has been well translated and much admired, has seemed a product of their own familiar culture rather than of the mythic America with its "miraculous immediacy of expression."

On the other hand, even those Italian intellectuals who have since become Communists have never, like some of our home-grown "liberals," judged our writers on the basis of their "progressivism," but always on the score of their attitudes toward experience and language. So that Faulkner, for instance, political reactionary though he may be, is for them, as for us, the best of our living writers; and Melville the greatest of our classics. There is something heartening in this core of agreement, which rises solidly amid the swirl of our peripheral differences. It is obvious how sympathetic, under the circumstances, the Italians must have found the critical work of Matthiessen, who perhaps alone in America tried to combine in quite their own way a regard for the claims of poetry and a program of political action. If Lawrence is the Virgil of the Italian Descent into Hell, Matthiessen is the Cato of their ascent toward the imagined Earthly Paradise of a new view of man as the master of a society "in which there is an organic unity between culture and the world of work."

It was not until 1946, however, that Pavese discovered Matthiessen, in a post-war era of new possibilities and disappointments. Right up through the war years, the anti-Fascist Americanists had continued to publish side by side with the pro-Fascists under the aegis of Lawrence. The culmination of this ill-assorted united front was the anthology *Americana,* in which Cecchi and Vittorini collaborated, their contradictions concealed amid the quotations from *Studies in Classic American Literature,* and the pictures of American whores, gangsters, and mountains.

In 1943, to be sure, the 24-year-old critic Giaime Pintor had written a review of that anthology, in which he had separated out the confused tendencies* in a brilliant piece of exposition that had to wait until 1945 to be published (it can be read now in a corrected version in the collection of Pintor's essays called *Il sangue d'Europa*). Pintor himself died at the end of 1943, blown up by a German mine while attempting to pass into occupied Italy to join the partisans; but his essay remains the classic discussion of the two discoveries of America. "Cecchi has scrupulously collected a museum of horrors, where he has isolated diseases and decadence, and recognized a world in which it is impossible to trust; while we have heard a voice profoundly sympathetic to us, that of true friends and our first contemporaries. . . . Bureaucratic corruption, gangsters, and economic crisis, all has become nature in a growing body. And that is the whole story of America: a people that grows, that covers with its unbroken enthusiasm the errors it has already committed, and with great good will risks future errors." The true religion of this America is the "exaltation of man," and its so-called materialism, even its love of money, is a front for this abstract fury, "the impulse toward man which animates American youth. And all the weary aesthetes who think of themselves as contemporaries of Pericles . . . the journalists who have taken upon themselves the 'defense of the West' . . . impose on American civilization the stupidity of a phrase: materialistic civilization." It is this despised

---

*The confusing of the two views again has resulted from more recent Communist attempts to sponsor a higher anti-Americanism. At a meeting of the "Charlie Chaplin Cinematographic Society" in 1952, I was handed a leaflet in which a quotation from Pavese (one of his unfriendliest) was combined with a lengthy comment by Ilya Ehrenburg, the whole headed with the famous title of the pro-Fascist Cecchi, *America amara.*

and vital America, which "has no cemeteries to defend," that has invented a new kind of fiction and perfected a new medium, the movies, thus "instituting the first colloquy between the great masses of the world and a unified culture."

Needless to say, Pintor is aware of the possibility that his "anti-Romantic" America, center of resistance to a Romantic Germany which "celebrated the revolt of the myth against man," may itself be a myth, a local name and habitation for a state of mind. "In our words dedicated to America," he concludes his essay, "much may be ingenuous and inexact, much may refer to arguments perhaps extraneous to the historical phenomenon of the U.S.A. in its present form. But it matters little: because, even if the continent did not exist, our words would not lose their significance. This America has no need of a Columbus; it is discovered within ourselves; it is the land which is approached with the same faith and the same hope by the first immigrants and by whoever has decided to defend at the price of pains and error the dignity of the human lot."

Hier oder nirgends ist Amerika— once more! As soon as the self-conscious words are said, a myth is dying; and if it is possible to write about the Italian discovery of America, it is because a dream has become history. The older books on our country continue to be reprinted; the scattered essays of an earlier period are gathered together; the shop windows are full of American novels, and the translations continue. Everybody translates American books (even my doctor is working on a popular handbook about babies), but translation is no longer a passion, merely a habit or even an industry; and no longer is the latest book from the United States picked up with a sense of furious haste, as if somehow everything depended on it.

As early as 1947, Pavese was able to head a new essay, "The days are gone in which we discovered America!"; and the intellectuals, who just after the war were generally Communists and are now more and more merely disillusioned, have been explaining to themselves and everyone else for nearly five years now that they really translated American literature in order to find out what they themselves were not; that American books are no longer as good as they were in the 1930's;

that America, having lost Fascism as an ideal opponent, has lost its vitality; that the American G.I. has been Europeanized to the point of dissipating his "exotic and tragic straightforwardness"; etc., etc. Meanwhile, the more conservative writers who once "defended the West" against America have now discovered us as allies in a new "defense of the West." The very youngest generation is discovering new utopias, a few in Moscow, even more in the vanished Social Republic of Mussolini — but without real conviction or enthusiasm. It is, alas, a time for common sense: "Many countries in Europe and in the world are today laboratories where one creates form and style . . . and even one living in a monastery may say a new word."

One can foresee the discussion five thousand years from now, when the scraps of some of these documents are being dug out of Italian soil, as to whether there ever really was an America, or only a metaphor like Atlantis, a fable for poets . . .

CHAPTER FIVE

The "Good American"

I have been haunted, ever since my return to the United States from Italy, by the image of a typical discussion at the end of which, as inevitably as in a recurring dream, I find myself heated, shouting a little, defending America with a passionate self-righteousness I should like to disown. But it is a true recollection and I cannot disavow it. What *was* I doing, playing the earnest advocate, the patriot at bay — I who, by temperament and on principle, have always been a critic and dissenter, and who had hoped in Europe to open a dialogue based on fairness and moderation? I cannot say I was not forewarned. Before my departure, several friends had told me of their own experiences, of how they, too, had found themselves for the first time forced into the role of apologists and ambassadors extraordinary. But I did not take what they said quite seriously, understanding it as a figure of speech, a hyperbole to express their exasperation with European intellectuals.*

I was prepared to meet with frankness the Europeans who trotted out the conventional criticisms of our culture; to grant that some of us, many of us, indeed, are smug, boorish, conformist, contemptuous of what we do not understand, virtually cultureless. I was resolved not even to assert in protest what, I have long known — that the average European has as little living connection with his country's traditional culture as any

---

*I use "European intellectuals" in an extended sense on the basis of limited experience. My first-hand acquaintance with intellectuals abroad was largely confined to Italy, but I believe it applies, in one degree or another, to most of the other countries of Western Europe — though not, I should suppose, to Great Britain.

Midwestern farmer; for I knew that in Europe at least no one is proud of such ignorance, that the European is likely to be in regard to culture a pretentious hypocrite rather than a surly Pharisee. And this difference I was ready to admit was a European advantage.

I suppose I had not quite realized that the European intellectual would not, as we ourselves do, hate our failings in us, but rather hate us for those failings, taking our faults for our essence. And surely I assumed that no European would forget that he had, indeed, learned of our faults from us; that his current picture of our world had been transmitted to him by those American novelists, of the last century and this, for whom we share an admiration; so that the European observer notoriously sees, even when he visits us, only a fictional America, the world he has learned to expect from Melville and Hawthorne, from Dreiser or Sherwood Anderson or William Faulkner. I had hoped that the European intellectual, in this sense the heir of an American tradition of dissent, would think of us as a society almost pitifully eager to confess its faults, to measure and assess them in the world's eye.

I should have realized (and in a way did) that Europeans have an odd habit of reading our most poetic books as anthropological documents. I had seen in New York, for instance, several years ago, Sartre's melodrama, *The Respectful Prostitute,* and knew what happened when one took Faulkner's parochial symbols of universal human guilt and endurance as a factual account of life in the specific American South. But such disingenuous misunderstandings seemed to me then peripheral and comic.

At any rate, I did not quite understand how anyone could overlook the fact that the myth of a "Bitter America" (Emilio Cecchi, the inventor of the phrase, was a leading critic of our literature) was made in the United States by writers who are as real a part of us as the Snopses or Babbitts whom they have created, and who, by these very creations, bear witness to a vigor and freedom of the imagination which is also America.

I had even hoped that my own small heterodoxies might serve as evidence that not all Americans think alike out of ignorance or choice or abject surrender. But I soon realized that any unorthodox comment I might make would be taken solely as testimony against my country, though I might personally be credited with a courage to which I had no claim. Whatever willingness I disclosed in conversation with my European acquaintances to admit vice or inadequacy in American society was most often regarded not as a sign that America still fostered in some of us the critical intelligence but as an indication of almost superhuman virtue on my part. Such evidence of virtue would be greeted with overt praise, and not a little concealed contempt; for I would have become not only a hero but also an accomplice — my off-the-cuff comments carefully distorted and filed away among the anti-American stereotypes of my auditors. It is only too easy to become the "Good American" of the anti-American Europeans; all one has to do is to talk before them precisely as one has always talked among friends at home, critically, skeptically, bitterly.

But the "Good" in "Good American" has exactly the tone and weight of the same adjective applied to the "Good Jew" of the anti-Semite. One is good in so far as he is different — i.e., not really a Jew or an American, not really the unmodifiable legendary figure of contempt. The anti-Americanism of many European intellectuals has reached the stage where it is almost immune to facts. An automatic selector has been built into the stereotype, which thus becomes self-sustaining and everlasting. The lowest common denominator of tourist making his expected gaffes, the American soldier abroad hailing all foreigners with a "Hey, boy!" — these count because they fit. But the American intellectual, the writer abroad who rejects the label of expatriate, the very novelists who have won universal acclaim — these somehow do not matter, except as they are willing to testify to the depravity of their country.

Some Americans (especially the young, whose own America is as mythic as that of their European friends) submit to the role imposed upon them, flattered by the social success it brings, and by the sense of belongingness that costs only a willingness to bear witness on demand. But most American intellectuals will not abide so ignoble an exploitation; and they fall into the counter-strategy of patriotic defense. It takes only a little while to bring to the surface of one's mind the virtues of his society, which he has, behind all criticism, always taken for granted: its hostility to hypocrisy, its eternal discontent.

He finds quickly that most Europeans are not only ignorant of these virtues but choose to remain so. A sufficiently platitudinous comment on our simplicity and animal vigor, or on the nastiness of McCarthy, is perfectly acceptable. But a favorable remark on the structure of our courts, or an unfavorable one on such legendary victims of them as Alger Hiss or the Rosenbergs, brings forth the supercilious smile, the unspoken but unmistakable rejoinder, "Propaganda!" Even literary remarks may stir suspicion; a derogatory word about the style of Theodore Dreiser or the criticism of F. O. Matthiessen, an unfavorable comment on a Negro poet — and one is labeled an apologist or the dupe of apologists. It is at this point that the shouting properly begins.

One soon learns that it is unwise to be polite about the most hackneyed and apparently harmless observation. Grant without qualification that American soldiers are ignorant, unacquainted with *The Scarlet Letter* and *Moby Dick,* and your interlocutor will follow up by observing in a conspiratorial tone, "It's easy for us [*us!*] to understand how such barbarians can be persuaded to use germ warfare against Korean peasants!" Or admit the abuses of Congressional investigating committees, and you will be expected to grant that the United States has resigned from Western civilization. One must refuse the gambit, protest loudly from the start.

To be sure, shouting is undignified and it solves no ultimate problems; but it leads to some interesting disclosures, perhaps clears the atmosphere that stifles real discussion. When you have cried out at last in exasperation, "What's the matter with you people? Why has the blind criticism of America become for you an obligatory assertion of your independence, while criticism of Russia is considered evidence of cowardice and venality? Surely when you compare the two countries . . ." — your European opposite number does not even let you finish.

"Naturally, there is no comparison," he tells you. "The Soviet Union has nothing in common with us. But America, now! When we criticize America, we are criticizing ourselves. Culturally you represent the most advanced stage of what we are all fast becoming."

Now one knows that this is, in a sense, true. American serious literature among the intellectuals, American mass culture among the people, moves inexorably into Europe. The Americanization of cultural life on all levels is a complement to, perhaps a cause of, anti-Americanism.

"Why do you make your forecast so sadly?" you ask your European friends. "Under our system you will survive. You will be harassed by movies, television, the comic books; but you will be permitted to fight back and you may win in the end. Under the Soviet system of mass culture, you would have to choose among conformism, silence, or death!"

"Would the death of an intellectual be so terrible an event?" Your interlocutor gives you his most cynical and pityingly European smile.

Here is the giveaway, the clue to why anti-Americanism has become a psychological necessity to many Europeans. The self-distrust of the intellectuals, their loss of faith in their function and in the value of their survival, blends with the Marxist dogma that one's own bourgeoisie (if you are a bourgeois, yourself!) is the worst enemy. Conditioned by this principled self-hatred, the European intellectual finds it hard to forgive America for being willing and able to let him live; and even harder to forgive himself for knowing that he could be, in our "McCarthy-ridden" land, if not happy at least unhappy in his customary way. Both these resentments he takes out on a mythicized image of all he hates, which he calls America.

It should be clear that even as self-hatred such a feeling is impure. For the European intellectual ends up via his anti-Americanism hating in himself and his world only what can be called "America," which is to say, "the Other." In the end, anti-Americanism of this type permits the European to indulge simultaneously in self-hatred and self-righteousness. So handy a psychological device is not readily surrendered.

Yet unless it be surrendered, unless the European intellectual learns to see the menace as well as the promise of his future not in a legendary America but in his actual self, self-pity will answer self-righteousness on both sides of the Atlantic — and we will delay yet longer in taking up that dialogue between the European and American intellectual upon which the solution of our problems, cultural and political, in part depends. Perhaps for now a real basis for disagreement is all we can hope to find; but certainly it is better for us to shout at each other in the same world rather than to smile condescendingly from our several nightmares.

CHAPTER SIX

Roman Holiday

It is difficult really to believe in Passover in Rome. By the time I had set out with my two older sons in search of matzos and a community Seder, Holy Week was at hand, and the streets were full of tourists: the Germans (back in force this year) carefully avoiding every eye and speaking only to each other; the seedy herds of Austrians following their guides from crowded bus to crowded bus; the Americans resting between churches at chic sidewalk cafés. It was no use to remind my boys that, after all, the Last Supper was a Seder, too; nothing could redeem the sense of moving in loneliness against the current that flowed toward the great basilicas, the celebration of the Tenebrae, the washing of the feet, and the final orgy of Easter Sunday when half a million foreigners and Romans would stand flank against flank, the visible body of Christendom awaiting the papal benediction.

It does not matter that scarcely any Roman will confess to a belief in religious dogma — that Rome is also a city of anti-clericalism, with a statue of Giordano Bruno presiding over its busiest market; what is *not* believed is always and everywhere the same. And into each house before Easter is past, the priest will come with holy water and a blessing (only the most ferocious Communist will bar his way) to wash believer and non-believer clean for the new year. The rhythms of the year, the rhythms of life itself, are the rhythms of the Church; and to be outside those rhythms as an American and a Jew is to be excluded as no one can ever be in America, where one's loneliness is what he shares with all his neighbors.

Yet the history and legend of Rome belong also to the Jews.

115

My sons and I travel down the Corso where the *ebrei* were once forced to race against asses; we skirt the Forum whose furthest limit is the Arch of Titus, with its image of the defeated Jordan borne on a stretcher; and my oldest boy asks me if it is true that no Jew is permitted to walk under that memorial to the fall of Jerusalem. I tell him that this was once a commonly held belief, and that, for all I know, the Orthodox may still hold it; and I go on to recount the legend of how the Golden Candlestick of the Temple fell from the hands of a triumphal Roman procession into the Tiber. My sons argue about whether it was an accident or an act of God, and they make up a story about finding it again, gold in the black mud.

But by this time the modern Roman Synagogue stands behind us, dignified and ugly, "built," as the guidebooks say, "in an imitation Assyro-Babylonian style" — and my mind has wandered off to the melancholy gossip I have heard lately about the former Chief Rabbi who has become a Catholic. I saw him once in the halls of the University where he now lectures, distrait and melancholy — or perhaps it is only that I expected, *wanted,* him to seem so.

An East European type, certain unofficial informants tell me, despised by the "old Roman" members of his congregation, he was left to bear the brunt when the Nazis came, to face the problem of raising the ransom they demanded. Almost all of the rich Jews were in hiding, my informants go on to explain, so that in the end it was the Pope who put up the money. Then, the war over, the aristocratic members of the congregation returned and began to conspire against their somewhat shabby leader, who therefore. . . . God knows whether any of it is true; but that the story itself should exist is enough to confirm my melancholy.

But today there are wreaths in front of the Synagogue, eight or ten of them draped with the Italian tricolor, their green leaves already dusty and turning brown, for they have been standing out since March 24, anniversary of the mass reprisals in the Ardeatine Caves, when sixty or seventy Jews, along with nearly three hundred other Romans, were killed by the Nazis. The monument to the dead, surmounted by the cross and the Jewish star, is brutally impressive (the Romans have never lost their flair for celebrating death); but more moving are the occasional small plaques on nondescript apartment houses — memorializing some individual victim who once lived there. His fellow-tenants, though they may have stolen his furniture once he was dead, will never forget him.

It is better to concentrate only on the dead. We stand beside the wreath and try to ignore the jaunty youngster who approaches us with a "Shalom" and offers to show us what is left of the "old synagogue" on a lower level. He speaks the sort of American a hep kid would have picked up from our soldiers, and his approach is precisely that of a street peddler offering to sell you something or change your money.

I try to tell my children something about the Ardeatine Caves, but I do not know the details they ask (What does the overhanging slab weigh? How old was the youngest victim?); and, anyhow, it is time to meet R. at the Portico of Octavia. More history. One part of the ancient portico has become the atrium of the church of Sant'Angelo, where for hundreds of years the Jews were forced on each Sabbath to hear a sermon urging conversion. Across the front of the church, in Hebrew and Latin, an inscription still thunders against the outcast and stiff-necked people. Beyond lies the old Ghetto; and, since R. has not yet arrived, we walk through the narrow, sodden streets, where my boys are impressed by the smell of filth and oppression. I do not tell them that all the poorer quarters of Rome share equally that ghetto smell.

In a little square that opens with typical suddenness around a fountain, a woman smiles at us hopefully and says, "Shalom." When we answer, "Shalom," we are surrounded by six or eight young men who appear out of nowhere. Each of them is the twin of the boy before the Synagogue; each has a genuine Swiss watch or Parker 51 pen to sell. My children haggle with them enthusiastically, and they ask us about America; until, even more suddenly than they materialized, they have all disappeared. We see only the soles of feet flashing down a twisting alley. Then we understand, for a cop is riding past, winking at us good-naturedly.

Meanwhile R. has come, and we discuss getting tickets for the community Seder. He knows, he says, a certain kosher butcher shop where one can buy tickets from a man named Polacco; he has this on excellent authority. So we go on to the butcher shop, where no one will confess to having heard of *our* Polacco. "Naturally," the butcher tells us, wiping more blood off his hands onto an already sufficiently bloody apron, "there are many Polaccos. Which one, is the question, and what do we want him for anyway? Tickets for the community Seder? Naturally, there are several Seders. Which one, is the question? Right or left, or — "

Right or left? In our bewilderment, R. and I consult each other in English; and someone taps me on the shoulder, draws me aside: a middle-aged man with a loud, impatient voice, who unexpectedly speaks excellent English. He is sure we would only be interested in the most Orthodox celebration. "Naturally, where you don't have to worry about the food!" He turns aside to consult an elderly man with a beard who has been pretending all along not to be with him; I think they are speaking Yiddish, but they whisper and I can't be sure. "The price will be only — " The tickets are already in his hand, and he presses them enthusiastically into mine.

"But isn't there another?" I ask.

His face loses a little of its not quite plausible friendliness. "Another Seder? Yes, there is one, not so kosher, for the younger men, *very* young — " He looks me up and down carefully, estimating my age. "Twenty-, twenty-five-year-olds. If anyone wants such company!"

"But isn't there one," I insist, "officially sponsored by the Synagogue?"

He regards me now with open contempt. "Officially sponsored? Children! A Seder sung by school children — " He walks off, followed by his accomplice with the beard, who looks back at us scornfully.

"Aha!" the butcher puts in at this point, "you want the children. It's the Polacco *School* you want, not Polacco!"

But R. isn't satisfied. He turns suspiciously on the butcher. "The *other* butcher, isn't he Polacco?" By this time, we do not know how many real or imaginary Seders there are, or what lies we may not be told in the interests of one faction or another.

"Him? He's my brother. We're Terracini."

It had to be Terracini! Not that it isn't a common enough name among Italian Jews: Terracina, Terracini — there must be at least twenty-five in the Rome telephone book, including the dealer in Catholic church supplies; but R. and I are momentarily taken aback. Terracini is also the name of the Communist Senator who was one of the leaders of the recent rioting in the Parliament. That very day a session has ended with the Communists hurling inkbottles at the president of the Senate; and, the day before, R. watched Terracini himself banging his desk with a stick in concert with his colleagues, so that the roll call would not be heard. . . . And it was Terracini, too, who a couple of months before explained away at a meeting of Roman Jewish intellectuals the anti-Semitic trials in Prague, denouncing as a Nazi and hireling our friend Professor T., who rose to challenge his lies.

But at last we have found the Polacco School, a *yeshiva* across the Tiber from the Synagogue, and Terracini is forgotten. The tickets and the matzos are being sold next door to each other; and the children are so delighted at reaching the end of our quest that we are not even disturbed at the curtness with which the young women in charge treat us. Never have they been so busy, so important! "Speak up! Speak up!" They have no time to waste over our indecision.

While we try to figure out the difference between Swiss matzos and regular matzos, we are good-naturedly but efficiently mauled by the large crowd, which struggles for first place with elbow and knee in the approved Roman style. They even look just like Romans, my children insist sadly; they don't look like Jews at all. And the matzos are called *azzime,* and they, too, are different in texture and shape from what we are used to. Even the Pesach wine (we buy everything in sight, flour, meal, wine; there will be complaints when we get home, but who cares!) turns out to be the customary *vino bianco* from Frascati, not the syrupy red stuff to which the children have been looking forward. But later we are all relieved and happy, balancing the awkward packages in our arms; we smile with a new and perilous sense of having found a community as we pass others carrying similar packages.

Next door, the lady in charge is delighted to see us; there will be another American at the Seder, she tells us, a woman with a small child. We will be like manna to them, for neither of them can speak anything but English. The Seder will be wonderful, *wonderful!* If we listen we can hear the children practicing now. It is true; we can just make out their voices, faint and sweet. We are pleased to be so wanted; and as we depart enthusiastically, the friendly *signora* assures us that the rabbi himself will be there. It is to be the next night, and the children can hardly wait.

Perhaps the rabbi *was* there, after all: we could never find out. It is true that there was at the head table a fine-looking, white-bearded old man, very genteel; but he could equally well have been an Italian Senator (even Terracini!), and he seemed throughout the celebration as bored as everyone else. The "American" woman turned out to be a South African who did not have a child at all, and she regarded the R.'s and us with dim hostility from the start. We arrived too early, of course, though we had allowed a half-hour past the announced time; and so we began under the terrible burden of shame borne by the first guest. The children from the school were already at their prayers, dressed in the Italian student uniform; but the white-draped tables which formed a square around their long crowded one were empty; and the teacher who led them glanced up from his book to us with what seemed to me a look of annoyance.

It was hot, and I walked up and down outside with R., watching the arrival of the other paying guests. They turned out to be mostly very old ladies, who drove up in expensive cars and were helped trembling up the steps by their chauffeurs. If they participated at all in the Seder, beyond nibbling a little from each of the plates set before them, I certainly could not tell. They were quite obviously only performing an act of charity.

Three young men came in at the last minute, dark and reticent, but obviously more at home than we, though they confessed later to being Americans. They seemed quite familiar to me, the kind of good Jewish boys who refuse invitations to dinner because they have promised their mothers to keep kosher. After the Seder, they told us in horror about the heterodoxies of the Roman Synagogue, about which I can remember only the fact that it celebrates Bat Mitzvah, the equivalent of Bar Mitzvah but for girls. Imagine it!

The Seder service itself was badly cut and extremely dull, despite the real charm of the children (there was one girl with the black, ugly-beautiful face of a Bedouin) and the freshness of their voices. The only emotion I could sense was the anxiety of the teacher that they get through it all without too horrible a blunder. The sacrifice was just a bone on a plate, the egg only something to eat; and the earnestness of the performing children (even the littlest ones did not squirm noticeably until the end) was canceled out by the apathy of the paying guests. It was a relief when the voice of the young Bedouin broke and they all giggled; or when the pregnant young wife of the teacher, who sat at the head of the table, reached over to slap her own child, distinguished from the others by not wearing a smock.

Three buxom waitresses in pink uniforms trimmed with the shield of David dashed frantically about with bowls of water for washing, herbs for dipping, etc., but they never managed to get anything to us on time, chiefly because the old ladies took so long waving them away; and we were often passed by completely, to the distress of my boys.

The meal itself was served somewhat more efficiently, though, naturally, not until everything was satisfactorily cold. It was a completely Roman, non-Paschal meal: broth with *pasta,* slices of roast veal, and finally artichokes *alla giudea,* which is to say, Jewish style; for the Jews have long been famous as restaurateurs in Rome, and this is their most notable contribution to the local cuisine. It was somehow the last disconsolate touch. Whether the school children had the same fare or not was difficult to discern, for they did not eat off china, like the guests, but from a single metal bowl, like the setting in a prison or a Dickensian workhouse.

There was more singing after the meal, of course; and for this the parents of the children were let in, ruddy-faced working people, ruddier with washing and the excitement of seeing their offspring perform for the rich. They sat across from us

on wooden benches against a farther wall, looking at the pale
old ladies and parchment-yellowish rabbi-senator, not in hostility, but like representatives of a different species. Over their
heads, a sign read in Hebrew: *With a strong hand!* And it
would have taken a Strong Hand, indeed, to have brought us
all out of Egypt together.

From this point on, the ceremony was speeded up until I
could no longer follow it in the *Haggadah* I had brought along;
the children had long since lost interest. Finally, the weary
little students were permitted to sing one song in Italian and out
of tune: the *"Chad gadya,"* into which they flung themselves
with obvious relief, while their parents beamed in approval
and the old ladies tried hard to smile. Only then the teacher,
who had conducted and prompted in suppressed anguish all
evening, rose to explain the symbolism of the egg, the herb,
the bitters; but conversation was general on all sides, and the
chairs of the children creaked. Only his wife listened to him,
earnestly, one hand resting lightly on her swollen belly —
poised for the quick slap if her own child grew restive.

Afterward, the old ladies and the bearded gentleman shook
the hand of the teacher, who bowed gratefully like a superior
servant, while the children trotted off, chattering, on the arms
of their parents. I was ashamed to look at my wife or the
R.'s, and I wanted even to apologize to my sons; but they
were content, after all, for they had been able to wear their
new skullcaps with the initials that their great-grandmother
had sent them, and they had drunk two glasses of wine apiece.
Next year in Jerusalem!

There was not a bus or streetcar in sight. The Communist
trade unions had called a strike for that day in protest against
the new election law passed by the Demo-Christians despite
inkwell-throwing and desk-banging. When we had come down
to the Seder, there had still been some transportation available; but now everyone had decided to enjoy the stoppage with
that frightening good humor with which a Roman crowd greets
any disorder. They stood in groups on the street corners josh-
ing each other about getting home, or sat at the tables of
sidewalk cafés cursing the government of the priests. All the
old ladies had long since been whisked back to the fashionable

quarters by their chauffeurs, and no one was left who knew it was Pesach.

We could not even find a taxi, and the R.'s decided to walk. *"Gut yontif,"* we called to each other as we parted, but we did not believe in it. After three-quarters of an hour, during which the children grew wearier and crankier, a bus came lumbering along which would carry us within a mile of our house. On the long ride home, my wife and I argued bitterly, chiefly because I, for some reason I can no longer recall, refused to admit how miserable the whole evening had been. Finally, I was yelling so loud that the two other passengers were watching me, delighted to be so entertained. Despite it all, the children had fallen asleep, and had to be awakened for the hike home; but they were surprisingly cheerful.

We had almost arrived, when someone hailed us. It was an American girl we knew and her Italian husband, both Jewish, both very young, and determinedly liberal.

"A big day," I said, thinking wearily of the holiday.

"The strike, you mean," he answered. "We really tied them up tight! This should be a lesson for De Gasperi and the Vatican, too." He seemed as enthusiastic about it as if he had arranged it all himself.

What was the use of arguing? "We're just coming from a Seder," I said to change the subject.

"A Seder! I'll bet." He laughed, hoping it was a joke.

"No — no — I'm serious. And tomorrow we're having another — a *real* one at home, so the kids will really understand it."

At that his wife could no longer bear it. "How can you do it?" she cried in horror, turning from me to my wife in search of an ally. "Do you mean to say that in this day and age you tell your children — " she could hardly manage to say it — "you teach them that we're the *Chosen People?*"

CHAPTER SEVEN

Looking Backward:
America from Europe

The end of the American artist's pilgrimage to Europe is the discovery of America. That this discovery is unintended hardly matters; ever since Columbus it has been normal to discover America by mistake. Even in the days when it was still fashionable to talk about "expatriation," the American writer was rediscovering the Michigan woods in the Pyrenees, or coming upon St. Paul in Antibes. How much more so now, when the departing intellectual does not take flight under cover of a barrage of manifestoes, but is sent abroad on a Fulbright grant or is sustained by the G.I. Bill. The new American abroad finds a Europe racked by self-pity and nostalgia (except where sustained by the manufactured enthusiasms of Stalinism), and as alienated from its own traditions as Sauk City; he finds a Europe reading in its ruins *Moby Dick,* a Europe haunted by the idea of America.

The American writer soon learns that for the European intellectual, as for him, there are two Americas. The first is the America of ECA and NATO, a political lesser evil, hated with a kind of helpless fury by those who cannot afford to reject its aid. The second is the America invented by European Romanticism — the last humanistic religion of the West, a faith become strangely confused with a political fact. To the European, the literature of America is inevitably purer, *realer* than America itself. Finding it impossible to reject the reality of death, and difficult to believe in anything else, the European is perpetually astonished at the actual existence of a land where only death is denied and everything else considered possible. Overwhelmed by a conviction of human impotence, he regards with horrified admiration a people who, because they are too naïve to understand theory, achieve what he can demonstrate to be theoretically impossible.

From Europe it is easy to understand the religious nature of the American belief in innocence and achievement; to see how even the most vulgar products of "mass culture," movies, comic books, sub-literary novels are the scriptures of this post-Christian faith — a faith that has already built up in Western Europe a sizable underground sect which worships in the catacombs of the movie theaters and bows before the images of its saints on the newsstands. A hundred years after the *Manifesto*, the specter that is haunting Europe is — Gary Cooper! Vulgar, gross, sentimental, impoverished in style — our popular sub-art presents a dream of human possibilities to starved imaginations everywhere. It is a wry joke that what for us are the most embarrassing by-products of a democratic culture, are in some countries almost the only democracy there is.

It seems to me that it has become absurd to ask whether a democratic society is worthwhile if it entails a vulgarization and leveling of taste. Such a leveling the whole world is bound to endure, with or without political guarantees of freedom; and the serious writer must envision his own work in such a context, realize that his own final meanings will arise out of a dialectical interplay between what he makes and a given world of "mass culture." Even the Stalinists, though they thunder against American jazz and cowboy suits for children, can in the end only kidnap our vulgar mythology for their own purposes. The sense of an immortality here and now, so important to American culture and parodied in Forest Lawn Cemetery, finds its Soviet counterpart in the mummification of Lenin or the touting of Bogomolets; while our faith in progress and achievement finds an *ersatz* in the Five Year Plans and the statistics doctored to assist belief. In its Russian form, what is possible in America has become compulsory, an unofficial rite has been made an orthodoxy. And even in our own country there have been occasional attempts to impose optimism (and eventually, one can only suppose, youth and naïveté) by law.

Yet, for us, hope has never become *just* official, a mere camouflage for actual exploitation, though indeed two generations of writers just before us believed so; and it was their sense of having alone penetrated our hoax of prosperity and happiness that nourished their feelings of alienation. The error of such writers was double (such errors, naturally, do not preclude good writing; being *right* is, thank God, optional for the writer). Not only was the American *mythos* real and effective, the very opposite of the hypocritical and barren materialism it seemed; but also everywhere, down to the last layer of babbittry, there existed beside this belief its complement: an unspoken realization of the guilt and terror involved in the American experience. In his sense of lonely horror, the writer was most one with everyone else.

Precisely the uncompromising optimism of Americans makes every inevitable failure to accomplish what can only be dreamed an unredeemable torment. Among us, nothing is winked at or shrugged away; we are being eternally horrified at dope-addiction or bribery or war, at things accepted in older civilizations as the facts of life, scarcely worth a tired joke. Even tax evasion dismays us! We are forever feeling our own pulses, collecting statistics to demonstrate the plight of the Negro, the prevalence of divorce, the failure of the female organ, the decline of family Bible reading, because we feel, we *know,* that a little while ago it was in our power, new men in a new world (and even yet there is hope), to make all perfect. How absurd of our writers to have believed that only they were pained at the failure of love and justice in the United States! What did they think our pulp literature of violence and drunkenness and flight was trying symbolically to declare? Why did they suppose that the most widely read fiction in America asks endlessly, "Whodunit? Where is the guilt?"

I think we are in the position now to understand that the concept of the "alienated artist" itself was as much a creation of the popular mind as of the artist. It is no accident that Edgar Allan Poe is both the prototype of the American Poet as Despised Dandy, and the inventor of the most popular genres of "mass culture." The image of the drunken, dope-ridden, sexually impotent, poverty-oppressed Poe is as native to the American mind as the image of the worker driving his new Ford into the garage beside the Cape Cod cottage; together they are the American's image of himself. Poe, Crane, Fitzgerald — each generation provides itself with its own lost artist — and their biographies are inevitable best-sellers.

I do not mean to imply that the role of scapegoat is not actually painful for the artist; his exclusion and scourging is the psychodrama of us all, but it is played out in earnest. Poe was in a certain sense a poseur, but he died of his pose; and the end of Fitzgerald was real terror. I want only to insist that the melancholy and rebellious artist has always been a collaborator in American culture — that it is only when he accepts the political or sentimental half-truths of democracy, when he says *yes* too soon, that he betrays his role and his countrymen — and that the popular mind at its deepest level is well aware of this.

Of all peoples of the world, we hunger most deeply for tragedy; and perhaps in America alone the emergence of a tragic literature is still possible. The masterpieces of our nine-teenth-century literature have captured the imagination of readers everywhere, precisely because their tragic sense of life renews vicariously the exhausted spirit. In Western Europe, the tragic tension no longer exists; it is too easy to despair and to fall in love with one's despair. Melodrama, *comèdie larmoyante,* learned irony, and serious parody — these are the forms proper to the contemporary European mind. In the orbit of Communism, on the other hand, despair has been legislated away; justice triumphs and the wicked suffer — there is no evil except in the other. Some lies are the very stuff of literature, but this is not among them; it breeds police forces rather than poetry.

Only where there is a real and advancing prosperity, a constant effort to push beyond all accidental, curable ills, all easy cynicism and premature despair toward the irreducible residuum of human weakness, sloth, self-love, and fear; only where the sense of the inevitability of man's failure does not cancel out the realization of the splendor of his vision, nor the splendor of his vision conceal the reality and beauty of his failure, can tragedy be touched. It is toward this tragic margin that the American artist is impelled by the neglect and love of his public. If he can resist the vulgar temptation to turn a quick profit by making yet one more best-selling parody of hope, and the snobbish temptation to burnish chic versions of elegant despair, the American writer will find that he has, after all, a real function.

Indeed, he is needed in a naked and terrible way, perhaps unprecedented in the history of Western culture — not as an entertainer, or the sustainer of a "tradition," or a recruit to a distinguished guild, but as the recorder of the encounter of the dream of innocence and the fact of guilt, in the only part of the world where the reality of that conflict can still be recognized. If it is a use he is after and not a reward, there is no better place for the artist than America.

PART THREE

THE END OF INNOCENCE

CHAPTER EIGHT

Montana; or The End of Jean-Jacques Rousseau

Hier oder nirgends ist Amerika.
GOETHE

There is a sense, disturbing to good Montanans, in which Montana is a by-product of European letters, an invention of the Romantic movement in literature. In 1743 a white man penetrated Montana for the first time, but there was then simply nothing to *do* with it: nothing yet to do economically in the first place, but also no way of assimilating the land to the imagination. Before the secure establishment of the categories of the *interessant* and the "picturesque," how could one have come to terms with the inhumanly virginal landscape: the atrocious magnificence of the mountains, the illimitable brute fact of the prairies? A new setting for hell, perhaps, but no background for any human feeling discovered up to that point; even *Sturm und Drang* was yet to come.

And what of the Indians? The redskin had been part of daily life in America and a display piece in Europe for a couple of hundred years, but he had not yet made the leap from a fact of existence to one of culture. *The Spirit of Christianity* of Chateaubriand and the expedition of Lewis and Clark that decisively opened Montana to the East were almost exactly contemporary, and both had to await the turn of the nineteenth century. Sacajawea, the Indian girl guide of Captain Clark (the legendary Sacajawea, of course, shorn of such dissonant realistic details as a husband, etc.), is as much a product of a

new sensibility as Atala — and neither would have been possible without Rousseau and the beautiful lie of the Noble
Savage. By the time the trapper had followed the explorer,
and had been in turn followed by the priest and the prospector,
George Catlin in paint and James Fenimore Cooper in the
novel had fixed for the American imagination the fictive Indian
and the legend of the ennobling wilderness: the primitive as
Utopia. Montana was psychologically possible.

One knows generally that, behind the thin neo-Classical
façade of Virginia and Philadelphia and Boston, the mythical
meanings of America have traditionally been sustained by the
Romantic sensibility (the hero of the first American novel died
a suicide, a copy of *Werther* lying on the table beside him);
that America had been unremittingly dreamed from East to
West as a testament to the original goodness of man: from
England and the Continent to the Atlantic seaboard; from the
Atlantic seaboard to the Midwest; from the Midwest to the
Rocky Mountains and the Pacific. And the margin where the
Dream has encountered the resistance of fact, where the Noble
Savage has confronted Original Sin (the edge of hysteria: of
the twitching revivals, ritual drunkenness, "shooting up the
town," of the rape of nature and the almost compulsive slaugh-
ter of beasts) we call simply: the Frontier.

Guilt and the Frontier are coupled from the first; but the in-
habitants of a Primary Frontier, struggling for existence under
marginal conditions, have neither the time nor energy to feel
consciously the contradiction between their actuality and their
dream. Survival is for them a sufficient victory. The contradiction remains largely unrealized, geographically sundered;
for those who continue to dream the Dream are in their safe
East (Cooper in Westchester or New York City), and those who
live the fact have become total Westerners, deliberately cut off
from history and myth, immune even to the implications of
their own landscape. On into the second stage of the Frontier,
it is dangerous for anyone who wants to *live* in a Western community to admire the scenery openly (it evokes the Dream);
such sentiments are legitimate only for "dudes," that is to say,
visitors and barnstorming politicians.

But the schoolmarm, pushing out before her the whore,

symbol of the denial of romance, moves in from the East to marry the rancher or the mining engineer (a critical cultural event intuitively preserved as a convention of the Western movie); and the Dream and the fact confront each other openly. The schoolteacher brings with her the sentimentalized Frontier novel, and on all levels a demand begins to grow for some kind of art to nurture the myth, to turn a way of life into a culture. The legend is ready-made and waiting, and speedily finds forms in the pulps, the movies, the Western story, the fake cowboy song — manufactured at first by absentee dudes, but later ground out on the spot by cultural "compradors." The Secondary Frontier moves from naïveté to an elementary consciousness of history and discrepancy; on the one hand, it falsifies history, idealizing even the recent past into the image of the myth, while, on the other hand, it is driven to lay bare the failures of its founders to live up to the Rousseauistic ideal. The West is reinvented!

At the present moment, Montana is in some respects such a Secondary Frontier, torn between an idolatrous regard for its refurbished past (the naïve culture it holds up defiantly against the sophistication of the East, not realizing that the East *requires* of it precisely such a contemporary role), and a vague feeling of guilt at the confrontation of the legend of its past with the real history that keeps breaking through. But in other respects, Montana has gone on to the next stage: the Tertiary or pseudo-Frontier, a past artificially contrived for commercial purposes, the Frontier as bread and butter.

In the last few years, Montana has seen an efflorescence of "Sheriff's Posses"; dude ranches; chamber of commerce rodeos, hiring professional riders; and large-scale "Pioneer Days," during which the bank clerk and the auto salesman grow beards and "go Western" to keep the tourist-crammed coaches of the Northern Pacific and the Great Northern rolling. The East has come to see its ancient dream in action — and they demand it on the line, available for the two-week vacationer. What the Easterner expects, the Montanan is prepared to give him, a sham mounted half in cynicism, half with the sense that this is, after all, what the West really means, merely made visible, vivid. There is, too, a good deal of "play" involved, a not wholly unsympathetic boyish pleasure in dressing up and pulling the leg of the outlander, which overlays and to some degree mitigates the cruder motives of "going Western." But in Montana's larger cities and towns a new kind of entrepreneur has appeared: the Rodeo and Pioneer Days Manager, to whom the West is strictly business. There is scarcely a Montanan who does not at one remove or another share in the hoax and in the take; who has not, like the nightclub Negro or the stage Irishman, become the pimp of his particularity, of the landscape and legend of his state.

Astonishingly ignorant of all this, I came from the East in 1941 to live in Montana, possessing only what might be called the standard Eastern equipment: the name of the state capital (mispronounced); dim memories of a rather absurd poem that had appeared, I believe, in *The Nation,* and that began: "Hot afternoons have been in Montana"; some information about Burton K. Wheeler; and the impression that Montana (or was it Idaho?) served Ernest Hemingway as a sort of alternative Green Hills of Africa. I had, in short, inherited a shabby remnant of the Romantic myth; and, trembling on an even more remote periphery of remembering, I was aware of visions of the Indian (out of Cooper and "The Vanishing American") and the Cowboy, looking very much like Tom Mix. I was prepared not to call cattle "cows," and resolutely face down any student who came to argue about his grades armed with a six-shooter.

I was met unexpectedly by the Montana Face.* What I had been expecting I do not clearly know; zest, I suppose, naïveté,

---

*Natives of Montana, it is only fair to say, don't believe in, don't *see* the Montana Face, though of course they can describe the Eastern Face, black, harried, neurotic. It takes a long time before newcomers dare confide in each other what they all see, discover that they have not been enduring a lonely hallucination; but the unwary outlander who sets down for public consumption an account of what he has noticed before he forgets it or comes to find it irrelevant must endure scorn and even hatred. Since the first publication of this essay, I have been reviled for putting in print my (I had supposed) quite unmalicious remarks on the "Montana Face" by men who have never read the *Partisan Review* — indeed by some who, I suspect, do not read at all. Yet some of those most exercised have been quite willing to admit the inarticulateness, the starvation of sensibility and inhibition of expression, of which "the Face" is an outward symbol. To criticize the soul is one thing, to insult the body quite another!

a ruddy and straightforward kind of vigor — perhaps even honest brutality. What I found seemed, at first glance, reticent, sullen, weary — full of self-sufficient stupidity; a little later it appeared simply inarticulate, with all the dumb pathos of what cannot declare itself: a face developed not for sociability or feeling, but for facing into the weather. It said friendly things to be sure, and meant them; but it had no adequate physical expressions even for friendliness, and the muscles around the mouth and eyes were obviously unprepared to cope with the demands of any more complicated emotion. I felt a kind of innocence behind it, but an innocence difficult to distinguish from simple ignorance. In a way, there was something heartening in dealing with people who had never seen, for instance, a Negro or a Jew or a Servant, and were immune to all their bitter meanings; but the same people, I knew, had never seen an art museum or a ballet or even a movie in any language but their own, and the poverty of experience had left the possibilities of the human face in them incompletely realized.

"Healthy!" I was tempted to think contemptuously, missing the conventional stigmata of neurosis I had grown up thinking the inevitable concomitants of intelligence. It was true, certainly, that neither the uses nor the abuses of conversation, the intellectual play to which I was accustomed, flourished here; in that sense the faces didn't lie. They were conditioned by a mean, a parsimonious culture; but they were by no means mentally incurious — certainly not "healthy," rather pricked invisibly by insecurity and guilt. To believe anything else was to submit to a kind of parody of the Noble Savage, the Healthy Savage — stupidity as mental health. Indeed there was, in their very inadequacy at expressing their inwardness, the possibility of pathos at least — perhaps even tragedy. Such a face to stand at the focus of reality and myth, and in the midst of all the grandiloquence of the mountains! One reads behind it a challenge that demands a great, liberating art, a ritual of expression — and there is, of course, the movies.

The seediest moving-picture theater in town, I soon discovered, showed every Saturday the same kind of Western picture at which I had yelled and squirmed as a kid, clutching my box of jujubes; but in this context it was different. The children still eagerly attended, to be sure — but also the cowhands. In their run-over-at-the-heels boots and dirty jeans, they were apparently willing to invest a good part of their day off watching Gene and Roy, in carefully tailored togs, get the rustlers, save the ranch, and secure the Right; meanwhile making their own jobs, their everyday work into a symbol of the Natural Gentleman at home.

They *believed it all* — not only that the Good triumphs in the end, but that the authentic hero is the man who herds cattle. Unlike, for instance, the soldier at the war picture, they never snickered, but cheered at all the right places; and yet, going out from contemplating their idealized selves to get drunk or laid, they must somehow have felt the discrepancy, as failure or irony or God knows what. Certainly for the bystander watching the cowboy, a comic book under his arm, lounging beneath the bright poster of the latest Roy Rogers film, there is the sense of a joke on someone — and no one to laugh. It is nothing less than the total myth of the goodness of man in a state of nature that is at stake every Saturday after the show at the Rialto; and, though there is scarcely anyone who sees the issue clearly or as a whole, most Montanans are driven instinctively to try to close the gap.

The real cowpuncher begins to emulate his Hollywood version; and the run-of-the-mill professional rodeo rider, who has turned a community work-festival into paying entertainment, is an intermediary between life and the screen, the poor man's Gene Autry. A strange set of circumstances has preserved in the cowboy of the horse opera the Child of Nature, Natty Bumppo become Roy Rogers (the simple soul ennobled by intimacy with beasts and a virginal landscape), and has transformed his saga into the national myth. The boyhood of most living Americans does not go back beyond the first movie cowpuncher, and these days the kid without a cowboy outfit is a second-class citizen anywhere in America. Uncle Sam still survives as our public symbol; but actually America has come to picture itself in chaps rather than striped pants.*

---

*The myth of the Cowboy has recently begun to decline in popular favor, crowded out of the pulps by the Private Eye and the Space Pilot; and is being "secularized," like all archetypes that are dying, in a host of more or less highbrow reworkings of the archetypal theme: *Shane, High Noon,* etc.

Since we are comparatively historyless and culturally dependent, our claim to moral supremacy rests upon a belief that a high civilization is at a maximum distance from goodness; the cowboy is more noble than the earl.

But, on the last frontiers of Montana, the noble lie of Rousseau is simply a lie; the face on the screen is debunked by the watcher. The tourist, of course, can always go to the better theaters, drink at the more elegant bars beside the local property owner, dressed up for Pioneer Days. The cowhands go to the shabby movie house off the main drag and do their drinking in their own dismal places. And when the resident Easterner or the visitor attempts to pursue the cowpuncher to his authentic dive, the owner gets rich, chases out the older whores, puts in neon lights and linoleum — which, I suppose, serves everybody right.

But the better-educated Montanan does not go to the Westerns. He discounts in advance the vulgar myth of the Cowboy, where the audience gives the fable the lie, and moves the Dream, the locus of innocence, back into a remoter past; the surviving Cowboy is surrendered for the irrecoverable Pioneer. It is the Frontiersman, the Guide who are proposed as symbols of original nobility: Jim Bridger or John Colter, who outran half a tribe of Indians, barefoot over brambles. But this means giving up to begin with the possibilities that the discovery of a New World had seemed to promise: a present past, a primitive *now,* America as a contemporary Golden Age.

When the point of irreconcilable conflict between fact and fiction had been reached earlier, the Dream had been projected westward toward a new Frontier — but Montana is a *last Frontier;* there is no more ultimate West. Here the myth of the Noble Woodsman can no longer be maintained in space (the dream of Rousseau reaches a cul-de-sac at the Lions Club luncheon in Two Dot, Montana); it retreats from geography into time, from a discoverable West into the realm of an irrecoverable past. But even the past is not really safe.

Under the compulsion to examine his past (and there have been recently several investigations, culminating in the Rockefeller Foundation-sponsored Montana Study), the contemporary Montanan, pledged to history though nostalgic for myth, becomes willy-nilly an iconoclast. Beside a John Colter he discovers a Henry Plummer, the sheriff who was for years secretly a bandit; and the lynch "justice" to which Plummer was brought seems to the modern point of view as ambiguous as his career. The figure of the Pioneer becomes ever more narrow, crude, brutal; his law is revealed as arbitrary force, his motive power as — greed. The Montanan poring over his past comes to seem like those dance-hall girls, of whom a local story tells, panning the ashes of a road agent who had been lynched and burned, for the gold it had been rumored he was carrying. Perhaps there had never been any gold in the first place. . . .

It is in his relations with the Indian that the Pioneer shows to worst advantage. The record of those relations is one of aggression and deceit and, more remotely, the smug assumption that anything goes with "Savages." There are honorable exceptions among the early missionaries, but it is hard for a Protestant culture to make a Jesuit its hero. For many years the famous painting of Custer's Last Stand hung in the state university, where the students of history were being taught facts that kept them from taking Custer for the innocent Victim, the symbolic figure of the white man betrayed by crafty redskins that he is elsewhere. In Montana it is difficult to see the slaughter at Little Big Horn as anything but the result of a tactical error in a long warfare with whose motives one can no longer sympathize.

Driving across Montana, the conscientious sightseer who slows up for the signs saying "Historic Point 1000 Feet" can read the roadside marker beside US 2 at Chinook, which memorializes "The usual fork-tongued methods of the white which had deprived these Indians of their hereditary lands," "One of the blackest records of our dealings with the Indians . . ." Or at Poplar he can learn how the Assiniboines "are now waiting passively for the fulfillment of treaties made with 'The Great White Father.' "*

---

*I have since been told that these signs were composed by a self-conscious "rebel," who later accommodated to the ruling powers and grew rich; but such an account is itself an American Legend — and anyway the words of the "rebel" have never seemed inappropriate to legislator, road commissioner, or traveler on the highways.

It is at first thoroughly disconcerting to discover such confessions of shame blessed by the state legislature and blazoned on the main roads where travelers are enjoined to stop and notice. What motives can underlie such declarations: The feeling that simple confession is enough for absolution? A compulsion to blurt out one's utmost indignity? A shallow show of regret that protects a basic indifference? It is not only the road markers that keep alive the memory of the repeated betrayals and acts of immoral appropriation that brought Montana into existence; there are books to document the story, and community pageants to present it in dramatic form. The recollection of a common guilt comes to be almost a patriotic duty.

What is primarily involved is, I think, an attempt to *identify* with the Indian. Notice in the sentences quoted from highway signs the use of Indian terminology, "fork-tongued," "Great White Father" — the attempt to get *inside* the Indian's predicament. If the Pioneer seems an ignoble figure beside the Indian, it is perhaps because he was, as a Noble Savage, not quite savage enough; as close as he was to nature, the White Pioneer, already corrupted by Europe and civilization, could not achieve the saving closeness. "Civilization," a road sign between Hysham and Forsyth ironically comments, "is a wonderful thing, according to some people." The corpse of Rousseau is still twitching.

At the beginnings of American literature, Cooper had suggested two avatars of primeval goodness: Pioneer and Indian, the alternative nobility of Natty Bumppo and Chingachgook; and the Montanan, struggling to hang on to the Romantic denial of Original Sin, turns to the latter, makes the injured Chief Joseph or Sitting Bull the Natural Gentleman in place of the deposed Frontiersman.

But the sentimentalized Indian will not stand up under scrutiny either. "The only good Indian is a dead Indian," the old folk saying asserts; and indeed the Montanan who is busy keeping the living Indian in the ghetto of the reservation cannot afford to believe too sincerely in his nobility. The cruelest aspect of social life in Montana is the exclusion of the Indian; deprived of his best land, forbidden access to the upper levels of white society, kept out of any job involving prestige, even in some churches confined to the back rows, but of course protected from whisky and comforted with hot lunches and free hospitals — the actual Indian is a constant reproach to the Montanan, who feels himself Nature's own democrat, and scorns the South for its treatment of the Negro, the East for its attitude toward the Jews. To justify the continuing exclusion of the Indian, the local white has evolved the theory that the redskin is *naturally* dirty, lazy, dishonest, incapable of assuming responsibility — a troublesome child; and this theory confronts dumbly any attempt at reasserting the myth of the Noble Savage.

The trick is, of course, to *keep* the Indian what he is, so that he may be pointed out, his present state held up as a justification for what has been done to him. And the trick works; the Indian acts as he is expected to; confirmed in indolence and filth, sustained by an occasional smuggled bout of drunkenness, he does not seem even to have clung to his original resentment, lapsing rather into apathy and a certain self-contempt. The only thing white civilization had brought to the Indian that might be judged a good was a new religion; but one hears tales now of the rise of dope-cults, of "Indian Christianity," in which Jesus and Mary and the drug *peyote* are equally adored. Once I traveled for two days with an Indian boy on his way to be inducted into the Army; and, when he opened the one paper satchel he carried, it contained: a single extra suit of long underwear and forty comic books — all the goods, material and spiritual, with which our culture had endowed him.

On the side of the whites, there is, I think, a constantly nagging though unconfessed sense of guilt, perhaps the chief terror that struggles to be registered on the baffled Montana Face. It is a struggle much more difficult for the Montana "liberal" to deal with than those other conflicts between the desired and the actual to which he turns almost with relief: the fight with the Power Company or the Anaconda Copper Mining Company for the instruments of communication and the possibilities of freedom. The latter struggles tend to pre-empt the liberal's imagination, because on them he can take an unequivocal stand; but in respect to the Indian he is torn with inner feelings of guilt, the knowledge of his own complicity in perpetuating the stereotypes of prejudice and discrimination. In that relationship he cannot wholly dissociate himself from the oppressors; by his color, he is born into the camp of the Enemy.

There is, of course, no easy solution to the Indian problem; but so long as the Montanan fails to come to terms with the Indian, despised and outcast in his open-air ghettos, just so long will he be incapable of coming to terms with his own real past, of making the adjustment between myth and reality upon which a successful culture depends. When he admits that the Noble Savage is a lie; when he has learned that his state is where the myth comes to die (it is here, one is reminded, that the original of Huck Finn ended his days, a respected citizen), the Montanan may find the possibilities of tragedy and poetry for which so far he has searched his life in vain.

CHAPTER NINE

Come Back to the Raft Ag'in, Huck Honey!

It is perhaps to be expected that the Negro and the homosexual should become stock literary themes in a period when the exploration of responsibility and failure has become again a primary concern of our literature. It is the discrepancy they represent that haunts us, that moral discrepancy before which we are helpless, having no resources (no tradition of courtesy, no honored mode of cynicism) for dealing with a conflict of principle and practice. It used once to be fashionable to think of puritanism as a force in our lives encouraging hypocrisy; quite the contrary, its emphasis upon the singleness of belief and action, its turning of the most prosaic areas of life into arenas where one's state of grace is tested, confuse the outer and the inner and make hypocrisy among us, perhaps more strikingly than ever elsewhere, *visible,* visibly detestable, the cardinal sin. It is not without significance that the shrug of the shoulders (the acceptance of circumstance as a sufficient excuse, the sign of self-pardon before the inevitable lapse) seems in America an unfamiliar, an alien gesture.

And yet before the continued existence of physical homosexual love (our crudest epithets notoriously evoke the mechanics of such affairs), before the blatant ghettos in which the Negro conspicuously creates the gaudiness and stench that offend him, the white American must make a choice between coming to terms with institutionalized discrepancy or formulating radically new ideologies. There are, to be sure, stopgap devices, evasions of that final choice; not the least interesting is the special night club: the "queer" café, the black-and-tan joint, in which fairy or Negro exhibit their fairy-ness, their Negro-ness as if they were mere divertissements, gags thought up for the laughs and having no reality once the lights go out and the chairs are piled on the tables by the cleaning women. In the earlier minstrel show, a Negro performer was required to put on with grease paint and burnt cork the formalized mask of blackness; while the queer must exaggerate flounce and flutter into the convention of his condition.

The situations of the Negro and the homosexual in our society pose quite opposite problems, or at least problems suggesting quite opposite solutions. Our laws on homosexuality and the context of prejudice they objectify must apparently be changed to accord with a stubborn social fact; whereas it is the social fact, our overt behavior toward the Negro, that must be modified to accord with our laws and the, at least official, morality they objectify. It is not, of course, quite so simple. There is another sense in which the fact of homosexual passion contradicts a national myth of masculine love, just as our real relationship with the Negro contradicts a myth of that relationship; and those two myths with their betrayals are, as we shall see, one.

The existence of overt homosexuality threatens to compromise an essential aspect of American sentimental life: the camaraderie of the locker room and ball park, the good fellowship of the poker game and fishing trip, a kind of passionless passion, at once gross and delicate, homoerotic in the boy's sense, possessing an innocence above suspicion. To doubt for a moment this innocence, which can survive only as *assumed*, would destroy our stubborn belief in a relationship simple, utterly satisfying, yet immune to lust; physical as the handshake is physical, this side of copulation. The nineteenth-century myth of the Immaculate Young Girl has failed to survive in any *felt* way into our time. Rather, in the dirty jokes shared among men in the smoking car, the barracks, or the dormitory, there is a common male revenge against women for having flagrantly betrayed that myth; and under the revenge, the rather smug assumption of the chastity of the revenging group, in so far as it is a purely male society. From what other source could arise that unexpected air of good clean fun which overhangs such sessions? It is this self-congratulatory buddy-buddiness, its astonishing naïveté that breed at once endless opportunities for inversion and the terrible reluctance to admit its existence, to surrender the last believed-in stronghold of love without passion.

It is, after all, what we know from a hundred other sources that is here verified: the regressiveness, in a technical sense, of American life, its implacable nostalgia for the infantile, at once wrong-headed and somehow admirable. The mythic America is boyhood — and who would dare be startled to realize that the two most popular, most *absorbed,* I am sure, of the handful of great books in our native heritage are customarily to be found, illustrated, on the shelves of the children's library. I am referring, of course, to *Moby Dick* and *Huckleberry Finn,* so different in technique and language, but alike children's books or, more precisely, *boys'* books.

There are the Leatherstocking Tales of Cooper, too, as well as Dana's *Two Years Before the Mast* and a good deal of Stephen Crane, books whose continuing favor depends more and more on the taste of boys; and one begins to foresee a similar improbable fate for Ernest Hemingway. Among the most distinguished novelists of the American past, only Henry James completely escapes classification as a writer of juvenile classics; even Hawthorne, who did write sometimes for children, must in his most adult novels endure, though not as Mark Twain and Melville submit to, the child's perusal. A child's version of *The Scarlet Letter* would seem a rather farfetched joke if it were not a part of our common experience. Finding in the children's department of the local library what Hawthorne liked to call his "hell-fired book," and remembering that *Moby Dick* itself has as its secret motto *"Ego te baptizo in nomine diaboli,"* one can only bow in awed silence before the mysteries of public morality, the American idea of "innocence." Everything goes except the frank description of adult heterosexual love. After all, boys will be boys!

What, then, do all these books have in common? As boys' books we should expect them shyly, guiltlessly as it were, to proffer a chaste male love as the ultimate emotional experience

— and this is spectacularly the case. In Dana, it is the narrator's melancholy love for the *kanaka,* Hope; in Cooper, the lifelong affection of Natty Bumppo and Chingachgook; in Melville, Ishmael's love for Queequeg; in Twain, Huck's feeling for Nigger Jim. At the focus of emotion, where we are accustomed to find in the world's great novels some heterosexual passion, be it "platonic" love or adultery, seduction, rape, or long-drawn-out flirtation, we come instead on the fugitive slave and the no-account boy lying side by side on a raft borne by the endless river toward an impossible escape, or the pariah sailor waking in the tattooed arms of the brown harpooner on the verge of their impossible quest. *"Aloha, aikane, aloha nui,"* Hope cries to the lover who prefers him to all his fellow-whites; and Ishmael in utter frankness tells us: "I found Queequeg's arm thrown over me in the most loving and affectionate manner. You had almost thought I had been his wife . . . he still hugged me tightly, as though naught but death should part us twain . . . Thus, then, in our heart's honeymoon, lay I and Queequeg — a cosy, loving pair . . . he pressed his forehead against mine, clasped me around the waist, and said that henceforth we were married."

In Melville, the ambiguous relationship is most explicitly rendered; almost, indeed, openly explained. Not by a chance phrase or camouflaged symbol (the dressing of Jim in a woman's gown in *Huck Finn,* for instance, which can mean anything or nothing at all), but in a step-by-step exposition, the Pure Marriage of Ishmael and Queequeg is set before us: the initial going to bed together and the first shyness overcome, that great hot tomahawk-pipe accepted in a familiarity that dispels fear; next, the wedding ceremony itself (for in this marriage like so many others the ceremonial follows the deflowering), with the ritual touching of foreheads; then, the queasiness and guilt the morning after the *official* First Night, the suspicion that one has joined himself irrevocably to his own worst nightmare; finally, a symbolic portrayal of the continuing state of marriage through the image of the "monkey rope" which binds the lovers fast waist to waist (for the sake of this symbolism, Melville changes a *fact* of whaling practice — the only time in the book), a permanent alliance that provides mutual protection but also threatens mutual death.

Physical it all is, certainly, yet somehow ultimately innocent. There lies between the lovers no naked sword but a
childlike ignorance, as if the possibility of a fall to the carnal
had not yet been discovered. Even in the *Vita Nuova* of Dante,
there is no vision of love less offensively, more unremittingly
chaste; that it is not adult seems beside the point. Ishmael's
sensations as he wakes under the pressure of Queequeg's arm,
the tenderness of Huck's repeated loss and refinding of Jim,
the role of almost Edenic helpmate played for Bumppo by
the Indian — these shape us from childhood: we have no
sense of first discovering them or of having been once without them.

Of the infantile, the homoerotic aspects of these stories we
are, though vaguely, aware; but it is only with an effort that
we can wake to a consciousness of how, among us who at the
level of adulthood find a difference in color sufficient provoca-
tion for distrust and hatred, they celebrate, all of them, the
mutual love of *a white man and a colored*. So buried at a
level of acceptance which does not touch reason, so desperately repressed from overt recognition, so contrary to what
is usually thought of as our ultimate level of taboo — the
sense of that love can survive only in the obliquity of a symbol,
persistent, obsessive, in short, an archetype: the boy's homoerotic crush, the love of the black fused at this level into a
single thing.

I hope I have been using here a hopelessly abused word
with some precision; by "archetype" I mean a coherent pattern
of beliefs and feelings so widely shared at a level beneath consciousness that there exists no abstract vocabulary for repre-
senting it, and so "sacred" that unexamined, irrational re-
straints inhibit any explicit analysis. Such a complex finds a
formula or pattern story, which serves both to embody it, and,
at first at least, to conceal its full implications. Later, the
secret may be revealed, the archetype "analyzed" or "allegori-
cally" interpreted according to the language of the day.

I find the complex we have been examining genuinely
mythic; certainly it has the invisible character of the true archetype, eluding the wary pounce of Howells or Mrs. Twain, who

excised from *Huckleberry Finn* the cussing as unfit for children, but who left, unperceived, a conventionally abhorrent doctrine of ideal love. Even the writers in whom we find it attained it, in a sense, dreaming. The felt difference between *Huckleberry Finn* and Twain's other books must lie in part in the release from conscious restraint inherent in the author's assumption of the character of Huck; the passage in and out of darkness and river mist, the constant confusion of identities (Huck's ten or twelve names; the question of who is the real uncle, who the true Tom), the sudden intrusions into alien violences without past or future, give the whole work, for all its carefully observed detail, the texture of a dream. For *Moby Dick* such a point need scarcely be made. Even Cooper, despite his insufferable gentlemanliness, his tedium, cannot conceal from the kids who continue to read him the secret behind his overconscious prose: the childish, impossible dream. D. H. Lawrence saw in him clearly the boy's Utopia: the absolute wilderness in which the stuffiness of home yields to the wigwam, and "My Wife" to Chingachgook.

I do not recall ever having seen in the commentaries of the social anthropologist or psychologist an awareness of the role of this profound child's dream of love in our relation to the Negro. (I say Negro, though the beloved in the books I have mentioned is variously Indian and Polynesian, because the Negro has become more and more exclusively for us *the* colored man, the colored man *par excellence*.) Trapped in what have by now become shackling clichés — the concept of the white man's sexual envy of the Negro male, the ambivalent horror of miscegenation — they do not sufficiently note the complementary factor of physical attraction, the archetypal love of white male and black. But either the horror or the attraction is meaningless alone; only together do they make sense. Just as the pure love of man and man is in general set off against the ignoble passion of man for woman, so more specifically (and more vividly) the dark desire which leads to miscegenation is contrasted with the ennobling love of a white man and a colored one. James Fenimore Cooper is our first poet of this ambivalence; indeed, miscegenation is the secret theme of the Leatherstocking novels, especially of

The Last of the Mohicans. Natty Bumppo, the man who boasts always of having "no cross" in *his* blood, flees by nature from the defilement of all women, but never with so absolute a revulsion as he displays toward the *squaw* with whom at one point he seems at the point of being forced to cohabit; and the threat of the dark-skinned rapist sends pale woman after pale woman skittering through Cooper's imagined wilderness. Even poor Cora, who already has a fatal drop of alien blood that cuts her off from any marriage with a white man, in so far as she is white cannot be mated with Uncas, the noblest of redmen. Only in death can they be joined in an embrace as chaste as that of males. There's no good woman but a dead woman! Yet Chingachgook and the Deerslayer are permitted to sit night after night over their campfire in the purest domestic bliss. So long as there is no mingling of blood, soul may couple with soul in God's undefiled forest.

Nature undefiled — this is the inevitable setting of the Sacred Marriage of males. Ishmael and Queequeg, arm in arm, about to ship out, Huck and Jim swimming beside the raft in the peaceful flux of the Mississippi — here it is the motion of water which completes the syndrome, the American dream of isolation afloat. The notion of the Negro as the unblemished bride blends with the myth of running away to sea, of running the great river down to the sea. The immensity of water defines a loneliness that demands love; its strangeness symbolizes the disavowal of the conventional that makes possible all versions of love. In *Two Years Before the Mast,* in *Moby Dick,* in *Huckleberry Finn* the water is there, is the very texture of the novel; the Leatherstocking Tales propose another symbol for the same meaning: the virgin forest. Notice the adjectives — the virgin forest and the forever inviolable sea. It is well to remember, too, what surely must be more than a coincidence, that Cooper, who could dream this myth, also invented for us the novel of the sea, wrote for the first time in history the sea story proper.

The rude pederasty of the forecastle and the captain's cabin, celebrated in a thousand jokes, is the profanation of a dream; yet Melville, who must have known such blasphemies, refers to them only once and indirectly, for it was *his* dream that they threatened. And still the dream survives; in a recent book by Gore Vidal, an incipient homosexual, not yet aware of the implications of his feelings, indulges in the reverie of running off to sea with his dearest friend. The buggery of sailors is taken for granted everywhere, yet is thought of usually as an inversion forced on men by their isolation from women; though the opposite case may well be true: the isolation sought more or less consciously as an occasion for male encounters. At any rate, there is a context in which the legend of the sea as escape and solace, the fixated sexuality of boys, the myth of the dark beloved, are one. In Melville and Twain at the center of our tradition, in the lesser writers at the periphery, the archetype is at once formalized and perpetuated. Nigger Jim and Queequeg make concrete for us what was without them a vague pressure on the threshold of our consciousness; the proper existence of the archetype is in the realized character, who waits, as it were, only to be asked his secret. Think of Oedipus biding in silence from Sophocles to Freud!

Unwittingly, we are possessed in childhood by these characters and their undiscriminated meaning, and it is difficult for us to dissociate them without a sense of disbelief. What — these household figures clues to our subtlest passions! The foreigner finds it easier to perceive the significances too deep within us to be brought into focus. D. H. Lawrence discovered in our classics a linked mythos of escape and immaculate male love; Lorca in *The Poet in New York* grasped instinctively (he could not even read English) the kinship of Harlem and Walt Whitman, the fairy as bard. But of course we do not have to be conscious of what possesses us; in every generation of our own writers the archetype reappears, refracted, half-understood, but *there*. In the gothic reverie of Capote's *Other Voices, Other Rooms,* both elements of the syndrome are presented, though disjunctively: the boy moving between the love of a Negro maidservant and his inverted cousin. In Carson McCullers' *Member of the Wedding,* another variant is invented: a *female* homosexual romance between the boy-girl Frankie and a Negro cook. This time the Father-Slave-Beloved is converted into the figure of a Mother-Sweetheart-Servant, but remains still, of course, satisfactorily black.

It is not strange, after all, to find this archetypal complex in latter-day writers of a frankly homosexual sensibility; but it recurs, too, in such resolutely masculine writers as Faulkner, who evokes the myth in the persons of the Negro and the boy of *Intruder in the Dust.*

In the myth, one notes finally, it is typically in the role of outcast, ragged woodsman, or despised sailor ("Call me Ishmael!"), or unregenerate boy (Huck before the prospect of being "sivilized" cries out, "I been there before!") that we turn to the love of a colored man. But how, we cannot help asking, does the vision of the white American as a pariah correspond with our long-held public status: the world's beloved, the success? It is perhaps only the artist's portrayal of *himself,* the notoriously alienated writer in America, at home with such images, child of the town drunk, the hapless survivor. But no, Ishmael is in all of us, our unconfessed universal fear objectified in the writer's status as in the outcast sailor's: that compelling anxiety, which every foreigner notes, that we may not be loved, that we are loved for our possessions and not our selves, that we are really — *alone.* It is that underlying terror which explains our incredulity in the face of adulation or favor, what is called (once more the happy adjective) our "boyish modesty."

Our dark-skinned beloved will take us in, we assure ourselves, when we have been cut off, or have cut ourselves off, from all others, without rancor or the insult of forgiveness. He will fold us in his arms saying, "Honey" or "Aikane"; he will comfort us, as if our offense against him were long ago remitted, were never truly *real.* And yet we cannot ever really forget our guilt; the stories that embody the myth dramatize as if compulsively the role of the colored man as the victim. Dana's Hope is shown dying of the white man's syphilis; Queequeg is portrayed as racked by fever, a pointless episode except in the light of this necessity; Crane's Negro is disfigured to the point of monstrosity; Cooper's Indian smolders to a hopeless old age conscious of the imminent disappearance of his race; Jim is shown loaded down with chains, weakened by the hundred torments dreamed up by Tom in the name of bulliness. The immense gulf of guilt must not be mitigated any more than the disparity of color (Queequeg is not merely brown but monstrously tattooed; Chingachgook is horrid with paint; Jim is portrayed as the sick A-rab died blue), so that the final reconciliation may seem more unbelievable and tender. The archetype makes no attempt to deny our outrage as fact; it portrays it as meaningless in the face of love.

There would be something insufferable, I think, in that final vision of remission if it were not for the presence of a motivating anxiety, the sense always of a last chance. Behind the white American's nightmare that someday, no longer tourist, inheritor, or liberator, he will be rejected, refused, he dreams of his acceptance at the breast he has most utterly offended. It is a dream so sentimental, so outrageous, so desperate, that it redeems our concept of boyhood from nostalgia to tragedy.

In each generation we *play out* the impossible mythos, and we live to see our children play it: the white boy and the black we can discover wrestling affectionately on any American sidewalk, along which they will walk in adulthood, eyes averted from each other, unwilling to touch even by accident. The dream recedes; the immaculate passion and the astonishing reconciliation become a memory, and less, a regret, at last the unrecognized motifs of a child's book. "It's too good to be true, Honey," Jim says to Huck. "It's too good to be true."

CHAPTER TEN

Images of Walt Whitman

It is difficult to remember that *Leaves of Grass* is, in its conception at least, an anonymous poem. Even its author seems more than once in the course of thirty years of revision to have forgotten that fact; and certainly he became convinced before the end of his life that it was a guilty secret, to be hidden with all the resources of a furtiveness of which he liked to boast. The signed proem, the endless insistence upon the first person, the deliberate confusion of the Mask and the self — all these come to conceal the truth which the authorless title page of the first edition confesses: that the "Walt Whitman" of *Leaves of Grass* is a persona really created by the poems it fictionally creates. An "eidolon" Whitman preferred to call it in his own highfalutin vocabulary, an "avatara," or more simply, "My Fancy." At the end of his life, he confesses under this name the doubleness of image and self:

> Good-bye my Fancy!
> Farewell dear mate, dear love!
> I'm going away, I know not where,
> Or to what fortune, or whether I may ever see you again,
> So Good-bye my Fancy.

It is his farewell to his truest love, cherished with a passion beyond "amativeness" or "adhesiveness," and he will not admit finally that even dying can sever them.

> Yet let me not be too hasty,
> Long indeed have we lived, slept, filter'd, become really
>   blended into one;
> Then if we die we die together, (yes, we'll remain one,) . . .
> May-be it is yourself now really ushering me to the true songs,
>   (who knows?)
> May-be it is you the mortal knob really undoing, turning . . .

There is the real romantic madness in this (and the metaphysics which lies beyond it), the irrational conviction that made Balzac cry out on his deathbed for a doctor of his own inventing, and which leads Whitman to dream that he and his fictive "Walt" will share all eternity.

But we must not let the final metaphysics blind us to the initial assumption upon which the wit and pathos of the poems really depend. Emerson, who felt so deeply into *Leaves of Grass* in his first reading, knew its namelessness, realized that the poem's "Walt Whitman" could not really exist. "I did not know until I last night saw the book advertised in a newspaper that I could trust the name as real and available for a post-office," he wrote to Whitman; but he let the newspaper fact convince him, and opened a correspondence that could only end in comedy and equivocation. It was not, of course, "Walt" who answered but "Walt's" promoter, rubbing his hands together and bowing like a salesman over his shoddy goods. "Master, I am a man who has perfect faith. Master, we have not come through centuries, tastes, heroisms, fables to halt in this land today. . . ."

It sounds like an impersonation, even a parody, and in a sense it is. Later, Whitman was to learn to play his own eidolon with more conviction in reviews, introductions, and conversation; but never, except in his most intense poetic moments, could he help somehow travestying the beloved Fancy that possessed him only when it would. I do not share an admiration for Whitman's prose, which has for me generally the sense of pushing, thrusting — being by brute force Walt Whitman. The comparison suggests itself to the medium who feels obliged to fake at blank moments the real experience that fails him.

It is Whitman's own fault (and that of the disciples whom he suffered only too willingly) that metaphors of table tapping and the Beyond come so readily to our minds. One does not become a child of nature in the nineteenth century by attempting to eschew culture; one becomes, in so far as he fails, a *literary* version of the child of nature; and, in so far as he succeeds, a creature of subculture: of the world of "cosmic consciousness" and phrenology that lurks beneath the surface

of ideas proper. In the latter sense, Whitman is the Mary
Baker Eddy of American poetry; in the former, he is its Ossian;
and it is upon the literary analogy that I want to insist in order
to redeem him from animal magnetism to art.

Ossian and Chatterton, the examples of the faked antique,
the artificial "natural," of the higher hoax as Romantic poetry,
suggest themselves; and Ossian, at least, Whitman has confessed to feeling as a temptation to be resisted. Whitman
has actually much in common with such poets, especially the
sense (one suspects) that the seeming fraud is the real truth,
that the writer is truly possessed by the spirit he seems to
invent, but also the anonymity prompted by the desire both
to take in the reader and to establish the higher truth of the
impersonation. In the Ossianic poet only the fictive singer is
real; it is McPherson who does not exist — and if there is no
forger there can be no forgery. Whitman has the advantage,
to be sure, of playing a contemporary role, so that he is free
to drop the cumbersome device of the "translated" or "discovered" manuscript — and has only to become in public life
the person he invents, that is to say, to counterfeit himself
rather than the text.

It is tempting to the stern moralist to see Whitman as the
tragic victim of his own imposture. As the years and editions
went by, the name "Walt Whitman" crept from its place in
the poem to the spine of the book; and the anonymous author
almost irrevocably disappeared, lying, distorting, destroying
all evidence of any life outside the legend. Even his face
changed, along with his stance and costume, as he willed himself from photograph to photograph into the image of the
Rowdy, the Christ, the Workman's Friend, the Beard and the
Butterfly, the Good Gray Poet. The one portrait of the anonymous author, an indolent dandy with a pert beardlet, shocks
us. We tend to believe only what the poem tells us, that Walt
never dressed in black, that he is

> Of pure American breed, of reckless health, his body perfect,
> free from taint from top to toe, free forever from headache
> and dyspepsia, clean-breathed
> Ample-limbed, a good feeder ... bearded, calm, unrefined ...

The unexpected revelations of the autopsy ("the left suprarenal capsule tubercular . . . a cyst the size of a pigeon's egg") or the glimpses in the accounts of early acquaintances of the shy misfit who drank only water and was never "bothered up" by a woman — these affect us like slander: nature slandering art, the actual the mythical.

But Whitman was finally the master of the actual, achieving by sheer will the Mask he dreamed. It is revealing to see him through the letters of *The Wound-Dresser,* walking the wards of the Washington hospitals during the Civil War: oppressed by headaches, worried about his weight, fussing like an old grandmother with his jars of jam, secretly titillated by all those beautiful young men so touchingly maimed; and yet somehow *really* exuding the strength and health he did not possess, convincing and helping others by his mythic powers; and paying for it all finally, paying for the legend of absolute participation, the boast: "I was there!"

By the time he had invented the Good Gray Poet, he had burned away all of himself that was not the image. "The secret" at which he eternally hinted was now untellable; perhaps he had actually forgotten it. With the death of his mother, the anonymous poet (who had been, above all, that mother's boy) was dead; and Whitman's subsequent paralysis was a declaration, as it were, that his body was now quite simply the book — to be slipped into the blouses of young men, to lie next to their flesh in innocence.

> Or if you will, thrusting me beneath your clothing,
> Where I may feel the throbs of your heart or rest upon your
> hip . . .

The poem had become a man, but the man in turn had become the poem. If this is a "pose" or "fraud," it is not one which we can despise.

No, if we are uncomfortable these days with Walt Whitman, it is not because he pretended to be what he was not; our judgments are not so simple. "Above all to thine own self be true" was good enough advice in the mind of one surer than we are what *is* the self. It is because the motives of his masquerade were so literary and conventional, and the image of the poet he proposed himself such a ragbag of *Versunkene*

Kulturgüte, Rousseau, Goethe, George Sand, Carlyle, Emerson, and God knows what else, eked out with phrenology and Fourth of July rhetoric, that we hesitate to accept him. If Whitman were really the monster of health and sympathy he paints himself, really the solemn discoverer of a New Sex or even of a hypostasized America as his early followers came to believe, we should not abide him for a moment. It is the poet who feared literature, the sly old maid finally trapped by his own cunning, who is *our* Whitman; and the point of *our Leaves of Grass* lies precisely in the distance between the poet and his eidolon. If that distance did not exist, Whitman would have been laughed out of existence by the first sophomore who snickered at "There is all that lot of me, and so luscious . . ."

I remember not many years ago a black-bordered notice in *Furioso,* advising certain rejected contributors that Walt Whitman was dead! And it is true that *a* Walt Whitman, a series of Walt Whitmans, has been destroyed, leaving only the poet we were not sure for a while was there at all: the poet who peers slyly from behind his most portentous statements to tip us the wink:

> To begin with take warning, I am surely different from what you suppose;
> Do you suppose you will find in me your ideal? . . .
> Do you think I am trusty and faithful?
> Do you see no further than this façade, this smooth and tolerant manner of me?
> Do you suppose yourself advancing on real ground toward a real heroic man?

or who, in double irony, speaks as the persona doubting the reality of the Whitman who creates it: "that shadow my likeness" who goes "chattering, chaffering" about the business of earning a living. "How often," remarks the poetic image coolly, "I question and doubt whether that is really me." The continual trifling with the illusion in *Leaves,* the ambiguity of the "I's" and the shifting irony of their confrontations ("O take my hand Walt Whitman! What do you hear Walt Whitman?"): this is far from the rant of a naïvely egoistic poet; it is a mannerist device, subtle and witty. To remember that

Leaves of Grass is an anonymous poem is to notice that it is a humorous one.

This is a sense of Whitman long lost behind the constructions of those searching the poem for "a real heroic man," or hopefully taking its size for a guaranty of its epic qualities. But the lyrical impulse swollen to epic proportions (this is a discovery of our age) produces either conscious irony or unwitting absurdity. In Whitman there is much of both; the latter has been pointed out sufficiently by all but the most fervent apologists; the former has been noticed sympathetically in the past only by Constance Rourke. "At the same time he remained within a sphere which . . . had been defined in popular comedy, that of the acutely self-aware." Whitman was not unconscious of this, and his confession of his awareness should not be held against him as Esther Shephard has tried to do. "I pride myself on being a real humorist underneath everything else," he once remarked. And to someone who warned, "After all, you may end up as a comedian," he responded, "I might easily end up worse." And he did, poor Walt Whitman, he *did!* But this he foresaw, too.

> Nor will my poems do good only, they will do just as much evil, perhaps more,
> For all is useless without that which you may guess at many times and not hit, that which I hinted at . . .

Out of his image of himself, not only the living, wittily qualified eidolon of his best lines, but out of the ersatz of that eidolon provided by the poetry at its worst, out of ghostwritten adulatory reviews and memoirs there emerged a quadruple figure with a fictional life — the Prophet of the New Era, the Faith Healer, the Sexual Emancipator, the Democrat at Home. The "hot, little" subprophets of the first generation, Burroughs and O'Connor and Bucke, soon detached the image of the Prophet, confronting lines from *Leaves* with lines from the Upanishads, suggesting a comparison with that other notable carpenter's son, Jesus; defining the state in which the Mask of Walt possessed the poet with Dr. Bucke's "Cosmic Consciousness"; in short, turning Whitman's poem into the scriptures of yet another homemade American religion. "Has our age produced a Christ — a Buddha? Has it given us a New Bible? I believe that in Walt Whitman we have the Prophet of a New Era, and that in his Leaves of Grass we have a book that will one day become a Bible to many seekers after light . . ." Within a generation the converts to the New Belief, the Whitmaniacs at large, had become a standard literary type. What had the poet done to deserve it?

Certainly, there is in him a vagueness, a failure to distinguish the poetic experience from the velleities that surround it, which blurs out into religiosity. It cannot be denied that Whitman wrote at times the sort of indeterminately ambitious verse that has been defined as "spilt religion" — and those to whom "spilt religion" is the only acceptable kind can hardly be blamed for finding in him evidences of their kind of sainthood. It must be said, further, that Whitman exemplifies a modern mystery, a kind of "conversion" (or, perhaps, "possession": one scarcely knows what to call it), elsewhere found in Rousseau, in which a third-rate mind, sentimental, obtuse, and indolent, is illuminated with inexplicable suddenness by reading a phrenologist's report or the announcement of an essay contest in a local newspaper. But it is not the cosmos that inspires Rousseau or Whitman, not any Otherness — but precisely the dazzling vision of themselves. In their moments of ecstasy what is made flesh is not God but Jean-Jacques or Walt.

Whitman as Christ has fared ill in our age that moves toward the poles of orthodoxy or unbelief, and from either pole regards the religioid with contempt. The image of the Source of Radiant Health has not done much better. The more intellectual turn to the analyst's couch or the orgone box for renewal, and the vulgar have their own non-literary prophets. What Mary Baker Eddy does not sufficiently cover ("I am he bringing help for the sick as they pant on their beds"), Dale Carnegie has claimed as his birthright ("Do you not see how it would serve to have such a body and soul that . . . everyone is impressed with your personality?").

In his role of Sexual Emancipator, however, Whitman has had a more successful career. About exactly what *kind* of emancipation Whitman promises, there has been considerable disagreement, some finding in him the celebrator of paganism, a free heterosexual life; others (André Gide, for example) discovering comfort and reassurance for the homosexual, the normalizing of the abnormal; still others presenting him as the celebrator, if not the inventor, of what the Germans call the *Zwischenstufe,* what Edward Carpenter has translated as "the Intermediate Sex." As a deliverer of *verse* from sexual taboos, a forerunner of D. H. Lawrence, willing to be abused and abandoned to redeem the phallus and the orgasm to the imagination, Whitman deserves the credit he has been given. It is not, however, to the poems but to an image of Whitman that the legend of the Sexual Emancipator refers, to an image he himself sponsored of himself as the Defender of the Body against the overweening claims of the soul; as the Deliverer from Christianity with its antithesis of flesh and spirit and its distrust of passion; as the savior not of poetry but of *us.*

Those who would preserve this legend of Whitman as the spokesman for total physical love find themselves in the uncomfortable position of having to underestimate the role of homosexuality in his verse. Havelock Ellis is typical in this regard, brushing aside the homosexual sensibility as "negligible," and crying aloud that "Whitman represents for the first time since Christianity swept over the world, the reintegration, in a sane and whole hearted form, of the instincts of the entire man." In his own neo-Freudian terms, Ellis recapitulates the new-religious interpretation of Whitman as a beneficent anti-Christ. "Here is no thing of creeds and dogmas. Here is no stupefying list of 'Thou shalts' and 'Thou shalt nots' . . . To Whitman the Devil is dead, and the forces of good are slowly but surely working for the salvation of all." Reading for the "devil" God in any of the conventional senses of the word (He who says, "Thou shalt" and "Thou shalt not") one sees the master-clue to the Whitman imago as the God of the Godless, the Father of the Fatherless, the Son of the Mother. The anti-Christian meaning of Whitman explains the odd united front that gathered about him: the "religious" Dr. Bucke and the "irreligious" Colonel Robert Ingersoll joined with the Nietzschean André Gide in his worship. Only D. H. Lawrence has ever challenged Whitman's claim to this honor, finding in him a final failure of nerve: "Then Whitman's mistake. The

mistake of his interpretation of his watchword: Sympathy.
. . . He still confounded it with Jesus' LOVE, and with Paul's
CHARITY. Whitman, like all the rest of us, was at the end of
the great emotional highway of Love. . . . The highway of
Love ends at the foot of the Cross. There is no beyond. . . .
He needed to supersede the Christian Charity, the Christian
Love . . . in order to give his Soul her last Freedom. . . .
And he failed in so far as he failed to get out of the old rut of
Salvation." But one can hardly expect Lawrence to be fair,
since he coveted for himself the title of the anti-Christian
Christ.

To all other enemies of the superego as Church or State or
paterfamilias, culture or Europe or "literature," Whitman has
seemed a sufficient idol, the bearded but motherly papa. In
this sense, even his homosexuality is necessary, not publicly
proclaimed but "unconsciously" *there* for his disciples as for
himself. It is as the Patriarch who is not a father, and who has
no Father on earth or in heaven, that Whitman appeals to the
Socialist, the advocate of the New Poetry, the professional
American, the undefined Democrat. Not realizing the necessity to his myth of his impotence, his femininity, Whitman fell
into the error of inventing for himself six bastards when he
was accused of physically loving men; but it was a half-hearted
addition to the legend, imagined late and discounted even as
it was told by the most ardent of his disciples.

The true "sons" of Whitman are necessarily "spiritual,"
those legendary readers who have never, of course, really read
him, but who correspond to the legendary poet: the mechanic,
the bus driver, the wounded soldier, bound to him by a love
as pure as Dante's for Beatrice. How careful he is in separating
sex from sentiment (*Children of Adam*), and sentiment from
sex (the *Calamus* poems) — and how American! Too American, perhaps, for any of us to see; certainly, it is only García
Lorca, a stranger in New York, who invokes this image precisely:

> Beautiful, Old Walt Whitman your beard full of butterflies . . .
> your thighs of a virginal Apollo . . . you moaned like a bird
> with its sex pierced with a needle . . .
> You dreaming of being a river and sleeping like a river
> with that comrade who would place in your breast
> a tiny pain of an ignorant leopard.

It is the heartbreaking innocence of this aspect of Whitman which Lorca seizes, the unfallen tenderness of America behind the machine-ridden cities; and he contrasts him sharply with the corrupted of the cities, whose meanings are quite different:

> queers of the cities, with your tumified flesh and your sullied
>   thought . . .
> harpies, assassins of doves
> slaves of women . . .

"Sleep, Walt," the Spanish poet concludes, finding in his virginal poet an odd promise of salvation, "and let a black boy announce to the golden whites the arrival of the reign of an ear of corn."

Not many worshipers of Walt, however, have been willing to accept him as the prophet of so ritual and mystic a revolution (surely the allusion to the Eleusinian mysteries that makes Walt the Ceres to the "black boy's" Kore is deliberate). From the beginning, he has been claimed as the forerunner of a more real, a more political "freedom," and as history has defined that ambiguous term more and more diversely, each faction, asserting its right to some meaning of the term, has held aloft its own image of Whitman. There has always been, to be sure, a suspicion that Whitman's "democracy" might be merely a rationalization of "adhesive" love; and in Germany, for instance, what began as a struggle between the "Uranians" and the Social Democrats over whether Whitman prophesied the coming of socialism or the emergence of the third sex ended in a rather vicious debunking of the "Yankee Saint" by the Uranian party.

But Socialists have always clung to Walt, raising his eidolon beside that of Karl Marx, while to others he has seemed linked to Mazzini and republicanism in general, as he is imagined in that most improbable of tributes by Swinburne (who later qualified his admiration drastically):

> Send but a song overseas for us,
>   Heart of their hearts who are free,
> Heart of their singer, to be for us
>   More than our singing can be;
> Ours, in the tempest at error
> With no light but the twilight of terror;
>   Send us a song oversea!

For the English poet, at first only uncertain as to whether he admired Whitman more as the apostle of freedom or of "the great god Man, which is God," Whitman stood for a specifically American experience. But in other European minds, both those that approved and those that were horrified, he was associated with an image of revolt that knew no national boundaries; and he was especially confused with those other serenely bearded rebels, Tolstoy and Hugo, in a way that reveals in the case of all three how different is their common mask from their stubbornly divergent selves. To the Continental who saw him as "the American" and America as somehow unitary, his image was blended with such improbable fellow-countrymen as Theodore Roosevelt, the "professor of energy" (by Rubén Darío), or President Wilson (in post-World-War-I Germany, where it is said he was considered the real author of the Fourteen Points).

But strangest of Whitman's posthumous avatars was that of a Marxist saint. While the French had been discovering in the author of *Leaves of Grass* a Nietzsche-like patron of intellectual anti-Christianity and an ancestor of *symbolisme,* the Germans had been finding behind the poem a figure that Johannes Becher was to name, finally, *Bruder Whitman,* Brother Whitman, Comrade Whitman; and they turned him willy-nilly into a dangerous poet, a revolutionary, whom the Central European police, convinced by the myth, felt obliged to ban just after the First World War. The *facts* matter not at all: that Whitman was a supporter of capitalism despite certain cagey reservations; that he despised trade unions; that after his one long interview with a Socialist proselytizer he murmured only, "What a beautiful young man!" — all this counted for certain sober critics and commentators, but not for the rank-and-file Marxists who knew only that Whitman represented the "Future" and so did they! In a sense, they were right, of course; for the legendary person he had created and released had taken on a life of its own and could make strange conversions long after the poet's death.

In Russia, too, an imaginary Whitman was drafted into the ranks of the revolutionaries, and by 1917 had become in the popular mind an unquestioned ancestral figure, so that *Leaves*

of Grass was one of the first American books officially sponsored in translation by the Bolshevik government. But, even
before that, a poem by Whitman had been placed in the hands
of the Soviet troops fighting the American Expeditionary
Forces, as if to assure them that they, not the soldiers of the
United States, were "America" as Whitman had defined it.

> Then courage European revolter, revoltress!
> For till all ceases neither must you cease.

"To a Foil'd European Revolutionaire" is, as poetry, Whitman at his worst — and the poetry inspired by "Comrade
Whitman" does not rise above this example. Oddly enough,
the redefined Communist Whitman was reimported into the
United States, where along with translated Mayakovski, it
became the official standard for "Proletarian Poetry" as practiced with fervor and imprecision in the darker 'thirties. The
figure of Whitman that informed this kind of verse is classically
invoked in a poem by Ben Maddow called "Red Decision," a
brief citation from which must stand for all the rest:

> Broad-hearted Whitman of the healthy beard
> stiffen my infirm palate for this bread,
> whose gritty leaven shall embowel me
> to hold and nourish, with reasoning pity and force,
> past fear and comfort or tranquillity,
> in solemn hands, my tough majestic pen.

It is tempting and easy to mock efforts of this sort, which
are, after all, no worse than Swinburne or most of the other
poets destroyed by the image they chose to sponsor them.
Whitman is an almost impossible muse, but it has taken us a
long time to discover it. In recent years the Marxists have
found themselves in almost uncontested possession of the figure
of Whitman (challenged only by an occasional homespun
versifier from the hills) as the practice and piety of our younger
poets have shifted toward tradition and elegance; but for a
while they stood in apparent solidarity with all that was "new"
in American literature, with a whole horde of enthusiasts for
whom Whitman was not only the whole future of poetry, but
America itself.

The image of Whitman as the Bard, the popular voice, the

very definition of the United States arises from a profound ambiguity in the poet himself; for one of the names he called his Fancy, his Mask was "America." "I hear America singing . . . I celebrate myself and sing myself . . ." The image of Walt swells and is extended until it merges indistinguishably with the body of an imaginary continent, and the continent with the vision of comradeship, with "Democracy *ma femme.*" In the end, there are two wives of Whitman and the two are one: himself and his country: Walt Whitman *ma femme* and America *ma femme.* The French is not merely accidental and comical; it gives away the whole game.

Walt Whitman's America was made in France, the Romantic notion out of Rousseau and Chateaubriand of an absolute anti-Europe, an utter anti-culture made flesh, the Noble Savage as a Continent. And from the same sources Whitman derived the ideal of a national poetry, the belief that a country did not really exist until a poet discovered it for the imagination. The irony of such literary ideas is that they must pretend to be unliterary, anti-literary, the expression of a purely native and ingenuous humanism.

> Come, Muse, migrate from Greece and Ionia,
> Cross out please those immensely overpaid accounts . . .

But no European is long fooled by the pose of barbarity that Europe invented; Thomas Mann, for instance, who loved Whitman, identified his meaning with the *humanitas* of Novalis — and with the thought of Goethe himself.

We have come to understand that the only American writers who can transcend the European tradition are those who begin frankly from it; that the "pure" Americans endure becoming unconsciously stereotypes devised by Europeans weary of the burden of their culture. The unreality of Whitman's America — that is, of the European dream of America — is revealed in its need to be forever moved toward a vanishing horizon, to be defined as the Absolute West. It is never the known and experienced world, but always the dreamed one over the next ridge, beyond the next river: the world of a legendary innocence, of Experience as Innocence, where one can undergo all and remain virgin. It is for this reason that Whitman the

New Yorker was redreamed (in part by himself) as the poet of a "West" which he had not even visited when *Leaves of Grass* took shape. It is utterly misleading to remember Whitman as a populist, plein-air poet; for at his best he is a singer of urban life, like Baudelaire, dedicated to redeeming for the imagination the world of industry, the life of cities. It is not to field or farmland that he invites the Muse, but to the urban kitchen with its window opening on the view of factories:

> By thud of machinery and shrill steam-whistle undismay'd,
> Bluff'd not a bit by drain-pipe, gasometers, artificial fertilizers;
> Smiling and pleased with palpable intent to stay,
> She's here, install'd amid the kitchen-ware.

But this is a witty Whitman and a precise observer who jibes ill with the figure of the diffuse and humorless Tribal Bard that the all-American Whitmanites have tried to create. *Their* Whitman has been classically defined by Edgar Lee Masters. "It is not because Whitman is a better poet than Emerson that he may be called the father of American poetry. . . . It is because Whitman wrote for the American tribe and the American idea. . . . Whitman was the tribal prophet and poet. . . . Whitman had the right idea, namely, that poetry, the real written word, must come out of the earth. . . . It is no wonder that a man as sincere as Whitman, whose sincerity chose prosody without rhyme, meter or ornament, had to endure the sneers and chatter of New York critics . . . who often miss the important, the real and truly American art."

But, one wants to protest, all these ideas come precisely out of "books and erudition" — and it is no use pleading in self-defense that they are bad books and spotty erudition: the fear of New Yorkers (critics or Wall Street bankers, it scarcely matters), provinciality as true virtue, "sincerity" as the sole aesthetic criterion, the notion that rhyme and meter are somehow meretricious, the adulation of the "tribe." What good to point out that these are the dreams of the effete at their most exhausted, the last nostalgia of the hyper-aesthete for a mythic "natural." Such ideas die hard because they appeal to those haters of literature unprepared to appear under their true colors: "emancipated" puritans and social reformers, superpatriots and Communists who fear and distrust art but like to boast that some of their best friends are poets. When challenged to name one, they can always evoke Walt Whitman. Poor Walt! It is the final indignity: to have become the image of the anti-artist, of the poet as despiser of poetry, of America as an anti-culture.

It gets harder and harder to remember that once (only two wars ago!) his name was the rallying cry of the literary avant-garde; New Sex, New Society, and New Poetry: they seemed three persons of a single god, and Whitman was its prophet. *Poetry,* the magazine founded by Harriet Monroe, still carries a tag from Whitman; and in its pioneer days it evoked as a syndrome, anti-conventional and anti-bourgeois, T. S. Eliot, Pound, Whitman, Amy Lowell, imagism, free verse, Sandburg, Frost, and E. A. Robinson. Then and for a long time afterward, other little magazines were sponsoring with equal fervor new directions in social organization and in experimental verse. To this blur of enthusiasm the prophetic blur at the heart of the Whitman image corresponded exactly; he is the presiding genius of an alliance based on the single slogan: "Make It New!"

It was an alliance that could not survive its first victories; quite soon the Socialist new poet was regarding the converted Catholic novelist with hostility; the rediscoverer of metaphysical wit and classical form was watching warily the exponent of uncorseted dithyrambs; the advocate of escape from emotion was wondering how he had ever enlisted beside the enthusiasts of phallic consciousness. In an introduction to the *Selected Poems* of Ezra Pound, Eliot has put his own protest on record: "I did not read Whitman until much later in life, and had to conquer an aversion to his form, as well as much of his matter, in order to do so. I am equally certain — it is indeed obvious — that Pound owes nothing to Whitman. This is an elementary observation." Amy Lowell had already detached herself with a haughty statement: "Often and often I read in the daily, weekly and monthly press, that modern vers libre writers derive their form from Walt Whitman. As a matter of fact, most of them got it from French Symbolist poets." It was toward Walt's Communist kidnapers that she was

glancing, for she added: "The last ignominy to him would be
the usage of his words to tear down the governmental structure
that he loved." And she concluded with the coolest of snubs:
"It is perhaps sadly significant that the three modern poets who
most loudly acknowledge his leadership are all of recent foreign
extraction. . . ."

This is the beginning of an attack that does not end until
Whitman is transformed from a figure symbolizing the way
poetry must go to a half-comic image personifying the wrong
turning, the temptation to formlessness and disorder, the blind
alley of the pseudo-poet. Pound's offer of a negotiated peace
finds no supporters even among his own followers:

> I make a pact with you, Walt Whitman —
> I have detested you long enough.
> I come to you as a grown child
> Who has had a pig-headed father;
> I am old enough to make friends.

This is an entirely new resistance to *Leaves of Grass,* not
the protest of the anti-Jacobin and the genteel, the demurrer
of a James Russell Lowell or a Holmes, feeling the hungry
generations treading him down; not the horrified "scientific"
rejection of a Nordau or Lombroso, classifying Whitman as
insane — but the refusal of a poet by the very future on
which he had staked all. It is the liveliest minds that begin
to turn away from him, not only the reactionary wits like
Wyndham Lewis: "Walt Whitman was, I feel sure, the father
of the American Baby. . . . Walt showed all those enthusiastic habits we associate with the Baby. He rolled about
naked in the Atlantic surf, uttering 'barbaric yawps' . . . he
was prone to 'cosmic raptures.' . . . He was a great big
heavy old youngster of the perfect Freudian type, with the
worst kind of enthusiasm in the Greek sense of the word."
To begin with, it is against the Mask of Whitman that they
revolt, for they do not want the Son of the Mother for *their*
Father; they are after new ancestors, a tradition not of the
traditionless but of the traditional. But they find it hard to
believe that there is a genuine poet behind the distasteful persona. Only in Europe does Whitman continue to belong to
the young, to the creating writers; in the United States he

becomes the possession of those new philistines who love the
renewal of the day before yesterday — and of the more liberal-
minded scholars.

It is these scholars who have been in recent years creating
a legend of Whitman's fame, a rags-to-riches story of a slow,
but unbroken triumph over the reservations of the short-sighted
genteel; and in the interests of this legend they have failed to
record (perhaps they have not even noticed) the decline of
their poet's reputation among our best practicing poets. Yet
the *essential* fact about Whitman as a force in American poetry
is precisely what Gay Wilson Allen, for instance, does not
even hint at in his *Handbook:* that for the last twenty-five
years Whitman has been a chief whipping boy of many of our
best poets and critics.

The defeat of Whitman as the informing image of the Poet,
as our bearded Muse of the New, is ironically sealed by an
attempted celebration in Hart Crane's *The Bridge* of his figure
as the Meistersinger of America.

> *Panis Angelicus!* Eyes tranquil with the blaze
> Of love's own diametric gaze, of love's amaze . . .
> Our Meistersinger, thou set breath in steel;
> And it was thou who on the boldest heel
> Stood up and flung the span on even wing
> Of that great Bridge, our Myth, whereof I sing!
>
> .   .   .   .
>   My hand
>   in yours,
>   Walt Whitman —
>
>   so —

This is hardly Crane at his best. Even the characteristic incoherence is a faked, a second-rate incoherence — not a blending at incandescent temperature but an ersatz fusion; and the
attack on the failures of Crane's poem which followed its
publication centered on this passage and on the image behind
it. The *locus classicus* is the review by Yvor Winters that
appeared in *Poetry* for June 1930, asserting that *The Bridge*
at its best "carries the epic quality of the Whitmanian vision
(the vision of humanity *en masse* or undifferentiated) to the
greatest dignity and power of which it is, probably, capable,"
thus proving under the most favorable conditions "the impos-

sibility of getting anywhere with the Whitmanian inspiration. No writer of comparable ability has struggled with it before, and, with Mr. Crane's wreckage in view, it seems highly unlikely that any writer of comparable genius will struggle with it again."

Doubtless, one of the troubles with the "Cape Hatteras" section of Crane's poem is the falsification by Crane (probably even to himself) of his relation to the image of Whitman. The homosexual sensibility which they shared is ignored in favor of Whitman's legendary representativeness as an "American"; besides, Crane, attracted with one part of his mind to Eliot, is already ridden with doubts about Whitman's true worth. A letter to Allen Tate reveals his ambivalence. "It's true that my rhapsodic address to him [Whitman] in the Bridge exceeds any exact valuation of the man. . . . There isn't much use in my tabulating the qualified, yet persistent, reasons I have for my admiration of him. . . . You've heard me roar at too many of his lines to doubt that I can spot his worst, I'm sure." The myth and the poet had begun to come apart for Crane; and I suspect they cannot be put together by an act of will. Certainly, one has the impression that "Cape Hatteras" is not believed in but *worked up*.

Whatever the truth about these matters, the failure of *The Bridge* was interpreted not as Crane's failure, but as Whitman's. Tate, Blackmur, and others seconded Winters, and this judgment of the Whitmanian imago via *The Bridge* soon became a standard conviction of the "New Critics" — indeed, one of the few beliefs which actually are shared by that illassorted congeries. In Blackmur a typical contrast is added to complete the position: "Baudelaire aimed at control, Whitman at release. It is for these reasons that the influence of Whitman was an impediment to the *practice* (to be distinguished from the reading) of poetry, and that the influence of Baudelaire is re-animation itself."

What began as an "advanced" minority opinion has tended to become at least an important orthodoxy, if not *the* orthodoxy of the young, changing emphasis along the way so that Whitman is regarded not only as a bad "influence" but even as a bad poet, the founder of an inferior tradition. William

Van O'Connor sums up the position in his recent study, *Sense and Sensibility in Modern Poetry*. "But Whitman and his followers — like Robinson Jeffers, Vachel Lindsay, Edgar Lee Masters, Carl Sandburg, Stephen Vincent Benét and William Rose Benét, and later Paul Engle, August Derleth, Muriel Rukeyser, Ben Maddow, and Alfred Hayes . . . are not in the line of American writers who have deepened our knowledge of human motivation or action. They are, in so far as they are followers of Whitman, away from the tradition which runs from Hawthorne and Melville through James and Eliot."

Though such amalgams as this seem to me to exploit shamelessly the device of "guilt by association," I sympathize with Mr. O'Connor's effort to isolate the exploiters of what he calls "the historico-mythic equivalent of America." I, too, am repelled by those who do not make poems but manipulate a prefabricated theme and feel that by naming an undefined essence "America" they can turn it into a universal touchstone. I do not even object to setting the "Whitmanians" against whatever equivalent of the metaphysical-symbolist tradition can be found in our literature, except as such a contrast implies that one tradition guarantees, or another makes impossible, poetry. Whitman, at least, succeeds, whatever his assumptions, in being a poet more often than it is ever possible to remember; he is not *merely* his myth, either as he himself expresses it or as it persists in this line of spiritual descent.

I know why Mr. O'Connor and many others find it hard to admit Whitman's excellence; one does not easily come to love a poet who is used as a weapon against oneself and one's favorite writers. And Whitman has become precisely such a weapon in the hands of those who (Van Wyck Brooks is an example) condemn Eliot or Pound on the grounds that they have rejected all that Whitman affirms. It is vain to retort with the commonplace that "poetry affirmeth nought," for Whitman has taught us otherwise. Besides, it is turn and turn about; once the sides were chosen up — Baudelaire against Whitman; Poe, Melville, or Hawthorne against Whitman; Eliot against Whitman — warfare was inevitable. You cannot beat Whitman over the head with Eliot and be surprised when the process is reversed. Such conflicts have a certain strategic value so long as we remember that the causes for which they are fought are not really the poets who bear the same names, but merely their images, tricked out to horrify or allure. Whitman is no more devil than messiah. He is a poet whom we must begin now to rescue from parody as well as apotheosis.

We shall not return to the same Whitman from which we started; twenty-five years of dissent cannot be undone. It is to our *own* Whitman that we come back, and we come by our own roads, via authors whom Whitman would perhaps have despised. It is not from his friends that we ask letters of recommendation but from those who had no reason to love him, from Henry James, for instance, or from Gerard Manley Hopkins. Even Randall Jarrell has felt obliged to remind us (albeit ironically), in a recent admirable essay, that James was moved almost to tears in reading Whitman to Edith Wharton, and that Hopkins wrote to Bridges: "I always knew in my heart Walt Whitman's mind to be more like my own than any other man's living." One laughs a little remembering Yeats's account of how he scarcely listened to Hopkins, whom he met in his father's studio, because he was carrying in his own pocket *Leaves of Grass;* but one laughs wryly, for it is the joke of history which is always on *us!*

It is not to the life-affirmer we are returning, but to the elegiac Whitman, the poet of death. "Merging! And Death!" D. H. Lawrence wrote accusingly of Whitman. "The great merge into the womb. Woman. And after that, the merging of comrades: man-for-man love. . . . Woman is inadequate for the last merging. So the next step is the merging of man-for-man love. And this is on the brink of death. It slides over into death." But the case for the prosecution has become the case for the defense: another joke of history. Dismayed by an optimism in which we no longer believe, a self-assurance that seems to us obscene, we find with relief in *Leaves of Grass* that "blackness ten times black" which Melville once thrilled to discover in Hawthorne. We are pleased to find surviving the hearty eidolon, the melancholy poet who began writing stories about the poor boy flogged to death by a wicked teacher, to honor "the dusky demon and brother" whom Walt did not forget. It is his attackers who have defined for us the Whitman we can love; even such negative and furious onslaughts as those of Esther Shephard and Harvey O'Higgins have succeeded in destroying not the poet but the legend which obscured him.

How different the meaning of what such critics have found is for us than it was for them! Discovering among Whitman's papers the cardboard butterfly with which he faked the famous portrait; learning that the untainted American family of which he liked to boast was ridden with madness and disease; finding a host of proofs that the New Orleans love affair, the vaunted bastards were deliberate hoaxes — his debunkers were ready to write off Walt as "insincere." To them this seemed to destroy his validity as a poet-prophet, to reveal him as "only" a self-advertiser, a poseur, not original or a Democrat or even a lusty breeder. But those of us who know that poetry (God forbid that we should attempt to judge the *man!*) is precisely a matter of cardboard butterflies on real fingers, that the wit and tension of a poem depend on the distance between the given and the imagined, are grateful to Miss Shephard and Mr. O'Connor for having rescued Walt Whitman from "life" (i.e., the clichés of politics and pseudo-mysticism) and having restored him to art.

Our Walt Whitman is the slyest of artificers, the artificer of "sincerity"; and, if this sounds like a joke, there is no reason why even the greatest poetry cannot be a joke on someone, not excluding its author. It does not seem to me enough to say, as G. W. Stonier has in one of the more perceptive comments on Whitman, "His duplicity staggers. He was a fine poet and a charlatan," because this implies that his fine poetry is based on something other than his charlatanism. Whitman's trickery is essential, not accidental, to his poems. Like the mannerists, like Shakespeare, who is the greatest among them, he is a player with illusion; his center is a pun on the self; his poetry is a continual shimmering on the surfaces of concealment and revelation that is at once pathetic and comical.

His duplicity is, I feel, a peculiarly American duplicity, that doubleness of our self-consciousness which our enemies too easily call hypocrisy, but which arises from our belief that what we dream rather than what we are is our essential truth.

The Booster and the Pharisee are the standard caricatures of the American double man, and Whitman was both Booster and Pharisee. Condemned to play the Lusty Innocent, the Noble Savage, by a literary tradition that had invented his country before he inhabited it, Whitman had no defenses. The whole Western world demanded of him the lie in which we have been catching him out, the image of America in which we no longer believe; the whole world cried to him: "Be the Bard we can only dream! Chant the freedom we have imagined as if it were real!"

But he was not "America"; he was only a man, ridden by impotence and anxiety, by desire and guilt, furtive and stubborn and half-educated. That he became the world's looked-for, ridiculous darling is astonishing enough; that he remained a poet through it all is scarcely credible. He has survived his images; and at last the outlived posturing, the absurd ideas, the rhetoric borrowed and misunderstood fall away, until only the poetry remains, and the poet — anonymous in the end as they were in the beginning.

I and this mystery here we stand.

CHAPTER ELEVEN

Some Notes on
F. Scott Fitzgerald

I. *Nothing succeeds like failure*

The case of F. Scott Fitzgerald belongs first of all to the history of taste in our time. It is immensely difficult at the present moment to distinguish our responses to Fitzgerald's achievement from our self-congratulatory feelings about certain recent changes in our own literary standards. We are likely to overestimate his books in excessive repentance of the critical errors of the 'thirties — for having preferred Steinbeck or James T. Farrell for reasons we would no longer defend. Fitzgerald has come to seem more and more poignantly the girl we left behind — dead, to boot, before we returned to the old homestead, and therefore particularly amenable to sentimental idealization.

And so a fictionist with a "second-rate sensitive mind" (the term is Tennyson's description of himself, and evokes the tradition of late Romanticism in which Fitzgerald worked) and a weak gift for construction is pushed into the very first rank of American novelists, where it becomes hard to tell his failures from his successes. Who cares as long as the confetti flies and the bands keep playing! It is all to the good, of course, that hundreds of thousands of us require the reprinting of his books, actually read him again along with the recent Mizener biography. He had threatened for too long to remain a "case" about whom everyone merely *talks*. If we were only content with reclaiming an imperfect good writer, who achieved just once a complete artistic success, but who in every book at some point breaks through his own intolerable resolve to be charming above all and touches the truth!

But, Lord have mercy on us, we want a "great" writer. It is at once the comedy and tragedy of twentieth-century American letters that we simply cannot keep a full stock of contemporary "great novelists." In the novel, unlike recent poetry in which certain reputations have grown slowly and steadily, we have had an erratic market: reputations fantastically overpriced are in an instant deflated, and new booms are launched. From moment to moment we have the feeling that certain claims, at least, are secure, but even as we name them they shudder and fall. Who now mentions James Branch Cabell? And who can think of Dos Passos and Steinbeck without a twinge of shame for dead enthusiasms? Dreiser and Farrell find a few surly defenders — but even their granted merits seem irrelevant to our current situation. Whom have we left? Faulkner and Hemingway, and even now the stock of the latter has begun to fall; a thousand imitators reveal the weaknesses we had not seen, and the younger critics begin, to the shrill screams of Hemingway's contemporaries, the drastic revision. Into our depopulated pantheon, therefore, we impress Fitzgerald.

Who else? There are several reasons that impel the choice: we have reached the point from which the 'twenties, Fitzgerald's 'twenties, can be regarded with the maximum nostalgia; we readopt the hairdos, the songs — and the authors. We see him now as one who refused to whore after strange Marxist gods, our lonely St. Anthony, faithful to literature in the sociological desert. The versions of Fitzgerald that these estimates imply are perhaps not quite true, but they are believed in and will do. And yet the *essential* appeal of Fitzgerald is elsewhere — astonishingly enough, in his *failure*.

Mr. Schulberg in his recent novel has remarked that in America nothing fails like success; but of course the obverse is also true: among us, nothing succeeds like failure. We are, behind a show of the grossest success-worship, a nation that dreams of failure as a fulfillment. The Christian paradox of the defeated as victor haunts our post-Christian world. None of us seems *really* to believe in the succeeding of success, though we do not know how to escape from its trap; and it has become one of the functions of our writers to supply us with vicarious failures for our second-hand redemption.

Edgar Allan Poe provides the prototype, of course: dope, whisky, the shadow of madness, poverty and early death — and Fitzgerald is the perfect modern avatar. It is the Fall not of a King, but of an Artist, the disaffected son of the middle class, of us all, that we demand to stir our pity and terror. For the great quasi-literate public, Fitzgerald is providing right now the *tragic experience:* creating, in the great amphitheater without walls of articles in *Life,* abridgments in the *Atlantic Monthly,* paragraphs in the papers, and 25-cent reprints, a debased equivalent of what the Athenian found in the *Oedipus Rex.* When any American writer refuses to live into the conventional public myth, the people remake him, as even Poe was retouched by Griswold, who invented in malice the American Writer, and as Stephen Crane was lied and vilified into the image necessary to us all.

But Fitzgerald *willed* his role as a failure, for all his paeans to success. Long before his own actual crack-up, he dreamed it, prophesied it in his stories and novels; and if one cannot read his true desire in the fictional projections, Mr. Mizener's account of the life more than confirms the intimations. Mr. Mizener's greatest merit as a biographer is that he does not cut the fabric of Fitzgerald's life to his own views, but by balancing a half-dozen partial readings of his career permits still others (including this one) that do not suggest themselves explicitly to him. Instinctively, Fitzgerald hoarded his defeats like his truest treasures: his rejection as a young man by Ginevra King, his expulsion from Princeton, the imagined attacks of tuberculosis and the real ones (a disease in which the will is all), the cutting to pieces of his prized movie script by Joe Mankiewicz — and above all, the drinking.

II. *Booze done it!*

From the beginnings of Western literature, there has been a tradition of the flaw as essential to the writer, but at various times there have been various notions of the ideal charismatic weakness: blindness in the most ancient days, incest in the Byronic period, homosexuality in the *fin de siècle*. But in America the flaw has been pre-eminently drunkenness, from Griswold's Poe dead in the gutters of Baltimore to Schulberg's Halliday-Fitzgerald dying among the undergraduates at Dartmouth. It was quite another sort of culture hero, the battered John L. Sullivan, who said mournfully, "Booze done it!"; but the words make an appropriate epitaph for our typical writer.

Every writer in Fitzgerald makes his first staggering entrance loaded: McKiscoe in *Tender Is the Night,* "Four-eyes" in *Gatsby,* Wylie in *The Last Tycoon;* the profession is inseparable from the vice. It is, I suppose, because the 'twenties were the time when drinking became quite simply the American Character, or at least its public face, that Fitzgerald was so much at home in that world, unalienated from the general binge. Mr. Mizener's book makes quite clear the pathetic hollowness of Fitzgerald's claim to be a spokesman for the 'twenties in the formal sense, a kind of higher John Held, Jr.; and a quick, embarrassed rereading of *This Side of Paradise,* with its queasy panegyrics of "kissing" and "petting," reveals a writer far too naïve and principled to speak for a time without principle. And yet Fitzgerald and his audience were, until the 'twenties died, at home with each other; the American citizen as lush and the American artist as lush cried into the same beer. It was not that only Americans, or American writers, drank (there was always James Joyce, as Hemingway reminded Fitzgerald between drinks), but that for Americans it so much *mattered;* and that in the United States, before drinking could become an overwhelming habit, it had first to be forbidden. It is surely no accident that the protagonist of Fitzgerald's best book has, like his author, grown wealthy on Prohibition, the sensitive bootlegger as the last Romantic — the "great" Gatsby, for whom only the drunken writer turns out to mourn after his inevitable defeat.

The greatest drunken writer whom Fitzgerald created, however, appeared in none of his books — being, of course, Fitzgerald himself. A part of the apparent waste of Fitzgerald's life stems from his having invested most of his energy in composing himself; and his Collected Works have not been finished until ten years after his death. One cannot claim to have read him without having read *The Far Side of Paradise* or the letters and reminiscences collected in *The Crack-up*. It is the glory and the curse of the Romantic writer that his achievement cannot survive his legend without real loss. When the lives of Scott and Zelda are forgotten, or when they have become merely chronologies without the legendary distortions and pathos, his books will be less rewarding. Think of Byron, to whom his sins are as necessary as drunkenness and the madness of his wife are to Fitzgerald!

III. *Portrait of the artist as a young girl*

The obverse of the Romantic habit of living one's life as if it were a work of art is that of writing one's books as if they were autobiographies. Fitzgerald is wary in this respect, but his dodges are superficial and ineffective. In his later books, he resolutely refuses to use the writer or artist as protagonist or point-of-view character. Even in *The Last Tycoon*, where the writer Wylie is obviously the character through whom the story of Stahr *must* be told, Fitzgerald's resolve to keep the writer as character peripheral quite ruins any possibility of a coherent organization; and in the end Fitzgerald smuggles himself into the skin of Stahr and of the young girl through whom the events are seen. Nothing is gained, and a good deal is lost — organization, certainly, and consistency of characterization.

It is not by pretending that one's central character is a gangster or psychiatrist or producer that one avoids turning art into confession; it is a question of method and irony and detachment, the devices that made *Stephen Hero* into *Portrait of the Artist as a Young Man,* the devices that Fitzgerald never mastered.

Any one of Fitzgerald's novels will illustrate the point; but perhaps *Tender Is the Night* will serve best of all. Almost all the main characters (Nicole Diver, the female lead, is of course based on Zelda), whatever their outsides, turn out to be F. Scott Fitzgerald. Dick Diver, the protagonist, who seems from a distance the assured aristocrat, the obverse of the author, reveals on the first close-up the Irish lilt, the drunkenness, the tortured sensibility that are Fitzgerald's. The pretentious novelist (enter drunk, to be sure!), Albert McKiscoe, is Scott in caricature, his social insecurity, his pretenses, even the early success he feared and hated. Abe North, faintly disguised as a musician, is Ring Lardner; but Ring Lardner was Fitzgerald's favorite *alter ego,* in whom he liked to see the image of his own doom (exit drunk, of course!). One could do a marvelous movie with all these parts played by the same actor — a different stance, different costuming, and as the camera moves close: the same face.

Even the young moving-picture actress, Rosemary Hoyt, turns out to be a version of the author. She is Irish (always a clue), full of embarrassment and guilty pride at a too-sudden success, and quite indeterminate in her sex. Indeed, the book is shot through with a thematic playing with the ambiguity of sex: Dick Diver makes his first entrance in a pair of black lace panties, and homosexuals, male and female, haunt the climaxes of the novel. "Economically," Rosemary's mother tells her at one point, "you're a boy, not a girl." Economically! One recalls the portrait of Fitzgerald as the most beautiful showgirl in the Triangle Show.

I had felt all this before reading in Mr. Mizener's biography that in *The World's Fair,* an abandoned book from whose fragments the first part of *Tender Is the Night* is made, Rosemary was indeed a boy, who was to kill his mother according to the original plot. It has been observed by Malcolm Cowley that Fitzgerald has always a double vision of himself, as outsider and insider at once, the man of the world and the bumpkin gawking at him; but it has not been remarked that at the end of his writing career the outsider had become defined as the Young Girl, a kind of anima figure, desiring hopelessly the older man who is *also* Fitzgerald, himself double: in the eyes of the girl all power and glamor, in his own view aging and corrupt or at the point of death.

In his last two novels, the same relationship appears, and the same sort of character as narrator, a portrait of the artist as a breathless young girl, still virgin though not without experience. Each time the affair ends in a deflowering without love and an eventual desertion, Diver-Fitzgerald abandoning Rosemary-Fitzgerald for Nicole-Zelda, and Stahr-Fitzgerald leaving Cecilia-Fitzgerald for Kathleen; the protagonists choosing both times that Other Woman by whom Fitzgerald symbolizes the lure of death and destruction which is stronger even than self-love.

This constant impulse to confuse himself with his characters destroys first of all the consistency of the people in his books; but, even worse, it leads Fitzgerald into an indulgence in self-pity, which is the grossest manifestation of his prevailing sentimentality. He is sentimental about everything — Princeton, the First World War, sex (egregiously!), Skull and Bones, Gold Star Mothers — but especially about his own plight. Everywhere in his work there is a failure of irony and detachment that amounts finally to a failure of intelligence, an indulgence of the "second-rate sensitive mind."

Like most American writers, Fitzgerald had to work without an accepted tradition to sustain him or received standards against which to measure himself. All his life, he moved uncertainly between the demands of his own erratic sensibility and a desire to please a great, undefined audience — to be loved by everybody. Like one of his own epicene coquettes, he postured and flirted with all comers, trying to cling meanwhile to a virginity which became more and more a technicality. To be wanted and admired, he was willing to seem to say less than he meant, to appear merely chic; so that it is still possible to read even his best books with no understanding and much pleasure. How could he ever find time to learn how to put a novel together with skill! All his life, point-of-view baffled him, and he was forced to make his transitions with such awkward links as: "To resume Rosemary's point of view, it should be said . . ." or "This is Cecilia taking up the story . . ."

IV. *What terrible and golden mystery . . .*

And yet . . . there is always the style of the details, the glow and motion of the close of *Gatsby* or the opening of

Tender Is the Night, those wonderful approaches and fade-outs. There is always the naïve honesty of reminiscence, the embarrassing rightness of his adolescents. And there is the supreme negative virtue: Fitzgerald's refusal to swap his own lived sentimentalities for the mass sentimentalities of social protest that swamp the later Hemingway. Even the compulsive theme of the *femme fatale,* the All-American banality of woman as destroyer, is capable of subtleties forever beyond the "proletarian novel." When Fitzgerald treats social themes he is absurd; surely there appears in the overrated fragment, *The Last Tycoon,* the least convincing Communist in American fiction. But he resisted the temptation to end *Tender Is the Night* with Dick Diver sending his kids off to the Soviet Union, a close that might well have won him the plaudits he so needed in 1934.

But, beyond all this, one feels in his work a great theme, however elusive and imperfectly realized. It is not love, though love is superficially everywhere in his writing; nor is it Europe, though he lived there and set one book and many stories in the expatriate background. Though he was educated in Catholic schools, it is not religion. His books have no religious insights, only religious décor — the obsessive metaphor of the "ruined priest," a theatrical making of the cross to close a book, a belated Aubrey-Beardsley-ish priest. The sensibility of the Catholic in America becomes, like everything else, puritan: the devil, self-consciously introduced in *This Side of Paradise,* shrinks to an evil aura around a tart's head. There is in Fitzgerald no profound sense of evil or sin, only of guilt; and no gods except the Rich.

The Rich — there is the proper subject matter of Fitzgerald, as everyone has perceived: their difference from the rest of us, and the meanings of that difference. That "other woman" who is death is also wealth; the girl, like Daisy, with gold in her voice. Of course, the wealthy in Fitzgerald are not *real,* but that is precisely the point. Whether in declared fantasy like "A Diamond as Big as the Ritz" or in nominally realistic novels, they resemble veritable millionaires as little as Natty Bumppo resembles an actual frontiersman. But they are, at least — like that Cooper character and unlike the nasty rich in proletarian novels — myths rather than platitudes, viable to the imagination.

It is not just snobbishness that drew Fitzgerald to the rich, the boy from St. Paul dreaming his life long of an imagined Princeton. In all his writing, one senses Fitzgerald in search of an American equivalent to *les grands,* the aristocracy to whom the French writers were able to turn in their reversion from the grubby bourgeois world. Was there anywhere, in America or among Americans abroad, a native aristocracy to whom "style" was a goal and a dream? It is not money getters, but spenders, to whom Fitzgerald turned in his search for allies, out of a sense that the squandering of unearned money was an art, like writing, that squandering of an unearned talent; and that among the very rich there might be a perpetual area of freedom, like that in which the artist momentarily feels himself in the instant of creative outpouring.

The world where a penny saved is a penny earned is the world of anti-art. The lower middle class in particular, Fitzgerald felt, were the enemies of style. He wanted a class that knows how to *use* writers, or at least desires a kind of life in which the imagination would have a chance to live. It was a hopeless dream, and in the end Fitzgerald learned two things: first, that the rich, whatever the quality of their living, regard the artist not as an ally but as a somewhat amusing *arriviste;* and, second, that to live the life of high style is to remain a moral child, who destroys whatever does not suit his whim. To be "rich," in the sense he dreamed, is to refuse responsibility, to deny fate, to try (as in the terrible scene toward the close of "The Diamond as Big as the Ritz") to bribe God. There is implicit in such a life a doom as absolute as its splendor, and in this sense alone the career of the very rich is like that of the artist.

It is a vision atrocious and beautiful enough to be true, and it survives in Fitzgerald's work, despite the incoherence and sentimentality, with the force of truth. It is fitting that our chronicler of the rich be our prophet of failure. To those who plead that Fitzgerald could not face up to life and success, it can be said that at least he kept faith with death and defeat.

CHAPTER TWELVE

Dead-End Werther: The Bum as American Culture Hero

There are certain books in a tradition which, after a while, everyone stops reading but no one can stop writing. The less aware a novelist is of these books, the more he is likely to submit to their pattern; and this is one of the best reasons for insisting that writers be educated. *The Sorrows of the Young Werther* is such an archetypal book — the first anti-bourgeois bourgeois novel, the celebration of suicide as the only possible consummation for the young man afraid that sex may harden into marriage, a work of art become the occasion for mere success, and the very act of living turn imperceptibly into accommodation to the world of convention. The only airtight Bohemia is death.

Werther is also, in the guise of a story about "true love," an attack on the role of woman in the middle-class world: cake-eater and haver *par excellence,* able to use a bourgeois husband for security and a rebellious lover for spiritual satisfaction, to flirt with death and accede to life. It is an embarrassing book, particularly when one recalls that its author went on living at the expense of his character and of all his sad young readers not able to discriminate so nicely between art and life.

James Jones's *From Here to Eternity* (best-seller and improbable choice of at least one critic as our greatest recent novel) is the latest version of *Werther,* and this it is important to notice as no one seems to have done, bored or titillated by its use of obscene language, or led off too quickly into observations on "naturalism." I take it that when a critic says that

From Here to Eternity is in the tradition of "naturalism," he
means nothing more spectacular than that it is badly written in
a special and quite deliberate way. In a certain sense, this is
merely belaboring the obvious: even Hollywood in an all-star
production found no difficulty in producing a movie that was
stylistically superior to the book; indeed, the movie-makers are
too much the prisoners of their own technical excellence to do
anything else. Only bankruptcy could betray them into the
sloppiness that Jones has striven for with all the means at his
command, striven for *on principle*. This principle one might
just as well call "naturalism," though the incautious use of
the term has, I am aware, led to a ridiculous sort of civil war
among the critics. On the darkling plain which is literary
discussion, one army advances under a banner reading, "Art
Is Morality! Without Form Only Confusion! (*signed*) HENRY
JAMES"; while the other side rallies under the device, "Not
Art But Life! X (*Theodore Dreiser his mark*)."

I shall, therefore, try to make quite clear what I mean when
I say that James Jones's book is a "naturalistic" version of
Werther, in which the *poète maudit* appears a bugler, and the
aristocracy and middle classes are blended into the officers,
a scarcely human group that make the Noble Savages, i.e., enlisted men, bear off the sanitary napkins of their women while
they themselves infect their wives with venereal diseases they
have picked up wenching. In all the writings in the line of
Werther, there is a hopeless confusion between the class
struggle and the inability of a sensitive (artistic or quasi-
artistic) young man to adjust to *any* given world. This
is reflected in an attempt to find a style in intent a protest
against current conventions, in fact a challenge to the whole
concept of literature, to language itself. The Storm-and-Stress
style of Goethe, however paradoxical at its heart (an anti-
conventional convention), was at least a new style, a radical
one — the beginning of something; but the protestant, un-
buttoned prose of James Jones belongs to an already weary
mode that only ignorance can take for revolt, a mode compromised and, in a way it can never confess, slick. This is no
beginning but an end.

The name of that end is "naturalism," which is to say, any

combination of methods the defects of whose qualities are grossness, clumsiness, and the sentimentalizing of the given and those who live on most intimate terms with it. Opposed to it is what might just as well be called "formalism," which lapses at its worst into gentility, overelaboration, and the sentimentalizing of detached insight and of those most capable of exploiting it. To the formalist to write badly is a sin; to the naturalist it is a virtue.

Like arguments about manners and whether or not costume or ritual are important, this conflict over taste is felt to be essentially a *class* struggle, a clash between Ivy Leaguers and the descendants of slaveowners on the one side, and the sons of immigrants, proletarians, and poor farmers on the other; so that defections from one camp to the other are thought of as renegadism. It is a myth of the "proletarian" side (variously sustained by Lawrence and Hemingway and now Jones) that the difference is also a sexual one: those with *cojones* and a real joy in their natural functions versus the impotent, sterile, or genteelly homosexual, who won't even admit that they sweat.

Like many novels of its class, *From Here to Eternity* exists on one level as a work of criticism, stating a theory of what the work of art should be and providing an instance of that theory in practice. It is at its worst the victim of its own doctrine, "successful" according to its own lights — which is not to say "natural" or "free," since *any* theory (even an anti-theoretical one) is a trap, and the fear of complexity can be as crippling as the horror of simplicity. One does not write in a state of nature merely for having disavowed the high traditions of his culture; he becomes rather the victim of the lower ones: in *From Here to Eternity,* the note of elegiac self-pity out of *Portrait of the Artist as a Young Man* via *Look Homeward, Angel;* the compulsive detail and the merciless reproduction of overhead speech usually associated with Dreiser; Hemingwayoid hard-corny descriptions of the orgasm; and, above all, a kind of Jack London hallelujah-I'm-a-bum stance — "This ain't *art,* Jack, it's the real McCoy."

The material rendered in this conglomerate style ranges from the documentary "real" (descriptions of barracks life, the stockade, etc.), through masturbatory fantasies (all whores are beautiful, all officers' wives seducible, yet somehow pure), to sophomoric bull sessions reported dead-pan as "ideas." It is the authority of the documentation that is forever saving the book from its own ambitions. Its value as literature, slight, intermittent, but undeniable, lies in its redeeming for the imagination aspects of regular Army life never before exploited, and in making certain of those aspects (the stockade, for instance, our home-grown "concentration camp") symbols of the human situation everywhere.

The essential subject of the *Werther* novel is always innocence and decadence — what is innocence and how can it be preserved in a corrupt world? This is, of course, a subject peculiarly American; indeed, our country makes its formal début almost at the moment of the publication of Goethe's book, and the hero of the first novel written in the United States dies with that tearful story open on the table beside him. In *From Here to Eternity,* the long sigh is sighed again; one has the sense that the good world, the world of innocents, has just passed away. The book is an inglorious wake in honor of the good old days: before the Wobblies were defeated, before Eagle Scout Roy Rogers replaced the bum Buck Jones as the kids' idol, before the movies were commercialized (i.e., when you could still see pictures like *The Grapes of Wrath*), before the draftees descended on "Wahoo" and a man could get laid in peace. One phrase recurs like a theme: "They are a vanishing race." No more good old First Sergeants! No more real Thirty Year Men!

Yet, even though the Golden Age is gone, the world irrevocably lost to the middle classes (who supported Hitler in Germany and appear in their latest disguise as the commissars in Russia), there exists a saving remnant, Noble Savages untouched by the general degeneracy. These are the men who can be "killed but not eaten," beaten to death or driven into' exile, but never forced into apologizing for their revolt or becoming accomplices of the system that crushes them. These are the men whose lives prove the essential innocence of us all, if only "they" would leave us alone — the innocence of self-love and brute courage. The only sin in Jones's world is the belief in sin; and his ultimate villain is the Priest.

Dillinger is the archetype of the saved, but a whole company surrounds him: the misfit, the individual non-conformist, the bum. "In France we called it the Underground, which was a heroic term. Here we called it the under*world* but it was the same world and the same kind of people with the same purpose" — mutual defense against the bourgeoisie. Among the underground men, there is a hierarchy: those simply on the bum and in the county jails, those in the federal prisons, those in the Army as enlisted men, those in the Army stockades, and finally the winnowed few who make (via solitary confinement) Ward Two, the quintessential Good Place of Jones's vision. In this ultimate womb, from which a rebirth to freedom is possible, the absolute bolshevik is at home, the "super-arch revolutionary . . . a sort of perfect criminal type, very dangerous, a mad dog that loves underdogs." It is here that Prew, Jones's protagonist, feels himself one at last with Dillinger and Joe Hill and Big Bill Haywood and Buck Jones, one with "the old American tradition of woodsmen and ground-clearing farmers" — a remnant of toughness in a world gone soft, the only force that can save America.

It is in Ward Two that the prophet of Jones's book, Jack Malloy, speaks the novel's final wisdom: the denial of sin, the belief in reincarnation (that strange sentimental religion so attractive to those who believe there is always one more chance), the use of passive resistance; the turning of the defeated into a rock against which their conquerors will dash themselves to death. What Malloy has finally to offer turns out to be the way of Werther: suicide. "Every man has the right to kill himself. . . . It's the only absolutely inviolable right a man does have . . . the old Anglo-Saxon idea of 'freedom' came from that." The final innocence, the ultimate America, the true freedom is — death!

It is in terms of this desolate vision of freedom that the artist has to choose his role and style; and *From Here to Eternity* deals centrally with the education of an artist for this choice. But one must be careful of the word "artist"; Prew, who is careful to make a grammatical error in every sentence (in this, as in so much else, his author's man), is the poor man's creator, a bugler and one of the collaborators in the "Re-enlistment Blues," a "folk song" printed at the end of the book, and intended apparently to be a poetic distillation of the pathos of the whole fable. Jones should have left the words to our imaginations, for they turn out to be in fact bad in a way he could not have foreseen, palpably faked. What Prew as a *Lumpen*-intellectual learns is that he must not accommodate his talents to the world's accepted evil: not bugle where favoritism overrides merit; not box (another of his popular arts) for the reputation of the regiment or his own promotion; not become a flunky in jail, or an officer in the company, or a married man in life. He learns in short to become the poor man's bohemian, to know promotion and marriage and success as the lures that turn a man from the purity of death — but especially to distrust marriage. To marry is to accept complicity, to recognize one's participation in universal guilt, for women do not know enough to die. They are driven hopelessly to conform, that is, to live and make life possible by endless lying, to bear children and to bring them up, to lure strong men into the trap of status and responsibility.

The really "good" feelings of the book are of the innocent-homosexual variety: the camaraderie of the joint trip to the whorehouse (bursting into your buddy's room with a bottle of booze to see how he's doing), and the games in the tough ward of the stockade — allowing yourself to be butted and slugged by your comrades to test how long you can take it. The ruling passion of the novel (despite all the pursuit of "tail" and all the talk about it) turns out to be a desire to spit out teeth, to be beaten and scarred, to be hurt past endurance and to endure (all, of course, just among the boys) — to anticipate the promise of death that is to be the book's climax, when Prew turns deliberately into a rain of machine-gun bullets. It takes a great war in all its initial fury, the bombs and strafing of the attack on Pearl Harbor, to provide a fitting orgasm for the love that is death.

When the writer has learned to rebel and suffer, he is securely joined to those "who could not fight back and win, so they were very strict in their great pride of losing"; and he must then learn *how* to speak for them. The slogan of *"non serviam"* is not enough in itself, for the artist can misguidedly stumble from non-cooperation into a formalist religion of art which scorns and baffles the ordinary Joe. There are, it is indicated, three kinds of art: the commercialized art of frank conformity to the bourgeoisie, the art of the real rebels, and that of the false rebels, the "aesthetes." In the end, the aesthetes only *think* they are rebels; for their rebellion is worthless, either prompted by self-hatred or else made into an end in itself. Oftener than not the decadent rebel is a fairy, dedicated to softness and "conscious aimless beauty." He has no toughness to protect him from the threat of reprisal and the desire for luxury, so that often he passes from unwittingly subserving the middle classes to outright capitulation — even writing slick fiction under a pseudonym in order to keep himself in champagne and to support the plushy apartment where he can seduce young soldiers. The special rancor Jones feels toward the homosexual must be understood in terms of his own stake in the "platonic" love of buddies as the only passion which leads to no commitment to life or society.

But decadents are not only ambiguous sexually; they are also "intellectuals," which is to say, they talk too damn much. To be articulate is to be lost. "Clerks, kings, and thinkers" merely *talk,* but "truckdrivers, pyramid builders, and straight duty men" build and rebuild the world out of their tonguelessness. The clerks ("tall, thin boys with fragile faces": the Army equivalent of intellectuals) talking of Van Gogh and Gauguin lose sight of the true folk sources of art, the clues to a "basic simplicity." It is only the *real* artist, who can mingle unnoticed with the hard guys, the character who has read all the good books (making reading lists out of everything mentioned by Tom Wolfe or Jack London) but would rather die than admit it, who can produce "the song of men who have no place."

As Werther turned to Homer and Ossian and the Ballads in order to touch again the great innocent heart of Nature, so Prew-Jim Jones turns to certain "pure" movies made between '32 and '37, *Grapes of Wrath* and *Dust Be My Destiny,* the on-the-bum pictures with James Cagney, George Raft, and John Garfield (these slick productions he thinks of as not yet commercialized); plus the authentic blues, hillbilly songs, and jazz — perhaps Django Reinhardt also, the three-fingered gypsy guitarist, and Jack London, the American prototype of the artist as bum. Here he hopes to find that "basic artless simplicity" which will be able to crash through the lies of bourgeois art, reach everyone at that core of loneliness which is our only real togetherness.

Finally, in order to prove the innocence of his characters' motives (and his own), their absolute non-complicity, Jones has to prove also their inarticulateness, the tonguelessness of their art and his. For this reason he is driven to contrive (or, perhaps better, to endure) a style which at once speaks and assures us that its message is unsayable. The "basic simplicity" he seeks is so deep beyond words that only a stutter can convey any sense of it. For better or worse then, Jones stutters — and stammers and slobbers and mumbles, all with the utmost conviction, since the lack of slickness is his credentials, his passport into the Utopia of the Natural.

Needless to say, this notion is in the end self-defeating. The absence of positive style makes it possible for the kind of reader Jones most despises to use *From Here to Eternity* for cheap thrills and illegitimate satisfactions. Not the nameless and the defeated, but the very bourgeois who want their pornography in the guise of literature, read his tract as a "dirty book." Any book they can "understand," whose language is no more precise or whose feeling no subtler than their own, this public will use for their own ends; and what *From Here to Eternity* has become in their minds the moving-picture version reveals — at once mawkish and "hot," an orgy of vicarious passion and self-pity. This kind of fate only a high art can escape; and such an art must pass beyond simplicity and nature, beyond the range of perception of those for whom essentially it speaks. It is a baffling dilemma, perhaps a fatal one, but it cannot be sentimentalized out of existence.

CHAPTER THIRTEEN

Adolescence and Maturity in the American Novel

The years since 1940 have been for writers and critics in America a time of disenchantment, marking, one hopes, the passage from the easy enthusiasms and approximate ambitions of adolescence to the juster self-appraisal of maturity. We have been obliged to recognize not only that we have had most recently a narrowing down, if not an actual exhaustion, of the vein of invention and experiment in the novel; but also that much of the work of the earlier twentieth century which seemed a little while ago so exciting and important actually had only a temporary appeal and a parochial interest. It is not that we have not had in the last thirty years at least two novelists of major stature, but that our sense of a full-scale renaissance, of a continually dazzling level of accomplishment, has turned out to be an illusion. Ironically enough, we have come to a realization of our own limitations during the same period in which many Europeans have embraced the illusion we are leaving behind; so that we find ourselves often in the embarrassing position of having to insist upon the inadequacies of American work which critics abroad find it politic to overpraise.

One of the chief disenchantments of American criticism has been the disconcerting way in which the "great" novels of ten or fifteen years back have tended to disappear. Year by year we have greeted new works with enthusiasm, we have remembered them fondly; but looking back for them over our shoulders we have found them inexplicably turned to dust. The novels of Sherwood Anderson, for example, appear to us now incoherent and unconvincing; his diminished reputation rests on a handful of short stories which survive their sentimentality by fixing it precisely, and which can still move us though they seem alien to what we are at present doing. Sinclair Lewis we find it harder and harder to believe we could ever have taken for a serious writer. The figure of Babbitt remains in our mind, a caricature of attitudes to which we no longer respond; but Lewis himself we remember as a cartoonist, a journalist with neither poetic nor psychological depth, the author of a curiously provincial parody of *Madame Bovary*. John Steinbeck we continue to find appealing only where he is least ambitious: his stories about animals touch us, and his sentimental entertainment *Tortilla Flat* we recall with affection; but his attempts to deal with adult human beings in all their complexity, to judge society (in such a book as *Grapes of Wrath*), seem to us marred by maudlin social piety and turgid symbolism.

John Dos Passos has recently been writing books that no one reads; and even turning back to *1919* or *The 42nd Parallel* we feel that all the famous technical devices are no more than mechanical substitutes for poetry, subterfuges to conceal from us the fact that he cannot create a convincing character. James T. Farrell strikes us as a writer who attains occasional passages of genuinely passionate insight almost by mistake, swathing them in such endless stretches of doughy, earnest documentation that we find it hard to remember them. Thomas Wolfe appears to us now as appallingly overblown, a writer still to be responded to enthusiastically, but only at the one moment of adolescence to which his frantic rhetoric is appropriate; certainly he is not a writer for the mature. We tend now to see him backwards through *Raintree County*, that illuminating failure arising from what Wolfe had made of Joyce and Kinsey had made of sex. The early deaths of Lockridge and Wolfe, self-inflicted or merely endured, blur into a single symbol of the plight of the American writer who does not know how to grow old.

Another such symbolic death is that of F. Scott Fitzgerald, leaving unfinished what might have been his only completely adult book. Even our best writers appear unable to mature; after one or two inexpert attempts, they find a style, a subject and tone, usually anchored in their adolescent experience — and these they repeat compulsively, like a songbird his single tune. Ring Lardner is an especially pathetic example, trying to make of his ballplayers occasions adequate to his bitter vision.

In general, our writers have no history, no development; their themes belong to a pre-adult world, and the experience of growing old tends to remain for them intractable. It is merely one aspect of that compulsive veneration of youth, that fear of all which is not simply strong and beautiful, so important in our total culture. When our novelists do not manage to die young or to stop writing completely (plunging into alcoholism as into a dream of the Garden), they are likely simply to get worse, ending often in intolerable parodies of their own best work. Ernest Hemingway is the classic instance of such a development. One of the best writers of the twentieth century, a novelist of immense technical means, and indeed the inventor of a style that has changed the writing of fiction in the whole Western world, Hemingway has still been unable to progress. When he has attempted to move from evocations of lost youth, from studies of impotence and the failure of love, to be "positive" or socially aware, he has seemed merely unconvincing and forced. It is almost as impossible to imagine a Hemingway character having a child (dying in childbed is another matter) as it is to conceive of one of them going to a ballot box. His characters seem never really old enough to vote, merely to blow up bridges; as they seem never old enough to reproduce, merely sufficiently mature to make the motions of the act of love. In every sense except the genital one, they remain children; so that the controlling values of his books are a boy's notion of bravery and honor and devotion, tricked out in the child's images of bullfighting and big-game hunting and playing war. In the earliest and best work, *The Sun Also Rises, A Farewell to Arms,* and some of the short stories, these notions and these images are turned into a nostalgic, desolate poetry, bare and mannered at the same time. But all the novels since *To Have and Have Not* (which enjoys the singular distinction of having had *two* bad movies made from it — and richly deserves the honor) have been failures, more and more disheartening up to the complete fiasco of *Across the River and Into the Trees.*

The Old Man and the Sea returns to a level of technical accomplishment almost equal to the earlier work by stripping away all social implications and any attempt to deal with mature emotions. Hemingway is always less embarrassing when he is not attempting to deal with women; and he returns with relief (with what we as readers at least feel as relief) to that "safe" American Romance of the boy and the old man. The single flaw in *The Old Man and the Sea* is the constant sense that Hemingway is no longer creating, but merely imitating the marvelous spare style that was once a revelation; that what was once an anti-rhetoric has become now merely another rhetoric, perhaps our most familiar one, and that even its inventor cannot revive it for us.

For the youngest American readers, writers barely beginning, the brighter college students, Hemingway has come to seem irrelevant, a little boring; though his immense, diffused influence continues to manifest itself in all American prose writing — and indeed in our speech itself. An occasional direct imitation (Chandler Brossard's *Who Walk in Darkness,* for example) only makes the point more firmly with its inescapably old-fashioned impact. The youngsters of today are disgusted not only by the dated and ridiculous role which Hemingway, more and more frantically, plays in his own life, but also by his failure to project an adult love, an adult commitment, an adult courage — from which they might at least revolt with dignity. His breathless pursuit of wars, swordfish, and lions leaves cold a generation born older than he will ever get.

Generally speaking, our writers no longer go to Africa or the left bank to escape from the dullness of America to a world of pure Experience; they are tourists or art historians or government officials or the holders of grants and fellowships, but they are not Exiles. They may get drunk in Paris or find mistresses in Rome, but they no longer consider their drunkenness a utopia or their sexual adventures a blow for freedom. In the same way, Bohemia has died for them; I do not mean that there are no bohemias, but that they are now escapes *from* writing, not escapes to it from the pressures of bourgeois life. It is for this reason that F. Scott Fitzgerald, who represents the world of bohemia and expatriation as something done with, who presents the world of the 'twenties with the pathos of something already outgrown, with a sense of how naïvely, how *innocently* lost that generation must appear to our post-Dachau vision, is more sympathetic to us than the much more talented Hemingway, to whom the Cult of Experience remains not a lost frenzy of the years after the First World War, but his only faith.

I suppose it is the death of the adolescent faith in Life as Experience which has led to a complementary loss of the ingenuous faith in Literature as Experience. It was once enough for us to know, or believe (it turns out that we were dealing with a legend), that Sherwood Anderson one day suddenly walked out of the office in which he worked, throwing aside bourgeois security for Art and Life. This seemed then a sufficient guarantee of his "integrity" (it was once our favorite word) and of his excellence as an artist. And, alas, this Anderson believed along with the rest of us, so that much of his work remains abortive, because, trusting to Experience to do the whole job, he stopped precisely where he should have begun in real earnest. There was in those days a hopeless confusion between what made a man "good" (i.e., everything his bourgeois parents would have believed bad) and what made a work of art good; "social consciousness," "sincerity," "progressivism" were taken for aesthetic terms. To such a muddled understanding of the relationship between the truth of art, the truth of conscience, and the truth of facts, writers like Upton Sinclair, Sinclair Lewis, and Farrell owe their former successes and their present waning popularity. Hemingway himself, though primarily a stylist and interested only at a second remove in "life," was victimized by similar assumptions, which have led to his continuing pose as a *naïf,* a latter-day Mark Twain; and he has felt obliged to invent with great pains a style which seems to take no pains; as some American politicians invest a great deal of art in seeming to speak like the artless common man.

Even so important and courageous a literary pioneer as Theodore Dreiser appears to us now of drastically limited value, despite his ability to create a milieu with all the thick substance of reality itself. It is not merely a matter of his sentimental subjects, those eternally seduced women, or of the gross style interlarded with ladies'-magazine elegancies, nor even of his profound and utterly unsuspected stupidity (intelligence and style alike are optional for the writer — and any subject can be redeemed); but of his failure to develop, his entrapment by the belief that a work of art is equal to its raw materials, and that its moral value is equal to the code its author professes rather than what is *realized* in the text.

It is tempting to say that the central fact of our period is the death of "naturalism" and the decline in reputation of the novelists associated with its seeming triumph. But what has died is only a small part of what is commonly associated with the term: a certain moral obtuseness, political sentimentality and naïve faith in documentation. Much has survived: the breaking of certain taboos about subject matter; the demonstration that no experience is too humble or trivial for the novel; the elevation of a solidly specified environment to equal importance with plot or character; the revolution in the conventions of writing dialogue — all these will never be lost. Yet the contemporary American author no longer believes that a work of art can be judged primarily by its accuracy in reproducing ordinary speech or rendering literally the horrors of Chicago slums; for us, the reality, the value, of a work of art lies in its symbolic depth and resonance, not in the exhaustiveness of its data.

It is for this reason that a vital influence on the contemporary novel is Henry James, who not long since was disowned as too aristocratic, too elaborately trivial to be either a good writer or a true American. In his own day, of course, James was felt, indeed felt himself, in the forefront of the movement toward "realism," while we relish in him what is least like such fellow-realists as William Dean Howells. Our James is the impressionist, the conscious artist, who dared assert that a concern with form is not immoral; and in whom we have come to recognize great poetry, profound images of good and evil, under the slowly elaborated accounts of people who apparently never sweat or blow their noses, and who manage to make love over teacups rather than in bed. From James, our younger novelists (even the ones most impatient with him, most insistent on all he ignores) have learned that a novel is not what its author *says* happened in it, but what is really *rendered.* It is possible to feel now that the Jamesian example has been assimilated, even institutionalized, and that we must be moving on; but there is no way to go except through Henry James, and no writer among us can ever doubt again that a book is made of words rather than facts.

For technique, the newer writers have been able to find a master no further back than the beginnings of realism; but, for an exemplar of the poetic subject, they have had to search behind the Civil War, to the Melville of *Moby Dick,* in whom they have found a blend of secularized puritanism, factual solidity, and symbolic resonance, an erudition and naïveté that point beyond realism. There is a Melville whom one scarcely knows whether to call the discovery or invention of our time, our truest contemporary, who has revealed to us the traditional theme of the deepest American mind, the ambiguity of innocence, "the mystery of iniquity," which we had traded for the progressive melodrama of a good outcast (artist, rebel, whore, proletarian) against an evil bourgeoisie. In James, too, a similar theme is suggested and then almost lost in the embroidery of sensibility; but, having seen once our theme, we do not willingly surrender it or the attitudes proper to it: "the blackness ten times black," the obligation to say *no,* the practice of irony and the acceptance that does not cancel it out. In these, there is the possibility of development and fulfillment, a way out of adolescence.

Guilt and innocence, the mystery of iniquity — most of our present-day writers are not in any orthodox sense religious (though a few are, and many enjoy playing poetically with the counters of orthodoxy: Original Sin and Salvation and the Dark Night of the Soul), but almost all of them feel that there are deeper perceptions of man's plight than the brash optimism of a Rousseau. We remember only too well the generations who tried to convince us that all metaphors of human evil were mystifications, the inventions of priests and aesthetes afraid of "real life." Indeed, during the 'thirties, when American "realism" was captured by the Marxists, such concerns were banned by the exponents of the "proletarian," who preached that the only criterion of good and evil, as well as the true subject of fiction, was the Class Struggle. The record of the so-called "proletarian novel" in the United States is one of the most absurd episodes of our literary history. The names of the "revolutionary" writers who seemed to us in 1935 about to make a new culture are hard to remember: Robert Cantwell, Grace Lumpkin, Jack Conroy, William Rollins — one sees them occasionally in a list of witnesses before a Congressional investigating committee, or on the masthead of a Luce publication. Merely to recite the half-forgotten names and to invoke our old enthusiasm is to learn the lesson which makes us smile a little when we see in Europe today attempts at social realism, at what the French call *"littérature engagée."*

Yet once, even established writers rushed to give assurances that they had graduated from post-war cynicism, Hemingway writing *To Have and Have Not,* and Fitzgerald himself toying with the idea of having Dick Diver become a Communist; and those who would not conform were disowned. It is symptomatic of our new turning that the favorite writer of most of our young novelists now is precisely the author most despised, during the "proletarian" period, as reactionary, ghoulish, and cheaply spectacular — namely, William Faulkner. We do not, to be sure, read his grotesque poems of comedy and horror as realistic reports on the South; for us the truth of Faulkner's world is a symbolic truth; and across his gothic landscape is fought not the historical war between North and South, but the eternal war between the dream of nobility and order and the fact of disorder and failure and sorrow. Naturally, his images are American images and even regional ones: the Negro, the Indian, the ravaged and forgotten wilderness, the miserable mountain farm, the riderless horse disappearing into the night — but their meanings are the meanings of such objects in dreams and not in history, meanings immediately translatable for anyone anywhere. Beyond this, there is Faulkner's concern with rhetoric and form which intrigues us; his stubborn insistence on finding for each book (*The Sound and the Fury* is perhaps the best example) a language and structure so nearly impossible that he is always risking absurdity.

Faulkner and Melville and James: these are the American novelists who function as living influences today. There are others whom we honor, Hawthorne and Mark Twain and Hemingway, for instance; but they do not so directly determine the ambitions of the beginning writer, except as they also contribute to the psychological, symbolic, gothic tradition these define. The strengths of contemporary writing correspond to the strengths of this tradition, boldness of imagery, subtlety of insight, and especially the willingness to plunge deep below the lintel of consciousness; and the weaknesses to its weaknesses, a tendency to involution and hysteria, to a rhetoric that becomes pseudo-poetry at its weakest; and a weakness in dealing with women. The tradition which stems from Melville, James, and Faulkner combines an overall moral maturity with a failure to achieve mature attitudes toward sex; there is a vacuum at the heart of American fiction that James's nervous indirection, Melville's underground homosexuality, and Faulkner's comic anti-feminism cannot fill. But at least there is a tradition at last, compounded ironically by three traditionless and lonely writers; and, beyond them, our newer novelists look to European sources: to the Russian novel of the nineteenth century, especially to Dostoevsky; to Marcel Proust, whose influence blends with that of James; to James Joyce and Thomas Mann; and more recently to Franz Kafka, who seems almost an American writer in his symbolic gothicism and who projected, before we knew we needed it, a style able to reproduce the logical insanity of a German concentration camp or a Russian political trial.

It is a point worth noting that most of our younger writers do not insist upon their *difference* as Americans, feeling themselves sharers in the general development of Western culture; indeed, one of the things that makes us feel alienated from an Anderson, a Dreiser, a Sinclair Lewis is their almost willful cultural naïveté, their fear of the traditional. For we have come to believe that an ignorance of the past and of Europe is the poorest way to ensure our own particularity. In home-made, degenerate form all the clichés of post-Enlightenment thought appear in the work of those writers most set on repro-ducing "pure" American experience; while in James and Mel-ville the fruit of reading and study is an approach at once new and enriched by older sources.

Not all recent American writers, of course, fall into the post-naturalist camp I have been describing. The writers of books describing the Second World War have apparently felt them-selves immune to the shifts I have tried to indicate, and with creditable diligence and woeful lack of invention they have rewritten the typical novels of the war of 1917, changing only dates and place names; while, a few years back, another atavis-tic novel, James Jones's *From Here to Eternity,* won consider-able critical acclaim by reviving and exemplifying the pseudo-realist theory that to write honestly one must write badly, that Art and Truth are mutually exclusive. There survives and flourishes, in addition, the slick sentimental-realist school, represented by John Hersey's *The Wall* and the novels of Irwin Shaw, which manage to combine a banal liberal op-timism with a commercially successful style based on watered-down Hemingway.

But among those writers who, in the phrase of Henry James, have "no ambitions except the highest" the majority are more concerned with symbol than with statement, more drawn to-ward poetry than toward journalism. Their work tends to be the opposite of naïve — in fact, rather difficult; and they are read, therefore, by a relatively small audience as compared not only with the readers of historical romances, but even with those who admire the tough or sentimental pseudo-realists. It is one of the ironies of the present situation in writing that our better novelists are at the same time un-popular and un-experi-mental. Nobody nowadays is doing anything startling or new; the techniques that are being exploited are those that were revolutionary in the 'twenties; but the mass audience has stub-bornly refused to catch up. This is hardly cheering to our younger authors, who tend to be a melancholy lot, having neither the comfort of commercial success nor the thrill of feeling themselves a gallant vanguard. They have tended, in self-defense, to find themselves special audiences for whom they specifically write and by whose acclaim they live; and while this strategy serves a purpose in sustaining them, financially and spiritually, it has tended to create a situation in which we have a series of competing "academies" rather than a conflict of the academic and the anti-academic.

Since it would be impossible to mention more than a few writers of the younger generation without simply compiling a catalogue, I shall limit myself to discussing particularly only two of the competing "academies," the two which seem to me in certain ways most important: one associated with *Harper's Bazaar*, the other with *Partisan Review*. I pick *Harper's Bazaar* to stand for a whole group which includes *Mademoiselle* and *Vogue* and the ill-fated *Flair*, which attempted to be deliberately and whole-heartedly what the others had become partially and almost by accident, and which ended as a parody of itself and of the others. *Harper's Bazaar* is, of course, not primarily a literary magazine at all, but an elegant fashion magazine for women, read not only by those who can afford the goods it advertises but by many who cannot and who participate vicariously in its world of values, picking it up on the table of a beauty-parlor waiting room. Finding a story by, say, Truman Capote tucked away between the picture of a determinedly unbeautiful model and an ad for a brassiere, most of the readers of *Harper's Bazaar*, one assumes, must simply skip the meaningless pages; and, knowing this, the editors (writers, themselves, or friends of writers) know that they can print anything they please.

But the conjunction of Capote and high style is not as accidental as it seems at first glance. We have been evolving in recent years a new sort of sensibility, defined by a taste for *haute couture*, classical ballet, baroque opera, the rites and vestments of Catholicism — and above all for a kind of literature at once elegantly delicate and bitterly grotesque. This new kind of sensibility, although (or perhaps because) it is quite frankly a homosexual one, appeals profoundly to certain rich American women with cultural aspirations, and is therefore

sponsored in their salons and published decoratively in magazines that cater to their tastes. The development of new markets
for the young writer with this sort of sensibility has gone hand
in hand with the development of a kind of high bohemia,
which moves freely from New York to Venice to Capri to
establish a world that is international and anti-bourgeois without being political or sordid or sullen, like the older bohemias.

The most important writer of this group is Carson McCullers, the most typical Truman Capote (or his latest version,
called Speed Lamkin or whatever, since in this world of
evanescent youth the hungry generations tread each other
down with astonishing rapidity). One can take the latter as
almost a caricature of the type: the "queen" as American
author, possessing a kind of beauty, both in person and as an
artist, which belongs to childhood and early adolescence, and
which withers before it can ripen; Southern in origin and
allegiance; and gothic (a very refined gothic) in style, blending
Edgar Allan Poe and Ronald Firbank in an improbable
grafting.

Such writers also descend in a strange way from Faulkner,
who provides them with a ready-made *paysage moralisée,* the
landscape of the South as a natural symbol for decay and
brooding evil. To the distrust and fear of woman in Faulkner,
they respond according to their own lights; and what there is
in the older writer of the agonizedly male has already been
transmuted for them by two transitional writers, both women
and both immensely talented, Katherine Anne Porter and
Eudora Welty — who began the process of taming and
feminizing Faulkner (he has had only one truly male follower,
Robert Penn Warren, who falls outside the scope of my present
essay), making possible the ingrafting of Henry James which
produces the true Magnolia Blossom or Southern Homosexual
style: pseudo-magical, pseudo-religious, counterfeiting the
symbolism of Faulkner in a rhetoric and rhythm derived from
James.

I have used the word "counterfeiting" because I find this
kind of fiction often merely chic behind its pretense of being
subtle and advanced. Even Capote, who possesses considerable talent, has come more and more to *play* at being an

author, to act out for the benefit of his own kind of society the role of the elegant, sad, futile androgyne — half reigning beauty and half freak. His novel *Other Voices, Other Rooms* already represents a falling away from the slight authentic music of such an early story as "Children on Their Birthdays," and some of his most recent work seems more and more just décor — like the quasi-surrealist window dressings of certain Fifth Avenue shops.

There has been a tendency for this school at its periphery, where it touches, let us say, Princeton, to combine in a perhaps foreseeable way with the formal emphasis of the "New Criticism," and to find expression in the more studied Jamesian effects of a writer like Frederick Buechner; but its realest triumphs are achieved in the fiction of Carson McCullers. Her first novel, *The Heart Is a Lonely Hunter,* published when she was only twenty-two, is heartbreakingly wonderful; the melancholy Southern town, the deaf-and-dumb protagonists all make their meanings precisely, scene and symbol fused into a single poetry without strain. The subject of Miss McCullers' work is the subject of her whole group: the impossibility of reciprocal love, the sadness of a world in which growing up means only learning that isolation is the fate of every one of us. Her central characters, those ambiguous boyish girls (Frankie and Mick: the names make the point) who stand outside of everything, even their own sex, lost in a world of freaks — these are strange new heroes of our time.

The *Partisan Review,* around which the second "academy" tends to polarize, is quite another matter, though, indeed, its typical contributors sometimes appear (though not usually with their best or most characteristic work) in *Harper's Bazaar;* while a sensibility, shriller or icier, but not fundamentally different from that which informs the fiction of the ladies' magazines, manifests itself in such *Partisan Review* contributors as Tennessee Williams and Paul Bowles. But the impact, the very appearance of *Partisan* indicate a fundamental difference. It is not an advertising journal that has stumbled into printing advanced fiction, but a review which began as a "little magazine" and has managed (thanks in part to angels, but chiefly to the stubborn devotion of its editors) to become an institution without ever having achieved a large circulation. One of the strangest things about *Partisan Review* is that, though its readers have never numbered more than about 10,000, its name is confidently used in journals with 100,000 and 2,000,000 readers as a symbol for certain values which do not have to be further defined. Certainly, it is resented, hated, and sullenly respected by a much larger number of people than have ever read it.

In its beginnings, it attempted to combine an allegiance to *avant-garde* aesthetic ideals and radical politics; at first, it was quite frankly a Communist publication, though its editors quite soon broke from orthodox Stalinism as the enemy of free culture. Its contributors are characteristically unhappy with each other and with the magazine itself; and they would resent to a man being spoken of as a group, as I am doing now. But they *do* have a good deal in common, not the least of which is their uneasy feeling of independence from each other, the sense that it is only their past which binds them unwillingly together. In politics, for instance, they have grown far apart, becoming variously Anarchists, Trotskyites, Social Democrats, New Dealers, and even Republicans — but they have all of them the complicated political awareness of those who once lived inside of or close to the Communist movement.

They are "political" in the European sense of the word, a sense that does not even exist for most Americans. Not only do they have Marx, accepted or denied, in their blood, but also Freud in much the same way, as well as contemporary sociology, anthropology, and philosophy in general — so that they are likely to take sides passionately in arguments about, say, existentialism or other recent European ideologies. They share the fondness of the Southern group for James and Faulkner, but in some ways Kafka is closer to their hearts (Isaac Rosenfeld, for instance, made a major, not quite successful effort, to create a body of American work in his image), and they feel a real kinship with Dostoevsky and Tolstoy. Precisely because their cultural background is so complex, and also because they have almost all been forced somewhere between 1935 and 1940 to make a radical shift in their political allegiances and aesthetic ambitions, it has taken these writers a long time to grow up. Some critics have even found it comical or disheartening to learn that many *Partisan* writers spoken of as "young" are thirty or thirty-five or forty. But they are in truth, for the reasons I have tried to suggest, still young as writers when middle-aged as men, still *beginning* — not dazzling successes at twenty like Truman Capote. They have matured slowly, but they have matured; and this is exceptional in the American scene.

The best of the group is Saul Bellow, a novelist of exceptional talent and in many ways a typical figure. Like most of the writers I am describing, he is a second-generation Jew (this is important, for the Jews are just now taking a place of peculiar significance in American cultural life; and, as a history-ridden people in a history-less land, they stand in a different relationship to the past and to Europe than any other American group), an urban type, whose world is not the archetypal small town that from Twain to Sherwood Anderson and on to Faulkner has been the world *par excellence* of our fiction. Nor is his city the Big Town seen by the provincial, the bewildering un-home that has haunted the American literary mind from the moment of Pierre's wild trip to New York. Saul Bellow's Chicago (like the New York of Delmore Schwartz) is the only home of the essentially homeless, remembered not idyllically as the Garden but as the desert to which one woke at the moment of the Great Depression.

Bellow's controlling images and myths tend to be social ones; ideas, political and philosophical, are not something intrusive in his work, but the atmosphere, the very condition of life. He feels most deeply where his thought is most deeply involved, and his characters come alive where they are touched by ideas. It is for this reason that the most moving passages in his books are discussions, the interchange of opinions and theories as vividly presented as a love scene or a fight. But his books are never "problem" novels in the sense of the socially conscious 'twenties. Even *The Victim* (which remains in many respects my favorite), though it takes off from the problem of anti-Semitism, does not aim at establishing the smug sense of our own innocence and the other's guilt, but suggests in its muted fable the difficulty of being human, much less innocent, in a world of injustice.

With *The Adventures of Augie March,* Bellow has won for the first time the general recognition he has long deserved, though his two earlier books had won at least equal critical acclaim. Writers of this school have, I think, a special problem in reaching a mass audience to whom the commonplaces of their experience have an inevitable tinge of the remote and abstruse; and *Augie* is a deliberate attempt to break through to such a group out of the parochial world in which Bellow began. *Augie* itself is an uneven book, redundant and untidy, full of a strange tough-abstract poetry that becomes sometimes merely mannered; but it is held together finally by a versatile irony that moves from barely quizzical tenderness to wild burlesque. Ideally, the book should be read after the grey, tight, orderly *Victim* in order to understand the self-imposed limitations against which it is in revolt. In everything but self-understanding and control, it is a better book, richer, more ambitious, funnier, the saga of an improbable Huckleberry Finn: Huck as a metropolitan Jew, a wanderer through cities, fallen among Trotskyites and comedians of ideas as well as grafters and minor machiavellians — but Huck still, the apostle of non-commitment, moving uncertainly but inevitably toward the "happy ending" of un-success. It is an explosive book, a novel powered by the atomization of its own world; and the world fragmented in its humor and violence is the world of the *Partisan Review,* which Augie may never have had time to read.

There are other lesser, but still interesting, writers in this constellation: Lionel Trilling, whose single novel was not quite successful, but who in two short stories perfected a new kind of moral-critical fiction; Delmore Schwartz, a poet and fictionist who evokes the Jewish-American milieu with a studied limpness, half-irritating, half-intriguing; Mary McCarthy, the most wickedly witty of the group, who satirizes the ideas of the *Partisan Review* itself at the point where they tend to die into banalities.

It is because the fictionists of this group are capable of

seeing themselves with a characteristic irony, sad or brittle, because their world is complex and troubled enough to protect them from nostalgia and self-pity, that I see in them evidence of a movement toward a literature of maturity. Yet certain flaws endemic to the whole American scene reappear disconcertingly in the *Partisan* group and mar *Augie* itself. One feels sometimes that only the weaknesses of American literature survive from generation to generation; that the heritage of our writers is a series of vacuums, which by evasion or strategy they must bridge or by-pass.

One waits still, for instance, for the American writer who can render as successfully as, say, any second-rank French novelist of the nineteenth century the complexities and ambiguities of sexual passion, of — (how absurdly hard it is for the American writer to say simply "love") of *love*. The sentimental-love religion has died out of our serious fiction, leaving only a blank, a blank that the nympholeptic stereotypes which play the women's roles in Saul Bellow's book surely do not fill. Among certain *Partisan* writers, there has recently been an attempt to make out of Laurentian reminiscences and Reichian doctrines a new religion — not of love, of course, but of "full genitality"; yet this seems anything but mature.

Moreover, there appears to be a growing impatience inside the *Partisan* academy, superficially directed at the excesses of the newer criticism but actually aimed at the whole Jamesian cult of sensibility, and this threatens to end in a general scalping of all Paleface writers. Yet the urge toward this polar split between "honest crudity" and "elegant introspection" represents as deep a wound in the American aesthetic sense as the analogous distinction of Dark Lady and Fair Lady stands for in terms of our sexual consciousness. There is a kind of toughminded provincialism implicit in the whole position: an impulse toward "moral realism," a fear of "mystification" (i.e., of religion and metaphysics), which may at any moment explode in a reversion to the simplest Redskin celebration of pure experience.

Against this temptation, Dostoevsky and Tolstoy and Kafka might well be expected to serve as antidotes; but it is hard to say how seriously these writers are finally taken and how far they are merely "culture" in the vulgarest sense of the word, the souvenirs of literary tourism. The "tradition" which sustains the *Partisan Review* remains, in a characteristically American way, partial and *willed*. Its canon develops not organically out of a given cultural past, but by forced breeding out of what a few strong-minded men *happen to know*. It is hard to see how such a situation can be avoided in a society distinguished by the indifference of the many to the making of its taste, and by an unbridgeable gap between its productive present and its only viable literary past.

The America which has survived westward expansion and the mass immigration of the last century can no longer live, except nostalgically, on the puritan-colored metaphysical tradition that was still able to nurture Hawthorne and Melville and Henry James. It is not only that America is comparatively young, but that it no longer possesses even the meager past it has lived; that it has, indeed, deliberately and joyously cast off that burden, so that each new generation must improvise not only its fate but its history. This is, on the one hand, an opportunity but, on the other, a curse; and, opportunity or curse, it cuts us off from the European alternatives of Tradition and Revolt. To be sure, we use these terms frequently but somewhat comically to describe our pious allegiance to or disavowal of values some ten or fifteen years old; and our failure to confess this leads to the constant counterfeiting of new pasts and the restless revaluations that succeed each other among us with bewildering speed.

There has been in recent times a notorious attempt to invent a full-scale synthetic myth of an America of the Open Road to replace the defunct New England version of our country; but this was born as unreal as its predecessor has become, and, as it has grown less and less sympathetic to a second-generation, urbanized world, its sponsors have grown shriller and shriller. The sentimentality of the wholesale American Legend and its corresponding dream of an unlimited mass audience have not directly influenced most serious American writers; but, in their self-satisfaction at having resisted so second-rate a temptation, they are likely to fall prey to the subtler allures embodied in the exclusive little audience with its conviction of the superiority of its special taste. To write deliberately for the few, we have been learning, is as dangerous as writing for the many in a mass society. To shift from the latter aim to the former is to move from the child's desire to buy universal love with perfect obedience to the adolescent's resolve to compel universal recognition with perfect non-cooperation, a resolve that ends typically in complete submission to the mores of one's gang.

The mature writer must write, as he has always written, for neither mass nor sect but for that pure fiction, the ideal understander, for whom we no longer have a name but who was once called the "gentle reader." In traditional cultures, that non-existent perfect reader was postulated in a set of values represented imperfectly but hopefully by a self-perpetuating body of critics. In America, he has never been institutionalized, surviving only in the unwitting parody of the "genteel reader," which at the end of the nineteenth century we rejected with scorn in favor of a more democratic but less useful concept, the "average reader."

The plight of the American writer is at best difficult; aware that the greatest books of our literature remain somehow boys' books, he seeks a way toward maturity. But between him and a mature relationship with his past lies our contempt for what is left behind, the discontinuity of our history; between him and a mature relationship with his public lies the impossibility of institutionalizing values in a democracy which regards taste as a vestige of aristocratic privilege; between him and a mature relationship with experience lies the fact that the only universally *felt* American morality arises from the ersatz religion of sentimentalism.

It is no wonder that our novelists have shuttled between the utopias of form and formlessness, pretending alternately that a technical point-of-view is a sufficient substitute for a moral viewpoint and that reported fact is the equivalent of judged experience. The images of childhood and adolescence haunt our greatest works as an unintended symbolic confession of the inadequacy we sense but cannot remedy. Perhaps it is impossible to attain a mature literature without a continuing tradition in the European sense; for it may be that no individual author alone and in a single lifetime can achieve an adult relationship to his culture and his vision of it. But we can, of course, never have such a tradition, only the disabling nostalgia for one; and quite rapidly the whole world is coming to resemble us in this regard. The essential fact of literature in our age is its inevitable "Americanization," as mass culture advances and the old systems of evaluation go down with the political structures into which they were ingrafted.

In this sense, the Continental vogue of American fiction, which seems otherwise a merely fashionable exoticism or even sometimes a gesture of self-contempt and anti-intellectualism, represents the search of Western literature for its future. Even now, the writers of many other countries begin to stand to their own past in a relation as uneasy as our own; and in our novel they find raised nakedly at last the question that underlay the experimentation of the 'twenties, the "social consciousness" of the 'thirties, the search for formal security of the 'forties: "Can the lonely individual, unsustained by tradition in an atomized society, achieve a poetry adult and complicated enough to be the consciousness of its age?" To have posed that question for the world is the achievement of the American novel at the present moment.

INDEX

Index